Scapegoats

Scapegoats

Baseballers Whose Careers Are Marked by One Fateful Play

CHRISTOPHER BELL

McFarland & Company, Inc., Publishers

Jefferson, North Carolina, and London

Library of Congress Cataloguing-in-Publication Data

Bell, Christopher, 1968–
 Scapegoats : baseballers whose careers are marked by one
fateful play / Christopher Bell.
  p.   cm.
 Includes bibliographical references and index.

 ISBN 0-7864-1381-6 (softcover : 50# alkaline paper)

 1. Baseball — United States — History.   2. Baseball players —
United States.   3. Baseball — Defense.   I. Title.
GV863.A1B43   2002
796.357′0973 — dc21   2002013559

British Library cataloguing data are available

Cover photograph: Bill Buckner *(National Baseball Hall of Fame Library,
Cooperstown, N.Y.)*

Manufactured in the United States of America

McFarland & Company, Inc., Publishers
 Box 611, Jefferson, North Carolina 28640
 www.mcfarlandpub.com

To my mother, brother and
the men in this book

Acknowledgments

A heartfelt thanks: I would like to thank the Baseball Hall of Fame and the *Sporting News* for their invaluable assistance. Both organizations were instrumental in supplying me with important periodicals to complete this book. To my friends, Eleanor and Jerry Koffler, Damian Begley, and Jim Kaplan who took the time to read this manuscript. Finally, Spencer Garrett (grandson of Fred Snodgrass), Tommy Henrich, Charles Owen (son of Mickey Owen), Carl Erskine, Ralph Branca and Bobby Thomson for their wonderful stories of Ebbets Field and the Polo Grounds. Finally, to you, the fans, who, like me, have followed baseball. Without your help, this book would not have been possible.

Contents

Preface

When I first began research for this book in June of 2000, I knew that the next year, 2001, would be the sixtieth, fiftieth, and fifteenth anniversaries of the Yankees' comeback in Game 4 of the 1941 Fall Classic, the Giants' remarkable playoff win in 1951, the Red Sox's improbable triumph in the 1986 American League Championship Series, and the Mets' amazing rally in the 1986 World Series. All four events involved the winners of those contests. But what about the people who were unfairly blamed for losing those contests? I also realized that since I remembered those anniversaries, other baseball aficionados could also recount those same contests. Most of this book was completed by the winter of 2000, but I kept digging, probing, and looking at every possible angle on the subjects of this book. I was pleased to find more material on these men. I thought I knew everything about those nine contests; I was surprised and elated to discover that I did not.

Then in the spring of 2001, I spotted a book called *Heartbreakers* written by John Kuenster. I saw the Pulitzer Prize–winning photograph showing Ralph Branca atop the Dodger clubhouse steps at the Polo Grounds, and I immediately knew what the book was about — losing teams in important ball games. I thought someone had beaten me to the punch. I was wrong. I liked *Heartbreakers,* but this is an entirely different book. Whereas *Heartbreakers* looks at the teams that lost those games, my book focuses on the men who were blamed for the losses.

"Oh, No Mo!" read the back page of the *New York Daily News* on the morning of November 5, 2001. Mo is the nickname for Mariano Rivera, one of the most dominant relievers on one of the most dominant teams in the last five years, the New York Yankees. The name is appropriate, for Mo practically mowed down every batter he faced. Rivera entered the seventh contest of the Fall Classic between the Yankees and their opponents, the Arizona Diamondbacks, in the eighth inning fanning the D'backs, which left New York only three outs away from their fourth championship in a row and fifth in six years—something that had not been done since the Yankees achieved this feat in 1936 through 1939, and from 1949 to 1953.

The year the Yankees did not win the World Series was in 1997, when they were eliminated in the division series by the Cleveland Indians in five games. The Yankees actually led 2–1 in the ninth inning of the fourth contest, and were two outs away from advancing to the LCS, when Sandy Alomar, Jr., stepped to the plate and homered to tie the game at 2–2. The Indians eventually won the game 3–2 and the Series the next day. The pitcher who yielded the home run was Mariano Rivera.

But Rivera was in his first year as the closer for the Yankees in 1997. New York's previous closer and the 1996 World Series MVP, John Wetteland, was not retained by the Yankees and signed with the Texas Rangers. Since the division loss to Cleveland, Rivera had been superb in the post season as he had closed out the 1998, 1999, and 2000 Fall Classics. However, due to the loss of reliever Jeff Nelson, who signed with the Seattle Mariners, Rivera was not automatic, for the Yankee bullpen was not as deep as it had been in their previous championship years. He lost six games, and if he worked two days in a row, Rivera was not as sharp as he had been on his previous outings.

Now in the ninth inning of Game 7 of the 2001 World Series, with New York ahead 2–1, Arizona was only nine strikes away from elimination. Mark Grace, the longtime Chicago Cub who never made it to the Fall Classic in the Windy City, took a gamble and signed with the Diamondbacks over the 2000 off-season. The move paid off as Grace prepared to face Rivera in the top of the ninth inning in the seventh game of the World Series. Rivera's first pitch was up and inside; then Grace looked at Rivera's second offering and lined it into center field. After Grace reached first, he was replaced by outfielder David Dellucci. Catcher Damian Miller was sent up to do the obvious: bunt. And on an 0–1 pitch, Miller laid one down.

Rivera jumped off the mound and corralled the ball. Dellucci, running, was far from second, but Rivera's throw pulled Yankees shortstop Derek Jeter off the bag, and Dellucci was safe at second as the ball sailed into center field.

The Diamondbacks now had runners on first and second with no outs and gave their fans hope against the best reliever in baseball.

Jeter, injured earlier, hurt himself on the play, when he twisted his leg as he tried to catch Rivera's relay to second. The next batter, veteran second baseman Jay Bell, was sent up to repeat the obvious. Bell, a good bunter, squared his bat and tried to sacrifice Dellucci to third. On Bell's bunt, Rivera again jumped off the mound, and this time made an accurate throw to Yankee third baseman Scott Brosius to retire Dellucci. But wait — Bell was only halfway down to first and Brosius still had a play on Bell. Brosius, however, made no throw to first baseman Tino Martinez. The Diamondbacks still had men on first and second with only one out instead of two. A few seconds later, Midre Cummings went in to run for Damian Miller at second.

Tony Womack, the hero of the NLCS, was the next batter. After falling behind in the count, Rivera battled back and got two strikes on Womack. However, Womack, also a battler, connected on Rivera's fifth offering and doubled to right field to score Cummings and tie the game at 2–2 with Bell taking third on the play.

Craig Counsell, who scored the winning run to give the 1997 Florida Marlins their championship, was at the plate with runners on second and third. He, like everyone else in Arizona, was probably thinking the same thing: repeat his heroics by driving one up the middle to score a run. Rivera got one strike on Counsell, but on the next pitch he hit Counsell to load the bases. Rivera now had to retire two men to give his team a chance to win the World Series in extra innings, with the knowledge that Arizona's championship-winning run was 90 feet from home plate.

After Counsell took his place at first, Luis Gonzalez stepped to the plate. Rivera reached back and blew past Gonzalez for strike one, but on Rivera's next offering, Gonzalez connected and blooped a single into center to score Bell who trotted home from third with the winning run. The Arizona Diamondbacks had dethroned the New York Yankees to become the new World Champions. Rivera took the slow walk to the Yankee dugout, something he had not been accustomed to during the last three years. Fans immediately looked at Rivera's blown save that cost the Yankees their championship. Did Rivera lose the World Series? No, it was a team effort. Could Brosius have retired Bell at first? We will never know, but if he had there would have been two outs with a man on second instead of one out with men on first and second, which of course would have dictated a different strategy by Yankees manager Joe Torre. Regardless of Rivera's or Brosius' play, what should be noted is the Yankees' anemic offense in the World Series— .183. The Bronx Bombers bombed at the plate and were bombed by the Diamondbacks in Game 1, 12–2, and in Game 6, 15–2. And if not for the moves of Arizona manager Bob Brenley, who tinkered with his rotation by starting Curt Schilling in Games 4 and 7, both on three days' rest — a daring move — the World Series might have been over in five games.

Nevertheless, Rivera was charged with the loss. The question still remains: can Mariano Rivera come back as he did in 1998 after his blown save in the Division Series? Time will tell. Mariano Rivera is not alone; he is one of a few good, if not excellent, players despite one bad moment.

At one time or another, we, the fans, who have devoted our lives to following our favorite sports teams, have fantasized about being athletes. The thrill of performing in front of thousands of people in stadiums and being watched by millions more on television can bring notoriety, wealth, and adulation. However, there is another side to an athlete — a side that allows the possibility for the athlete to improve his craft for years, and then in one moment, to commit a misplay on the field that tarnishes the record he has amassed throughout his career.

John F. Kennedy wrote *Profiles in Courage*, a book about eight U.S. senators who, during one point in their political careers, acted on principle rather than political expediency, resulting in personal attacks and ostracism from the public and in the media. This work in no way equates the profession of an athlete to the enormous responsibilities of the men in the government. It is, rather, the story of nine baseball players who were sometimes ostracized by the public over one moment during their professional careers. As with the U.S. senators, the ostracism resulted from their doing their jobs. Among them:

Fred Merkle, a young man still in his teens, but destined to be branded a "Bonehead" for doing what many other ball players throughout the years have done.

Ralph Branca, an overpowering right-hander, whose dominance on the mound equaled that of Christy Mathewson, Rube Marquard, Babe Ruth, Bob Feller, and Dwight Gooden, but who will be forever associated with one pitch that delivered one of the most talked about home runs in baseball history.

Donnie Moore, who for years struggled to reach the big leagues, became the savior for his team, and a split second later was wrongly linked to the team's failure to advance to the Fall Classic. He descended into the depths of tragedy.

Bill Buckner, who performed so gallantly on the ball field for years despite being in constant pain. A contact hitter and throwback player, he played for the love of the game, but in one night was consigned to receive all the blame for the Red Sox's failure to win the World Series, even though Boston had another game left.

These players never sought a vote and their actions never affected us socially, politically, or economically — only emotionally.

The purpose of this book is not to dwell on the disappointments of a player's career. It is about the love of the game that each baseball fan feels when rooting for his or her beloved team and what happens when the fan takes the game too seriously, when we blame one ballplayer for the failure of an entire team to win the big game even though that ballplayer gave his heart and soul, blood and tears, for his entire baseball career. Some players are able to go on and have successful careers after giving up a pitch or making an error. Other players are not so lucky.

Out of the many strikeouts and putouts they made, we remember them for only one play or one pitch that resulted in many fans' minds in that ballplayer's day of infamy. Fans forget that baseball is a team sport, with each team consisting of 25 men and a manager. They also forget that the team's performance or the manager's decision could have drastically altered the game such that the ballplayer's day of infamy could have been avoided. Even after the event took place, some teams still had a chance to recover and win the game or championship.

Nevertheless, society continues to blame one person for a team's failure. As the saying goes, "If you can't fire the team, then you fire the manager." Or, "If your team does well and you can't win a championship, then find a scapegoat to blame for the loss." It is easy to blame one person for the loss of a championship; it makes us, as baseball fans, feel better. We can say that since we are not at fault when our team loses we can root for them again. We will feel bad for awhile, but since we did not do the deed, we can rationalize that if it weren't for that player's miscue, our team would have won and everything would have been okay.

First and foremost, each player in this book is a hero on the ballfield. Not for the home runs, base hits, perfect games, or no-hitters thrown. These men are heroes because after each player experienced disappointment on the baseball field, he tried to come back to the game, to show the fans that he was more than a player who had committed an error on the field or a pitcher who had thrown a home run pitch.

Other ballplayers could have been added to this book. For instance, in Game 7 of the 1960 World Series, New York Yankee pitcher Ralph Terry threw the home run pitch to Pittsburgh Pirates second baseman Bill Mazeroski. The Pirates won 10–9, became World Series champs, and gave baseball its first Series-ending home run. Two years later the Yankees again were in the Series, this time against the San Francisco Giants. Ralph Terry again started Game 7 and in the bottom of the ninth, the Yankees were ahead 1–0. The Giants had two men on and two outs when Terry threw a pitch to Willie McCovey, who swung and hit a line drive that looked like a sure base hit that would score two runs to win the Series. But Yankee second baseman Bobby Richardson snagged McCovey's line drive to save the game and give the Yankees the World Series title — sweet redemption for Ralph Terry and the reason he escaped a chapter in this book.

Curt Flood of the St. Louis Cardinals was regarded for years as one of the greatest defensive center fielders in baseball, but in Game 7 of the 1968 World Series against the Detroit Tigers, Flood misplayed a fly ball hit by Jim Northrop. The Tigers scored three runs and won the game and the Series. But a year later, Curt Flood would demonstrate an inordinate amount of courage off the field that had not been seen since the early days of Jackie Robinson. When Curt Flood refused to accept a trade to another team without his consent, he challenged the baseball establishment. His bold stance against baseball led to the revocation of the reserve clause which bound a player to a team forever unless that player was released or traded. Flood suffered financially and emotionally, and prematurely ended his career. Once reviled, he is now a hero. Ask any millionaire athlete. For any ballplayer who has been maligned as a result of one play or pitch, this book is for you.

CHAPTER 1

Fred Merkle

Frederick Charles Merkle became immortalized for one play, but unlike the rest of the players in this book, Merkle never threw a pitch that resulted in a loss or made an error on the field that cost his team a win during or near the post-season. Merkle's immortality came as a result of a hit that should have won a game. Merkle's blown play, or "Merkle's Boner," happened soon after the beginning of the twentieth century. Merkle's name lives on to this day even though there was no radio, television, or Internet to broadcast his mistake.

Merkle's father, Ernst John Karl Merkle, immigrated to the United States from Switzerland at age two to join Merkle's grandfather, Johann Ulrich Merkle, who arrived in America in 1866. After Merkle's grandfather died in 1872, Ernst John moved to Quincy, Illinois, and remained there until age 18, when he moved again, this time to Watertown, Wisconsin. Five years later, Ernst Karl Merkle married Anna Amalia Thielmann on August 4, 1887. The Merkles had four children. Their first child, Frederick Charles, was born on December 20, 1888, in Watertown, Wisconsin. Not long after Fred was born, the Merkles moved to Toledo, Ohio.[1] By the age of 16, Merkle, a big and strong young man, excelled as a pitcher and played football as a halfback. However, he chose baseball and for two years pitched semi-pro ball in Ohio and Indiana.

By 1907 Merkle was playing Class D ball for Tecumseh of the South Michigan League. For a time he played third base until later that season, when he was shifted to cover first base. He attracted the attention of the New York Giants who purchased his rights for $2,500.

Merkle managed to appear in 15 games for the Giants in 1907, batting .255 with 12 hits and 5 RBIs. In 1908 three teams— the New York Giants, Chicago Cubs, and Pittsburgh Pirates— vied for the National League pennant. John McGraw managed the Giants and fielded a team that was armed with pitching ace Christy Mathewson, known as "Big Six" in honor of the horse-drawn fire engines that roamed New York City during that era.[2] Mathewson was off to a good start, winning his first six games, but ran into a dry spell that started when Pittsburgh defeated Mathewson 5–1 on May 13.[3] Mathewson then lost five more games before finally defeating the Brooklyn Superbas (Dodgers) 1–0 on May 29. Though Mathewson found his stride and returned to his dominating form, McGraw used him too many times in 1908. The Giant right-hander would sometimes pitch on three and even two days' rest because McGraw felt he didn't have anyone else he could trust to win ball games. Mathewson would pitch on his regular scheduled day, and then he would pitch the next day if he was needed. Out of the 56 games Mathewson appeared in, he made 44 starts and completed 36 of them for a 37–11 record and a 1.43 ERA. However, Mathewson's many starts would cost the Giants later in the season.

The Cubs, winners of the previous two National League pennants, were still a formidable team. Their manager, first baseman Frank Chance from the famed infield that included second baseman Johnny Evers and shortstop Joe Tinker, also sported a pitching ace of his own: Mordecai "Three Finger" Brown, who would go 29–9 in 1908.

The Pirates were led by outfielder manager Fred Clarke. Pittsburgh matched the other contenders with pitching aces Nicholas Maddox, who went 23–8, and Vic Willis, who went 23–11. Clarke fielded a team that included famed slugging shortstop Honus Wagner, who would amass 201 hits and 109 RBIs and bat .354 in 1908. But Wagner, injured in 1907, announced that he would retire in 1908. It was speculated that Wagner's recent marriage was the basis for his retirement.[4] Wagner's retirement was short lived as National League President Frank Pulliam met with the Pirates shortstop and convinced him to come back for one more season.[5] Wagner relented and signed a one-year deal to play baseball in 1908. Ironically, with Wagner back in the lineup, the Pirates, who had won a few games during Wagner's absence, went on a losing streak and by the end of April, the Cubs led the Pirates by one game and the Giants by a game and a half.

The year 1908 marked Frank Pulliam's fifth year as president of the National League. A life-long bachelor who once served in the Kentucky legislature, Pulliam befriended Barney Dreyfuss, the owner of the baseball team in Louisville, Kentucky, who offered Pulliam a position with his ball club.[6] When Dreyfuss moved his team to Pittsburgh, Pulliam went with Dreyfuss. Although Pulliam was a shy and sensitive man, he became president of the National League as a result of a compromise between two other candidates: Nicholas Young, the current president, and Albert Spalding, the sports entrepreneur. Despite its prestige, Pulliam's tenure as president of the league was tenuous at best. His mettle was tested from the beginning as he clashed with John McGraw, whom Pulliam suspended after he hurled insults towards umpires, especially Bob Emslie, whom McGraw named "Blind Bob."

But it was McGraw's next act of defiance that drew Pulliam's ire.[7] In 1904, the New York Giants and Boston Red Sox each won the pennant in their respective leagues. McGraw, backed by Giants owner John T. Brush, refused to play in the World Series. Instead, the Giants raised a flag in Polo Grounds that read "1904 World Champions." Although Pulliam could not compel the Giants to play in the World Series in 1904, the Fall Classic returned the following year.

Yet 1905 did not dim the enmity between McGraw and Pulliam, as Pulliam suspended McGraw again. But the suspension was never enforced as McGraw went to court and won an injunction, thereby voiding the suspension. This festering antagonism that existed between both men reached its zenith in 1908. Throughout the summer of 1908, the Giants, Cubs, and Pirates distanced themselves from the rest of the league, as all three teams remained in either first, second or third place.[8] Merkle would only appear in 38 games, mostly as a pinch hitter and runner, and he had even fewer at bats than the year before. He ended the 1908 season at .268 with 11 hits, 1 home run, and 7 RBIs.

The stage for the controversial game involving Fred Merkle was set in a contest between the Pirates and Cubs on September 4. This incident would ultimately seal Merkle's and the Giants' fates three weeks later.[9] The Cubs came to Pittsburgh to play a three game series with the Pirates. Willis was chosen to stop the Cubs and "Three Finger" Brown, who had already defeated Pittsburgh four times that season. Both Willis and Brown were up to the task, for in the bottom of the tenth, the Pirates and Cubs were still knotted at 0–0. Pirate manager Fred Clarke started the inning with a single, and Tom Leach came up and sacrificed Clarke to second. Honus Wagner, the famed shortstop, singled to move Clarke to third. Pittsburgh's rally seemed to ruffle Brown, as he hit the next batter, Warren Gill, to load the bases. With the bases full of Bucs, Brown gathered himself and fanned Ed Abbaticchio for the second out, but Owen Wilson stepped up to the plate and hit Brown's first offering into center field. Clarke raced home with the apparent winning run, but as Gill headed for second base, he watched the ball go into center field, stopped a few feet short of the bag, and headed back to the clubhouse.

Chicago Cub centerfielder Jimmy Slagle saw Gill's shenanigans at second and threw the ball back to second baseman Johnny Evers who then stepped on the bag. Evers cited rule 5.9 which called a person out for not touching second after the winning run had crossed home plate on a base hit. But Evers' protest fell on deaf ears as Hank O'Day, the sole umpire of the game, informed Evers that he did not see the play at second base. He refused to reverse the call but Evers' tantrum had made its mark on O'Day. Although O'Day didn't reverse the call, he nevertheless promised Evers that if such a play happened again, he would enforce rule 5.9. The Cubs protested the game to National League president Pulliam who also upheld the score 1–0 to the Pittsburgh Pirates.

Regardless of the loss, the Cubs played good baseball in September, winning 17 out of 23 games before arriving at the Polo Grounds for a crucial four game series with the Giants set to begin on September 22. The Giants also played well in September, winning 18 out of 21 games and leading the Cubs by six percentage points. The Giants' record stood at 87–50, followed by the Cubs' at 90–53, and the Pirates' with an 88–54 record. Chicago swept the doubleheader from New York that day and now led the Giants by percentage points.

Scene: The Polo Grounds III

The Giants, synonymous with professional baseball since 1883, were originally called the New York Gothams. John B. Day and Frank Mutrie, co-owners of the original New York Metropolitans, formed the Gothams. The Gothams played their ball games at 110th between Fifth and Sixth avenues. Polo was actually played on this site by wealthy New Yorkers; thus, the Polo Grounds was born.

When Mutrie became the manager of the Gothams, he stocked the team with members of the Metropolitans. This fortuitous combination enabled the Gothams to win 85 out of 112 ball games. One day after the Gothams soundly defeated the Philadelphia Phillies, Mutrie was so ecstatic about the team's dominant play that he cried, "My big fellows! My Giants!"[10] And the team was officially called the New York Giants in 1885. The good times did not last, however, as the Giants lost their home when the City of New York booted the Giants from 110th and Fifth Avenue in 1889.

The Giants played some of their home games in New Jersey and Staten Island before the team settled on 155th–157th streets at the southern section called Coogan's Hollow, named after James J. Coogan, Manhattan's first borough president, who died in 1890. Although the ballpark was called Manhattan Park, the Giants renamed it the Polo Grounds for a second time (Polo Grounds II), even though Polo was never played at Coogan's Hollow. The Giants shared the field with the Player's League, who fielded

Fred Merkle: His failure to touch second base during a crucial game at the end of the 1908 season earned him the label "Bonehead." Although Merkle established a fine career, Bonehead stuck with him for the rest of his life. (Photograph courtesy of the National Baseball Hall of Fame Library, Cooperstown, N.Y.)

their team at the northern section of Coogan's Hollow called Brotherhood Park. After the Players League folded a year later in 1891, the Giants took over Brotherhood Park and renamed it the Polo Grounds III.

The Polo Grounds III was constructed of concrete and wood. Seating capacity was around 16,000, but if fans could not purchase a ticket, they could still view the games behind a rope in center field which held about 5,000 spectators, or on top of a cliff named Coogan's Bluff.

About 25,000 fans poured into the Polo Grounds on the next afternoon, September 23.[11] The game began like any other. Coincidentally, Hank O'Day, who had umpired the controversial game between the Cubs and Pirates three weeks before, was umpiring today's game between the Cubs and Giants. This time O'Day would have help from Bob Emslie, who would umpire the other bases.[12] McGraw chose Mathewson to face the Cubs. Chance countered with Jack Pfiester (full name Pfiestenberger), who was known as "the Giant Killer." Pfiester was not a good pitcher, but he seemed to have the Giants' number and turned into Cy Young whenever he faced the New Yorkers. True to form, Pfiester kept the Giants at bay. Meanwhile, Mathewson was up to the task, matching Pfiester zero for zero through four innings.

But in the top of the fifth, Chicago drew first blood. Tinker hit a ball that got past Giants rightfielder Mike Donlin, who had moved out of position. Tinker ran around the bases and by the time Giants center fielder Cy Seymour came up with the ball, Tinker had scored and the Cubs led 1–0.

The Giants countered in the bottom of the sixth. Herzog came up to the plate and hit the ball to Harry Steinfeldt at third. Steinfeldt fielded the ball, but made a wild throw that sailed past Chance at first and allowed Herzog to end up at second. Next, Bresnahan successfully sacrificed Herzog to third and Donlin made up for his fielding blunder as he singled home Herzog to tie the score at 1–1. After the Giants tied the game, both pitchers settled down and prevented any more scoring.

As New York was about the bat in the bottom of the ninth, a loud cheer swept through the Polo Grounds. Devlin responded to the fans' catcalls with a single to center field. The next batter, left fielder Moose McCormick, failed to sacrifice Devlin to second, and replaced Devlin at first.

Normally, Fred Tenney would have been the next batter, but Tenney woke up with a backache that morning and could not play. It was the first time that Tenney was out of the lineup all year. His replacement was 19-year-old Fred Merkle. Pfiester had fanned Merkle thrice that day, but on his fourth trip to the plate, with one out, Merkle hit a line drive that barely got by Chance at first. As the ball rattled along the right field foul line, the crowd exhorted McCormick on, who wound up at third. With runners on the corners, up came shortstop Al Bridwell, who wasted no time and singled up the middle past Pfiester. Emslie, umpiring at second base, dove out of the way, and managed to elude the ball.

As for Merkle, he was rounding first when McCormick crossed home plate with the apparent winning run. Suddenly Giants fans streamed onto the field to celebrate what appeared to be a 2–1 New York win. With the fans now on the field, Merkle, just short of second, stopped in mid-stride, turned around, and went to the Giants' clubhouse.

Merkle did what many other players—including Fred Clarke just three weeks before—had done. As the winning run crossed home plate on a base hit, the runner approaching second stopped short of the bag and returned to the clubhouse.

Johnny Evers, as he did in Pittsburgh three weeks before, searched for the ball to nullify the Giants' second run. Evers quickly informed Cubs centerfielder Art Hoffman to get the ball. Hoffman scrambled after it and got it despite the many fans that had descended onto the playing field, and threw the ball back to Evers. His relay sailed past Evers to Iron Man McGinnity, the Giants pitcher who also coached third base that day. He sensed something was wrong and grabbed the ball. Tinker then jumped on McGinnity's back and fought for the ball, but McGinnity freed himself and threw the ball into the left field stands.

In a mystery that remains to this day, Evers suddenly turned up with the ball on second.[13] If the ball was thrown into the left field stands, how could Evers get the ball back into the infield with the multitude of Giants fans that now occupied the field?

After McGinnity threw the ball in the left field grandstands, a Cub player (Floyd) Rube (Kid) Kroh, allegedly found the ball.[14] But where? No one knew for sure, but Kroh allegedly pried the ball from a fan in the stands and relayed the ball back to Tinkers who then relayed it to Evers.

Another version is that Evers got a ball from a ball bag. The Cubs second baseman began arguing his case with Emslie, but Emslie confessed that he ducked out of the way of Bridwell's single to avoid being hit by the ball and that he never saw the Merkle play at second. But Hank O'Day, the umpire who had ruled against the Cubs the last time on the same play, claimed he saw the incident and this time upheld rule 5.9 and called Merkle out for not touching second.

Thus, the score was still tied at 1–1. However, with the crowd celebrating what many fans thought was a Giants win, O'Day decided that the game could not go on, called it over due to the impending darkness and headed out of sight.

Slowly, word got to McGraw that Merkle was out because he had not touched second. McGraw was beside himself, for in his mind his Giants were being denied a win because of a cheap technicality. If Merkle was out, McGraw wondered, then why didn't Umpire O'Day wait until the crowd had dispersed and continue the game?

McGraw was sure that Pulliam would award the game to the Giants, but McGraw, who had feuded with Pulliam over the years, including in July of that season when the Giants' manager refused to play a game because he wanted to rest his players, lost the argument that night when Pulliam met O'Day in his downtown Manhattan office and sided with the umpire that Merkle was out at second. The game was still tied at 1–1.[15] The Giants and Cubs were scheduled to play each other the next day, and the disputed game could have gone into the top of the tenth tied at 1–1.

Not taking anything for granted, the Cubs arrived at one o'clock the next day to continue the tied ball game. The Giants, on the other hand, did not reciprocate. Manager Frank Chance thought that the Cubs should win on account that the Giants had forfeited the game. But New York was spared from the forfeiture when the umpires did not show up for the game at one o'clock either.

At the regular scheduled game, the Giants did not let yesterday's controversial defeat affect them. They beat the Cubs 5–4 to maintain their lead over Chicago by a few percentage points.

The Giants did not win many games after that. A doubleheader loss to the Cincinnati Reds, coupled with losing three times to Harry Coveleski of the lowly Philadelphia Phillies within a week, plunged the Giants into third place.[16] In the meantime, the Cubs won 4 out of the next 5 games to reclaim first place.

The Pirates would not go away, and swept the Dodgers and the Cardinals on October 2 to lead the Giants by a half game and Chicago by one full game. A day after the Pirates' doubleheader win, National League president Pulliam began hearing the arguments concerning the Merkle play on September 23. The matter was referred to the National League Board of Directors. Garry Herrmann of Cincinnati, Charles Ebbets of Brooklyn, and George B. Dovey of Boston headed the Board.

The Pirates then traveled to Chicago to play the Cubs for their last series of the season. The Pirates led the Cubs by .003 percentage points, but on October 4, the Cubs beat the Pirates 5–2 to virtually knock them out of the pennant race.[17] The Cubs tied the Giants for the pennant with the win. Pittsburgh's only hope hinged on the Board reversing the Merkle game, and the Boston Braves sweeping the last three games against the Giants.

Unfortunately for Pittsburgh, the Giants dashed the Pirates' hopes with a win over the Braves. New York won their two remaining games to end the last day of the season tied with the Cubs at 98–55. A day later, the

Board of Directors decided that the Merkle game would stand as a tie ball-game. Accordingly, if the two teams were deadlocked at the end of the season, the September 23 game would be replayed on October 8.

The tiebreaker was held to decide the winner of the National League pennant. Many Giants fans were already at the Polo Grounds, having camped outside the ball field earlier in the day. Fans who could not purchase a ticket that day still had the option to view today's contest at Coogan's Bluff. The rambunctious crowd was so uncontrollable that they managed to break down a section of the fence and push themselves in. In all, 26,000–40,000 plus fans witnessed the tie-breaking game.[18]

McGraw turned to Mathewson to pitch this important game against the Cubs; however, Mathewson had pitched nearly 400 innings over the course of the season and he was tired. But McGraw felt that he had to start his best pitcher to win this game. Mathewson assured McGraw that despite his tired arm, he would go as far as he could. Chance countered with "Giant Killer" Pfiester, but "Three-Finger" Brown was ready to relieve Pfiester if he were scored upon in the early innings.

Merkle, still affected by his base running mistake, did not play in the game.[19]

The Cubs did not score in the first inning, but New York did. In the bottom of the first, Pfiester hit Tenney in the leg, and walked the next batter, Buck Herzog, which moved Tenney to second. With two on and nobody out, the Giants had a chance to put the Cubs away in the first inning, but New York failed to capitalize as Pfiester struck out the next batter, Giants catcher Roger Bresnahan. Herzog wandered off first and was nailed by Cubs catcher John Kling.

Although Donlin doubled off Pfiester to score Tenny from second and Pfiester walked the next batter Seymour, Chance had seen enough. The Cubs' manager went to the pitching mound and replaced Pfiester with "Three-Finger" Brown.

Normally, the Giants could hit Brown. But on this day, he reverted back to his dominating form, retired the next batter, and got out of the inning with the Giants ahead only 1–0.

The Cubs struck back in the top of the third. When Tinker stepped to the plate, Mathewson signaled to Cy Seymour, who was playing in shallow centerfield, to move deeper in the outfield. Seymour refused. As fate would have it, Tinker lined Mathewson's pitch into deep center field. Had Seymour heeded Mathewson's warning, he might have caught Tinker's fly ball. Instead, Seymour made a desperate, futile attempt, and the ball sailed over his head. By the time Seymour came up with the ball, Tinker wound up with a triple. Kling came up and singled in Tinker to tie the game at

1–1. Brown sacrificed Kling to second. Mathewson looked like he would get out the inning when Jimmy Sheckard flied out for the second out, but he walked Evers and surrendered doubles to outfielder Wildfire Schulte and Chance. When the inning was over, the Cubs led 4–1.

The Giants made one last attempt to win the pennant. In the bottom of the seventh, Devlin and Moose McCormick both singled. Merkle, infamous on September 23, reached on Three Finger Brown with a walk. Giants fans began cheering to spur on the team.

With nobody out and the bases full of Giants, Mathewson, a good hitter, was scheduled to bat. Yet, in one of the few times he would do so while managing the Giants, McGraw took Mathewson out of the lineup for pinch-hitter Larry Doyle. Although Doyle was injured, he still tried to hit for Mathewson. McGraw probably wished he had left Mathewson to hit for himself as Brown easily retired Doyle. Despite Tenney's sacrifice fly to score Devlin from third, Brown induced Herzog to ground out to short and end the rally. The Giants had cut the Cubs' lead in half; but the comeback as well as the pennant was over.

Brown held on and Chicago won the game 4–2. For the third straight year, they were National League Champions.

The Cubs raced for their lives as a mob of Giants fans ran on the field. Some of the Cub players were even assaulted by the Giants fans and the Cubs needed a police escort to get back to their hotel.

The Cubs went on to win the World Series against Ty Cobb's Detroit Tigers. But perhaps turn about is fair play. Evers' questionable force-out of Merkle has been costly for the Chicago Cubs ever since. Chicago has appeared in seven World Series since 1908, and has lost them all. The first loss was to the Philadelphia A's in 1910, and the Cubs would lose to the A's again in 1929. The Cubs then lost to the Red Sox in 1918. Chicago returned to the Fall Classic in 1932, but the team lost that World Series to the Yankees, and would do so again in 1938. Finally, Chicago would lose two more World Series to the Detroit Tigers in 1935 and 1945. Since then, the Cubs have not appeared in the Fall Classic. The team has appeared in the postseason by winning the National League Eastern Division in 1984 and 1989 and the Wild Card in 1998.

John McGraw, to his credit, never blamed Fred Merkle for costing the Giants the National League pennant in 1908. For the rest of his life, McGraw believed that the 1908 pennant was stolen from him. McGraw even raised Merkle's salary and convinced him to stay on the team when he wanted out of baseball.

But McGraw's generosity did little to assuage Merkle during the off season as he lost weight and sank into a deep depression.[20] When he returned the next season, Giants fans did not let him forget the incident either. They labeled Merkle "Bonehead," and joked, "So long, Fred, don't forget to touch second."

Despite the jeers that greeted him when he stepped up to the plate, Merkle became the starting first baseman for the Giants the following year. In 144 games, Merkle collected 148 hits, 4 home runs, and 70 RBI's.

Merkle's best year was 1912 when he appeared in 129 games, batted .309, and again collected 148 hits, 11 home runs and 84 RBI's. Merkle did this in the dead ball era, a period when home runs were as common as Halley's Comet.

Merkle got to play in the World Series when the Giants won three straight pennants from 1911 to 1913, but the Giants never won in those years, losing to the Philadelphia A's in 1911 and 1913 and to the Boston Red Sox in 1912. In 1916, Merkle was traded to the Brooklyn Dodgers for catcher Lew McCartey.[21] That year, Brooklyn won its first pennant and misfortune followed Merkle there as the Dodgers lost the Series to the Red Sox and a pitcher named Babe Ruth.

The next year Merkle was sold to the Cubs for $3,500, and when Chicago won the pennant in 1918, it looked like Merkle, playing in his fifth Series in six years, would finally win a championship.[22] But as we all know, Ruth and the Sox beat the Cubs, and Merkle was on the losing side again. After the 1920 season Merkle left the Cubs and played four years at first base for Rochester in the International League.[23] In 1925, Yankee manager Miller Huggins brought Merkle back to the major leagues to serve as a player-coach. In seven games he was used as a right-handed pinch-hitter. Yet Merkle still could not shake his past. While he was coaching an exhibition game, a fan yelled "Bonehead!" Merkle gritted his teeth, but never responded to the insult. Huggins, on the other hand, went to Merkle's defense and chastised the fan. The next year, Merkle's one at bat qualified him to be on the Yankees' roster in the World Series. Merkle's bad luck continued unabated as the Yankees lost the series to the Cardinals. In 1927, he was dropped as a coach for Art Fletcher, a former teammate of Merkle's with the Giants.[24] That year the Yankees swept the Pirates in the World Series. As for Merkle, he signed on to manage the Reading Internationals in the winter of 1927. However, he lasted only four months as the manager — a bad team and the inability to communicate with his players led to Merkle's dismissal.

Two years later, he was managing the Class D team in Daytona-Ormond when one of his players called him "Bonehead." Merkle left the field and never managed again. Merkle, married with two daughters, settled in Ormond, Florida. He used his losing share in World Series games to invest in real estate. Unfortunately, that venture was short-lived as the Depression forced many entrepreneurs to foreclose, and Merkle lost most of his money in real estate. He managed to obtain work with the WPA on a county bridge project and also found work as a physical instructor.[25] Merkle avoided many of his baseball contemporaries and would not grant interviews to any sportswriters. He faulted the sportswriters for hyping the incident that led people to label him "Bonehead."

Merkle's assessment is correct, for the day after the controversial game on September 23, this article appeared in the New York Times: "Censurable stupidity on the part of player Merkle in yesterday's game at the Polo Grounds between the Giants and Chicago placed New York team's chances of winning the pennant in jeopardy. His unusual conduct in the final inning of a game perhaps deprived New York of a victory that would have been unquestionable had he not committed a breach in baseball play that resulted in Umpire O'Day declaring the game a tie."[26] The Times article also said that it was Manager Chance who seized the opportunity to nullify the run. As we all now know, it was Johnny Evers who was the real person who should be given some credit for knowing the rule book.

Merkle spent his days at the Ormond Oaks Club playing bridge and golf. Even in his retirement, Merkle could not escape the unfair moniker that was applied to him. One day during the 1930s, Merkle and his family were attending church services in Florida when a visiting minister announced to the parishioners that he was from Toledo—the hometown of the "Bonehead Merkle." Merkle rose with his family and left the church.[27] But there were decent people in Florida who were sympathetic to Fred Merkle. A local editor arranged an agreement with the Daytona Beach sportswriters not to mention Merkle's mistake in their columns.[28] More importantly, Merkle's fortunes began to change after World War II when he became a partner in a firm that manufactured fishing equipment.[29]

In 1949, the Brooklyn Dodgers met the New York Yankees in the World Series. Members of the 1916 World Series team were invited to the first game of the Series. Everyone showed up except Merkle. Dodger announcer Red Barber was doing a story on the team and went to Florida to see Merkle. Merkle told Barber that he and his family were hurt by the many people who still referred to him as "Bonehead." Barber finished his story and sent it to Merkle. Barber did not hear from Merkle until the next year at a New York Giants Old-Timers game. At the game, Merkle, in a brand new suit, accompanied by his daughters, saw Red Barber and thanked him for the column that informed readers that Merkle wasn't at fault for costing the Giants the pennant in 1908.[30]

Despite a few jeers from the fans calling him "Bonehead," Merkle was received warmly by the majority of the 35,073 Giants fans at the Old-Timers game. He enjoyed himself immensely that day as he reminisced with old teammates such as Larry Doyle. Merkle was heard to have said, "It makes a man feel good to hear such cheers after all these years. I don't think I'll forget. I expected so much worse."[31]

Merkle's seclusion was over as he began to travel more and more to other baseball events such as the Daytona Beach Islanders Class D baseball team's games of the Florida State League. Merkle then became an instructor, tutoring youngsters on the fundamentals of baseball. After Merkle finished his first day as an instructor, he was moved to tears.

And the good times began to roll on, but time was running out on Fred Merkle. On January 14, 1956, Merkle made his last public appearance at an old-timers game for the March of Dimes. Riding in an open automobile, he was graciously received by all of the fans. Afterwards, Merkle sat down and again reminisced with other old-time baseball players who were present for the occasion.[32]

Six weeks later, on March 2, 1956, Merkle died of natural causes, though many people believed that Merkle died prematurely on September 23, 1908. The play was a bum rap, for none of Merkle's contemporaries who were on first base ever bothered to touch second if a runner had crossed the plate with the winning run.

Fred Merkle is a hero and he should be given credit for coming back the following year after the controversial play in 1908 and for taking all that abuse from the sportswriters and fans who continued to call him "Bonehead" during his career and after his playing days. In his 14 full seasons in the major leagues, Merkle's lifetime .273 average is comparable to the lifetime averages of such Hall of Fame shortstops as Pee Wee Reese (.269) and Phil Rizzuto (.273).

Merkle is still remembered to this day for one play and though rule 5.9 no longer exists, "Merkle's Boner" is still told within the annals of the game. Looking back on the episode, if umpire O'Day had not been intimidated by Johnny Evers to enforce a rule that many ball players had broken, Merkle's name would not have lived on.

National League president Pulliam could have ordered the disputed game to continue the next day, or to count the run even though the rule was on the books, since the rule was not enforced during the disputed game between the Pirates and Cubs on September 3. Thus, two different rules were allowed within a span of three weeks that left devastating consequences on the 1908 pennant race and on the life of Fred Merkle.

Seventy-five years later, former American League president Lee McPhail did what Pulliam should have done. On July 24, 1983, George

Brett hit a two run home run off of Yankees reliever Rich "Goose" Gossage in the top of the ninth. The Royals led New York 5–4, or so they thought. Yankee manager Billy Martin protested the amount of pine tar on Brett's bat, claiming that it exceeded 18 inches, which was against the rules.

The umpires measured Brett's bat on the back of home plate which measured 18 inches. The amount of pine tar exceeded the width of home plate and the umpires ruled that Brett was out. Brett went ballistic and the Yankees won the game 4–3.

However, after a national outcry, McPhail over-ruled the umpires. Brett's home run stood and the Royals again led 5–4. New York and Kansas City finally finished the game on August 18, 1983, when both teams had an off day in the schedule. The Yankees went down in the bottom of the ninth and the Royals finally won the game 5–4.

The Merkle incident would also take its toll on Frank Pulliam, who would be criticized in the press for his indecision. Pulliam suffered a nervous breakdown before committing suicide a year later.

The Giants themselves began to break down, as New York lost key games during the stretch run after September 25 to allow the Chicago Cubs to tie them. If they had won at least one of those games against Coveleski, who only managed one victory prior to facing the Giants, Fred Merkle's failure to touch second base would have been an afterthought.

And finally, to this day, many people wonder how Johnny Evers actually came up with the ball that Al Bridwell hit to score the winning run when Iron Man McGinnity threw the ball into the left field stands.

CHAPTER 2

Fred Snodgrass

Our next story also involves the New York Giants, but this time, the player is Fred Snodgrass. In 1849, Larkin and Amelia Snodgrass, Fred's grandparents, migrated to Ventura, California, from Kentucky.[1] Their third son, Andrew Snodgrass, grew up in Ventura, and eventually became sheriff of the town. Later, Andrew married Addie Elizabeth McCoy, who gave birth to their son Fred Snodgrass, born on December 19, 1887, in Ventura, California. As a boy, he traveled with his mother, who owned and operated a series of hotels in Los Angeles. It was in Los Angeles that young Fred Snodgrass spent his formative years playing sandlot baseball at Spring Street School. Fred and his friends would play baseball with a tennis ball and substitute their fists for baseball bats. Tennis balls were used because baseballs were priced at ten cents—a princely sum in those days—and Fred and his friends would hang out at Shutes Park catching foul balls, so they could use real balls for their games. Fred attended Los Angeles High School and starred on the baseball team. After graduating Snodgrass entered St. Vincent's College, now Loyola Marymount College, on a baseball scholarship where, in 1905, the team won the Inter-Collegiate Championship.[2]

The St. Vincent's College baseball team got to train with the New York Giants in three exhibition baseball games during spring training. John McGraw, the New York Giants manager, umpired the games between the two teams.

Snodgrass' days as a student at St. Vincent's College were numbered. While still a student he was asked to try out for a professional baseball team in Los Angeles. Though he played only one game as a catcher on the professional team, Snodgrass was classified as a professional ball player; thus he became ineligible to play with St. Vincent's College. A year later, he quit school and went to work for a moving company. But Snodgrass was not through playing baseball.

In February 1908, John McGraw went to Los Angeles, California, to attend the horse races. McGraw was visiting a mutual friend in Los Angeles when he inquired about Fred Snodgrass, whom McGraw remembered from the game two years before.[3]

McGraw could not forget Snodgrass, since both men quarreled during the game. Snodgrass' bravado endeared him to McGraw, who saw a little of himself in Snodgrass. Besides Snodgrass' gumption, McGraw was also impressed with his catching skills for St. Vincent's College.

Word got back to Snodgrass that McGraw was looking for him, and later both men met at the hotel where McGraw resided. At the meeting, McGraw asked Snodgrass if he still wanted to play ball. Snodgrass, who was playing semi-pro ball on Sundays for the Hoegee Flags, told McGraw that he was interested in playing ball, but that the Three-I League in Peoria, Illinois, had already offered him a contract.

McGraw then produced a contract to play for the Giants for $150 a month and asked Snodgrass to mull over his offer. Snodgrass decided to accept McGraw's offer, signed with the Giants, and went with the team to Marlin, Texas, for spring training.[4]

Snodgrass made his major league debut for the New York Giants on June 13, 1908. Though he appeared in only six games that year, Snodgrass, along with the rest of the Giants, witnessed the Merkle incident on September 23.

Snodgrass played thirty games in 1909 and spent most of the year on the bench. The New York Giants tailed off that year, finishing the 1909 season in third place, eighteen and a half games behind the Pittsburgh Pirates who won the pennant that year. The highlight of the 1909 World Series was the matchup between Honus Wagner of the Pirates and Ty Cobb of the Detroit Tigers, but it was Wagner's Pirates who bested Cobb's Tigers in seven games.

In 1910, Snodgrass was still a third-string catcher when McGraw approached him about playing the outfield. Snodgrass, tired of riding the bench, jumped at the opportunity and batted .321 with 127 hits, 44 RBIs and 2 home runs.

The Cubs won the pennant in 1910, but they lost the World Series to the Philadelphia Athletics. The following year the Giants won the pennant. They, too, would lose the World Series to the Athletics. During this time Snodgrass became a full time player with the Giants and batted .294 with 154 hits and 77 RBIs.

The Giants of 1912 were still a formidable team. Rube Marquard and Mathewson each won 26 and 23 games, respectively. The big surprise came from rookie Jeff Tesreau, who won 17 games and led the league with a 1.96

ERA. First baseman Fred Merkle, second baseman Larry Doyle, and catcher Chief Myers (a Cahuilla Native American), all hit over .300 to power the Giants' offense.

The Giants took over first place in mid–May and although they faltered late in the season, they managed to hold off a last minute charge by the Chicago Cubs and won the pennant with a 103–49 record.

Their opponents were the Boston Red Sox, who won the pennant with a 105–47 record. Boston was led by player-manager Jake Stahl. Stahl fielded a lineup that included Smokey Joe Wood who won 34 games that year.

Wood was joined in the rotation by 20 game winners rookie Hugh Bedient and Buck O'Brian. Boston also fielded a lineup that included Duffy Lewis in left field, Harry Hopper in right field and Tris Speaker in center field, who batted .383 that year with 222 hits. Their faithful fans were called "The Royal Rooters," and they were led by Ed "Nuff Ced" McGreavey.

The World Series began in New York on October 8. The Series would alternate between ballparks, so games 1, 3, 5, and 7 would take place at the Polo Grounds and games 2, 4, and 6 would take place at Fenway Park. In Game 1, Wood defeated Tesreau and the Giants 4–2.

Many people were surprised that McCraw did not start Mathewson in Game 1. Instead, Mathewson started in Game 2 at Fenway Park. Boston mayor John F. Fitzgerald, grandfather of John F. Kennedy, threw out the first ball of the game.[5] After seven innings the Giants trailed the Red Sox 4–2, but in the top of the eighth, New York scored three runs to take a 5–4 lead. But that lead was short-lived as Boston tied the score on Art Fletcher's error, his third of the game and New York's fifth overall.[6] The Giants regained the lead in the ninth, but lost it when Beals Becker, substituting for Snodgrass in center field, misread a fly ball hit by Tris Speaker.

Speaker wound up on third and scored when Art Wilson, substituting for Giants catcher Chief Myers, could not handle the relay at home. Thus, the game was tied again at 6–6.

Both teams failed to score in the tenth inning and in the eleventh, umpire Silk O'Loughlin decided to call the game a tie on account of darkness. The next game would be replayed the next afternoon at Fenway Park.

In Game 3, Marquard defeated Boston starter Bucky O'Brian 2–1 to tie the series at a game apiece. The play of the game occurred in the bottom of the ninth with New York holding a 2–1 lead. Boston had a scoring threat with men on first and second with two outs when Giants rightfielder Josh Devore made a game-saving catch off the bat of Boston catcher Forest Cady. Boston rebounded to win the next two games.

In Game 4 held at the Polo Grounds, Wood struck out eight Giants, walked none, and defeated Tesreau again, this time by the score of 3–1. In

Game 5 held at Fenway Park, Mathewson allowed five hits that day; unfortunately, two of those hits were back-to-back triples in the bottom of the third by Harry Hooper and Steve Yerkes, which, along with Larry Doyle's error, gave the Red Sox all the runs they would need as Bedient tossed a three hitter and edged Mathewson 2–1. With these two wins, Boston led New York in the Series three games to one. In Game 6, Marquard rescued the Giants at the Polo Grounds as New York broke the game open with a five-run first inning outburst. Boston only managed two runs off of Marquard, who held on and won the game 5–2.

Wood was scheduled to face Tesreau for the third time in the Series. Boston fans were confident that Wood could wrap up the Series with a win. But, before Wood could start the game, the Royal Rooters were attempting to take their usual seats. The Boston front office did not plan on a tied contest in Game 2, and the Royal Rooters were given their pavilion seats for only three games. The pavilion seats for this game were available to anyone on a first come, first served basis. The Rooters, synonymous with Boston baseball since 1897, were misled into thinking that their usual seats were automatically reserved for them. The Rooters became indignant and felt slighted when they discovered their seats were occupied, and were asked to leave by the Boston Red Sox. The Rooters would not budge, so the police were called to restore order. The Rooters staged a riot which delayed the game.[7] Wood, who had warmed up before the melee, could not loosen up and his arm stiffened. The Giants took advantage of Wood's ineffectiveness and scored six runs in the top of the first. Boston manager Jake Stahl removed Wood after the first inning. This time, Tesreau went on to defeat the Red Sox 11–4 and the Series was tied at three games apiece. Stahl's managerial move would prove fortuitous the next day.

Since Game 2 ended in a tie, an eighth contest was needed to crown a world champion. Boston won the coin toss and the final game was played at Fenway Park.

Scene: Fenway Park

The American League, which was formed in 1901, consisted of eight teams. The Boston baseball club, a founding member of the league, began its historic run as the Boston Somersets, named after its owner, Charles Somers.[8] The Boston Somersets played their home games at the Huntington Avenue Grounds, which had about 9,000 seats.

The next year, Somers sold the Somersets to Henry Killileu, whose stewardship lasted for two years. In 1904, the team, now known as the Pilgrims, was purchased by General Charles Taylor, who gave the team to his son John.[9] It was John Taylor, who, in 1907, affixed Red Stockings on the players' uniform. Henceforth, the team was called the Red Sox.[10]

By 1910 John Taylor wanted to sell the Red Sox. Taylor knew that a new ballpark would increase the value of the team, so in June of 1911, Taylor desired a new ballpark to be built between Lansdowne and Jersey streets near a swampy area called the Fens. Taylor would again etch his name in baseball lore as he gave the ballpark its famous name when he said, "It's in the Fenway Section, isn't it? Then name it Fenway Park."[11]

Construction began in September of 1911 and was completed seven months later in April of 1912 with the seating capacity around 27,000. Rain washed out the first two games of the 1912 season, but the Red Sox opened their new ballpark by defeating the recently named New York Yankees (formerly the Highlanders) 3–2.

But Fenway Park did not make headlines the next day, for the *Titanic* had sunk after hitting an iceberg on its maiden voyage from Southampton, England, to New York five days earlier. Throughout the week, readers were inundated with news about the *Titanic*.

The Royal Rooters did not show up and cause any havoc for Game 8. Instead, about 1500 Giants fans flocked to Fenway Park to support the National League champs. All told, 17,034 fans witnessed the first extra game in World Series history.[12] Mathewson was chosen to oppose Bedient in the eighth and final game.[13]

The Giants made their bid to win the Series in the top of the third. Josh Devore reached Bedient for a walk and scored on Giants rightfielder Red Murray's double.

New York tried to pad their lead in the fifth when Doyle hit a long drive to right field, but Harry Hooper speared the ball just short of the fence to rob Doyle of a home run. Meanwhile, Mathewson had shut down the Red Sox through the first six innings. With one out in the bottom of the seventh, Stahl blooped a single and Mathewson walked Boston shortstop Heinie Wagner. Fenway Park began rooting for a hit to tie the game. Mathewson momentarily silenced the fans at Fenway as he retired Forrest Cady on a pop out to Fletcher for the second out.

Stahl then sent Olaf (Swede) Henriksen to pinch-hit for Bedient. Mathewson quickly got two strikes on Henriksen, but on the next pitch, Henriksen swung late, yet he managed to slap the ball past Buck Herzog who dove in from third. Stahl scored on the play and the game was tied 1–1. Mathewson prevented any more damage when he retired Hooper on a fly out.

Stahl summoned Wood to the mound to preserve the tie game. This was the first time Wood and Mathewson, two dominant pitchers of their era, faced each other in the Series.

Wood, shellacked by the Giants in the previous day's game, reverted back to his winning form and shut down the New Yorkers in the eighth and ninth innings. Mathewson was equal to the task and shut down the Red Sox in the eighth. However, with one out in the bottom of the ninth, Stahl came up to the plate, tore into a Mathewson fast ball, and nearly hit it out of Fenway Park for a home run. The ball landed near the fence just out of the reach of Murray's glove for a double, but Stahl did not score as Mathewson retired Wagner and Cady to get out of the ninth unscathed.

The game entered the tenth inning and became the first sudden death contest in World Series history. Wood retired Snodgrass for the first out. Then Red Murray came up and bounced a double into the left field stands. Giants fans thought that Murray's hit should count as a home run, which was the rule of the day, but the home run was nullified because both clubs agreed at the start of the Series that if a ball bounced into the stands it would count as a double.

Merkle then followed with a single to score Murray with the go ahead run and the Giants reclaimed the lead 2–1. Wood retired the next batter to keep the Red Sox deficit at one run. When Mathewson took the mound, he needed just three more outs to give the Giants the world championship. For Merkle it would be sweet vindication for his base running mistake four years earlier, but as we have seen, Merkle was never the recipient of good luck.

In the bottom of the tenth, Clyde Engle was the first batter. Mathewson got two quick strikes by Engle and on the next pitch, Engle lofted a harmless fly ball into right-center. Murray, the rightfielder, was near the ball, but the center fielder Snodgrass controlled the traffic in the outfield and yelled, "I got it!" Murray obliged, but Snodgrass did not have it and dropped the ball. Engle, running on the play, ended up at second. Mathewson, irate, stepped off the mound to settle down. He was a bit rattled as Harry Hooper stepped up to the plate and tore into Mathewson's first pitch. Snodgrass shook off his error on the previous play, raced back, and made a tough catch. Engle was so sure that Hooper had gotten a hit that he nearly ran past third and had to scamper back to second to avoid being doubled off.

Despite Snodgrass' brilliant catch, Mathewson did not settle down as he walked the next batter, Steve Yerkes, on four pitches.

The next play would haunt the Giants forever. Tris Speaker came up to bat and on Mathewson's first pitch, Speaker popped up into foul territory along the first base line. Merkle had the easiest chance to make the play and Mathewson also had a chance to catch the ball. Instead, Mathewson

Fred Snodgrass: Errant yes, but wrongly accused of losing the 1912 World Series, as his teammates failed to retire Tris Speaker on an easy pop fly. Speaker would then single to set up the winning run which gave the Red Sox their championship. (Photograph courtesy of the National Baseball Hall of Fame Library, Cooperstown, N.Y.)

called "Chief, Chief!" Myers, who was farther away from ball than either Mathewson or Merkle, lunged for the ball, but could not catch it, and the ball dropped harmlessly in front of Mathewson, Merkle, and Myers.

Some baseball fans wondered if Mathewson acted on instinct by calling on Myers to make the play, or if he mistrusted Merkle because of his failure to touch second in the playoff game in 1908.

Whatever the reason, Speaker took advantage of his new life at the plate and singled in Engle to tie the game at 2–2. Devore, now playing in right field, made a mistake by throwing home, and Yerkes easily pulled up at third. McGraw ordered Mathewson to walk Duffy Lewis to set up the double play to get out of the inning. Up came third baseman Larry Gardner who spoiled McGraw's strategy by jumping all over Mathewson's fast ball and hitting it into deep right field. Devore caught the ball and made a futile attempt to throw out Yerkes, who tagged up from third and scored the winning run. Boston won the game 3–2 and were world champions.

Decades later, Fred Snodgrass spoke about the fateful play.[14] "Now understand, this was the last game; this was the absolute payoff. The Giants had scored their run and all they needed was to hold it. The score: two runs for the Giants, one for Boston. Engle was up batting for Wood. I was in centerfield and we were scared to death that Matty was going to walk him. Engle hit a towering fly. I was really in the territory of Jack Murray, who was playing in right, but as we played it on the Giants, the center[field] got the call. I called for the ball first and Murray yelled, 'Squeeze it, Snod.' Now that was a matter that could have happened one thousand times, one million times. It was a fly ball. Because of overeagerness, or overconfidence, or carelessness, I dropped it. It's something I'll never forget."

McGraw, as he did in Merkle's case, never blamed Snodgrass for losing the Series. He, like everyone else, knew that if Speaker's foul ball had been caught, the game would have gone into the top of the eleventh tied at 2–2. Plus, if Fletcher's three errors in Game 2, along with that of Giants catcher Art Wilson, who failed to hold onto the ball at home plate which allowed the tying run to score and knot the game at 6–6, cost New York a win, the Giants could have won the Series in seven games.

Instead, McGraw raised Snodgrass' salary by a thousand dollars the next year. But the sportswriters were not as understanding of Snodgrass' error, which became known as the "$30,000 Muff." Thirty thousand dollars was the sum that separated the winner's share from the loser's share. The *New York Times* headline the next day read *Sox Champions on Muffed Fly*.[15] *Snodgrass drops easy ball, costing his teammates $29,524.00. Boston winning 3–2.* The paper went on to say, "Write in the pages of World Series baseball history the name of Snodgrass. Write it large and black. Not as a hero;

truly not. Put him rather with Merkle, who was in such a hurry that he gave away a National League championship. Snodgrass was in such a hurry that he gave away a World Championship. It was because of Snodgrass's generous muff of an easy fly in the tenth inning that the decisive game in the World Series went to the Boston Red Sox this afternoon by a score of 3–2, instead to the New York Giants by a score or 2–1."

What was more startling was that the sportswriters brought up Fred Merkle's name in conjunction with Snodgrass', thus keeping Merkle's base running error alive. As the evidence shows, both men were not entirely responsible for losing the pennant or the world championship.

The fans would not forget either. In 1914, the Boston Braves were making their legendary run for the pennant. The Braves were in last place on July 4, then caught fire and staged a remarkable comeback and took over first place on August 25th. But the Braves were not through with New York as both teams exchanged first place throughout September. The pennant race brought out the fans and forced the Braves to abandon their small ballpark at the South End Grounds for the more spacious Fenway Park.

One game that stood out for both teams took place at Fenway Park.[16] New York was trailing the Braves by four runs when the Giants rallied to tie the score. Braves starter George Tyler took out his frustration on Snodgrass by throwing at his head each time he stepped to the plate.

On Snodgrass' fourth trip to the plate, Tyler hit Snodgrass, causing both players to exchange a few unpleasant words. The Boston fans began taunting Snodgrass and Tyler got into the act when he threw the ball in the air and dropped it — a snide reminder of Snodgrass' World Series error two years earlier. The crowd roared with approval, but Snodgrass shot back by thumbing his nose at the fans when he took the field in the bottom of the inning.[17]

The Braves fans would not back down. They taunted Snodgrass again and added insult to injury by pelting him with more food and other debris. Boston mayor James M. Curley got into the act by marching onto the field and demanding Snodgrass' removal from the game. Umpire Bill Klem refused. It should be noted that Snodgrass played a shallow center field and he was the first person to leave Fenway Park when the game was over.

The Braves lost the game, yet they won the war as the team denied the Giants a fourth straight pennant and outdistanced New York by 10½ games.

Ironically, Snodgrass, who was given his unconditional release by the Giants midway through the 1915 season, signed on with the Boston Braves. Snodgrass left the major leagues a year later after his one full season with the Braves and played one year for Vernon of the Pacific Coast League. At the end of the 1917 season, Snodgrass was informed that his salary was to be cut by 50 percent. Snodgrass refused to sign and began a holdout.

The issue was never resolved, so Snodgrass, who liked to say that *he* was the first to hold out over a contract dispute, quit baseball and went back to California to start his farming career.

In eight plus seasons, Snodgrass batted a respectable .275. Snodgrass, like Merkle, played in the dead ball era. In 1920, baseballs were wound tighter, thus home runs became much easier to hit. Nevertheless, Snodgrass was a good ball player during his day. He once commented: "I was never a sensational ball player, but I used my head out there. I used to study the hitters and when a man came to bat, I knew exactly where to play him."[18]

When he died on April 5, 1974, his obituary in the *New York Times* read: "Fred Snodgrass, 86, Dead. Ballplayer Muffed 1912 Fly."[19] But Fred Snodgrass was more than a man who dropped a fly ball. After leaving baseball, he was able to go on with his life and became a stalwart citizen of Oxnard, California. In Oxnard, he became a successful rancher and businessman, and he was the first person to sell electrical appliances in the town. He also served on a number of boards, including the Alta-Mutual Co., Saticoy Water Co., and Ventura Frozen Foods. Later he became the director of the Bank of A. Levy, a position he would hold for forty years. Snodgrass also was heavily involved in the community. He became the mayor and a city councilman of the town. He even brought the Giants to play baseball in Oxnard, which was a big deal to the town in those years. Snodgrass still loved the game, barnstorming with Babe Ruth in Japan. More importantly, Snodgrass never regretted his playing career despite his error in the World Series.

Still, customers and strangers would ask Snodgrass about his error in the 1912 World Series. One day Snodgrass was in a store when he dropped an egg. Someone blurted out, "Dropped one again, Fred?" Despite the remark, Snodgrass was never bitter about that error that created his fame or infamy, depending on one's point of view, for the rest of his life.[20] Snodgrass himself said that if he hadn't dropped the ball in the World Series, no one would remember him. But people did remember him, and until the day he died, Snodgrass received three or four requests per week for his autograph, which he knew was a direct result of his error in the 1912 World Series. Snodgrass, a gentleman to the end, dutifully fulfilled each request.

CHAPTER 3

Mickey Owen

The Giants would play in two more World Series in 1913 and in 1917. America entered World War I in 1917. After the war, the Giants would not return to the series for four more years. The Giants remained a dominant force in baseball during the early twenties and mid-thirties, winning seven pennants and three World Series titles.

During those years, the Giants shared the headlines with their American League counterpart, the New York Yankees. The Yankees, with their new star player, Babe Ruth, faced the Giants in the World Series from 1921 to 1923. The Giants won the World Series in 1921 and 1922 and the Yankees won it in 1923. Like the Giants, the Yankees became a dominant force in baseball during the 1920s and 1930s, thanks to Ruth and men like Lou Gehrig, Waite Hoyt, Lefty Gomez, Joe DiMaggio, Bill Dickey and Tommy Henrich. The Yankees were more successful than the Giants as the Bronx Bombers won eleven pennants and eight World Series.

America also thrived during the 1920s until the stock market crash of 1929 signaled the end of the Roaring Twenties. The Depression soon followed and crippled America as hundreds of thousands of men and women were unemployed. Two things kept the public from thinking so much about the Depression: movies and baseball. Later, Americans were concerned about entering World War II, which had started in September of 1939.

Arnold Malcolm "Mickey" Owen was born on April 4, 1916, in Nixa, Missouri. His father, Horace Owen, a navy seaman, married his mother Gertrude, a school teacher, shortly before he was born.[1] At age seven, the Owenses moved to Los Angeles, California. There was no television and radio was still in its infancy, so Owen and his friends would occupy their time playing baseball in the warm California weather. This love for baseball led Owen to the minor leagues in southern California. It was there that Owen was discovered by Charlie Barrett, who scouted for the St. Louis Cardinals.

In 1935, Owen moved back to Missouri and began his stint in the minor leagues. Owen played for Springfield in the Western Association. A year later, he moved up to Columbus in the American Association.[2] Owen progressed quickly through the minor leagues and joined the St. Louis Cardinals and their famous "Gas House Gang" in 1937. That year Owen appeared in 80 games where he batted .237 with 54 hits, no home runs, and 20 RBIs.

Then, in 1938, Owen's first full season in the major leagues was a productive one, as he batted .267 with 106 hits, 4 home runs, and 54 RBIs. Owen's average slipped a bit during the next two years, and at the end of the 1940 season, he was sold by Cardinal general manager Branch Rickey to the Brooklyn Dodgers for $100,000 and two minor league players, catcher Gus Mancuso and John Pinter.[3]

Baseball, like America, will always remember 1941. Franklin D. Roosevelt was inaugurated for an unprecedented third term as president. Americans were still divided on World War II as Charles Lindbergh, the hero of the first cross-Atlantic flight from New York to Paris in 1927, was involved in the America First Movement to keep the United States out of World War II. On December 7, the Japanese attack on Pearl Harbor ended all the debates and America entered the war the next day.

Before that event took place, baseball witnessed two incomparable feats, which still stand to this day. With the retirement of Lou Gehrig in 1939 due to complications from Amyotrophic Lateral Sclerosis, a disease that cripples the motor skills, Joe DiMaggio, in his sixth year with the Yankees in center field, now carried the team. The first feat took place during the spring and summer of 1941. On May 15, DiMaggio singled off of Edgar Smith of the Chicago White Sox. He kept getting hits for ten, twenty, thirty, and forty straight games.

On July 2, DiMaggio hit a three-run home run to break the all-time hitting streak record of 44 straight games set by Wee Willie Keeler in 1897.

Fifteen days later, Al Smith of the Cleveland Indians induced DiMaggio to hit two hard grounders to Ken Keltner at third base. Keltner fielded the ball cleanly and promptly threw out DiMaggio each time. In the seventh, DiMaggio grounded out to Lou Boudreau at shortstop and the streak was over at 56 games. DiMaggio's hitting streak remains to this day.

The second feat of the 1941 baseball season was Ted Williams' pursuit of .400. Williams, in his third year for the Boston Red Sox in left field, had the highest average which stood slightly above .400 most of the summer. Yet, as the season wound down, Williams' average began to slip. Finally on the last day of the season, his average stood at .3995. Mathematically, it would round up to .400.[4]

Williams had the option to sit out a doubleheader with the Philadelphia A's to protect his .400 average or play and risk losing it. Williams, the greatest hitter to ever play the game, got into uniform and collected six hits in eight at bats and wound up with a .406 average.

The Yankees and Red Sox were at the top of the American League, but the Yankees won 41 games during DiMaggio's hitting streak and won the pennant on September 4th, a full seventeen games over Boston. The Yankee record stood at 101–53.[5] Joe DiMaggio led all Yankees with a .357 average. Joe jolted 193 hits, 39 home runs and 125 RBIs. Leftfielder Charlie Keller batted .298 with 151 hits, 33 home runs, and 122 RBIs and rightfielder Tommy Henrich batted .277 with 149 hits, 31 home runs, and 85 RBIs.

Pitchers Lefty Gomez and Red Ruffing each won 15 games, along with Marius Russo and Spud Chandler who chipped in with 14 and 10 games, respectively. Joe McCarthy managed the 1941 Yankees.

In the National League, the Brooklyn Dodgers (100–54) outlasted the St. Louis Cardinals (97–56) and won the pennant by 2½ games.[6] Center fielder Pete Reiser hit .343 to win the batting title and led the team with 184 hits, 14 home runs, and 76 RBIs. Dixie Walker contributed, batting .311 with 165 hits, 9 home runs, and 71 RBIs. Dolph Camilli batted .285, knocked out 151 hits, 34 home runs, and 120 RBIs. Joe Medwick batted .311, banged out 171 hits, with 18 home runs, and 88 RBIs.

The Dodgers pitching staff was led by both Kirby Higbe and Whitlow Wyatt, who each won 22 games. Curt Davis chipped in with 13 wins and reliever Hugh Casey won 14 games for the National League champs.

Yankee Stadium hosted the first game of the World Series. Most people think Game 4 was the turning point of the Series. The fourth contest was important, as we shall see, but Game 1 was just as significant.[7]

Yankee second baseman Joe Gordon homered off Dodger starter Curt Davis in the bottom of the second. The Yankees added two more runs in the fifth and seventh innings. Meanwhile, Yankee starter Red Ruffing held the Dodgers to only one run through six innings. His only blemish was to Mickey Owen, who in the top of the third, tripled and then scored on a ground out. In the top of the seventh, a Yankee error put Cookie Lavagetto on first. Up came shortstop Pee Wee Reese who singled.

With runners on first and second and no outs, Dodgers manager Leo Durocher sent up Lew Riggs to pinch-hit for Owen. Riggs made Durocher look like a genius when he singled in Lavagetto and the Dodgers trailed the Yankees by a score of 3–2.

The Dodgers were in good shape as Brooklyn had men on first and second, and still there were no outs. Durocher then sent Jimmy Wasdell to bat for Brooklyn starter Curt Davis. Durocher had given Wasdell the bunt sign, but Wasdell popped up in front of the Yankee dugout. Red Rolfe charged in from third and caught the ball for the first out. Reese saw that Rolfe had abandoned third, so he took off for the bag. Shortstop Phil Rizzuto also saw what transpired, and raced toward third, arriving there just in time to receive Rolfe's throw and tag out Reese for an unconventional double play.

The play was a rally-killer. Momentum shifted back to the Yankees as Red Ruffing retired Dixie Walker on a groundout at second base to end the inning. The Dodgers had another chance in the ninth when they put runners on first and second with one out, but Ruffing induced Herman Franks to hit into a double play to end the game. The Yankees held on and won the game 3–2.

In Game 2, Whitlow Wyatt of the Dodgers gave up single runs in the second and third innings before settling down. Yankee starter Spud Chandler kept the Dodgers in check until the sixth, when Brooklyn scored two runs to tie the game at 2–2.

In the top of the seventh, Dixie Walker reached first base on an error. Chandler then conceded a single to Billy Herman. Yankee manager Joe McCarthy went to the mound and replaced starter Spud Chandler with Johnny Murphy. After Murphy fanned Reiser for the first out, Dolph Camilli singled home Dixie Walker to put the Dodgers ahead for good. Brooklyn won the game 3–2 to tie the series at a game apiece.[8]

The scene switched to Brooklyn as the Dodgers hosted Games 3, 4 and 5 of the World Series. Ebbets Field, described by Brooklyn Dodger fans as an intimate and warm ballpark, became a house of horrors for the Dodgers over the next seventy-two hours.

Russo, pitching for the Yankees, and Fitzsimmons, pitching for the Dodgers, tossed shut-out ball for over seven innings. With two outs in the top of the eighth, Russo came up to bat and lined the ball off of Fitzsimmons' leg and broke his kneecap. The ball nestled into the glove of Pee Wee Reese for the third out. Fitzsimmons would have to leave the game, and would never again be the same pitcher. The Yankees took advantage, tagging reliever Hugh Casey for two runs. In the eighth, the Dodgers could only cut the lead in half with a run. Russo held on and the Yankees won the game and led the Series 2–1.[9]

Scene: Ebbets Field

This ballpark that seated just below 35,000 is still remembered today, forty years after it was razed to become a housing project. If a tree grew in Brooklyn, then it is a safe bet that Ebbets Field bloomed throughout the borough for 45 baseball seasons.

But before the beloved "Bums of Flatbush" set foot onto Ebbets Field, the Dodgers began as the Brooklyn Trolley Dodgers of the American Association from 1883 to 1889. In 1890, the Trolley Dodgers moved to the National League. By then, the team was known as the Brooklyn Bridegrooms, in honor of six recently married ballplayers.[10]

That year, the Bridegrooms, who had played their home games at Washington Park since its inception, moved to Eastern Park. The team returned to Washington Park in 1898 because of poor attendance at Eastern Park.

Washington Park was situated at Fourth Avenue between Third and Fifth streets. The ballpark seated about 16,000, and just like the other stadiums of that era, a rope in the outfield separated the fans and allowed spectators to view the game in the bleacher section.[11] Also in 1898, Charles H. Ebbets took over the team that was now known as the Brooklyn Superbas. It was Ebbets who fourteen years later constructed the beloved ballpark that bore his name on a garbage dump called "Pig-town" for $750,000.

Ebbets broke ground on March 5, 1912, and the ballpark was completed within one year.[12] The first game at Brooklyn's new home took place between the Superbas and the newly named Yankees in an exhibition game on April 9, 1913. The ballpark where Hilda Chester rang her cowbells along with the Brooklyn Dodger Sym-phony was located at 55 Sullivan Place and bounded by Bedford Avenue, Montgomery Street, and St. McCeaver Place.[13]

On that day, a newspaperman asked Charles Ebbets what the name of Brooklyn's new ballpark would be. Charles Ebbets was said to have renamed the field Washington Park until a newspaperman suggested that he should name it Ebbets Field. Charles Ebbets seemed amused by the suggestion and said, "All right, that's what we'll call it, Ebbets Field."[14]

At first Ebbets Field seated only 25,000, a figure that Charles Ebbets had in mind when he envisioned such a ballpark. The dimensions were 419 feet from left field, center field stood at 450 feet, and right field stood at 301. The fences in left and center field were 20 feet high, but in right field the fence stood at 9 feet.

The Superbas thrived in the new ballpark as the team went to the World Series in 1916 and in 1920. But they suffered sixteen losing seasons throughout the 1920s and most of the 1930s. During this time, the team and Ebbets Field took on different looks. First, the team was renamed the Robins, in honor of its manager, Wilbert Robinson. When Wilbert Robinson was forced to leave the team after 1931, the team became the Brooklyn Dodgers.

Left field was shortened to 365 feet by 1940. Center field stood at 400 feet and right field stood at 297 feet. A scoreboard was constructed along with the left field stands that increased the attendance by 9,000. A right field fence stood about twenty feet atop the many signs that adorned Ebbets Field, such as Coca-Cola, Botany Ties, Gem Blades, and the famous advertisement from Abe Stark that would award a suit to a batter who hit the sign. Baseball was not the only sport played on Ebbets Field. Boxing matches also took place at Ebbets Field from 1910 to the 1930s. The Brooklyn Football Dodgers played there from 1930 to 1944.[15]

Though Brooklynites witnessed many facets of Ebbets Field, baseball fans wanted to see post-season play, and there was light at the end of the tunnel starting with Brooklyn's first night game on June 15, 1938.[16] Brooklyn's future seemed bright as the team finished in third place in 1939 and second place in 1940 before finally reaching the National League summit in 1941.

The 33,813 fans filed into Ebbets Field to witness Game 4, one of the most talked about games in the history of the Brooklyn Dodgers.[17] The Yankees scored a run off of Kirby Higbe in the first inning. In the top of the fourth, Keller led off the inning with a double. Higbe then walked Bill Dickey, and Gordon followed with a single to load the bases. Higbe momentarily stymied the Yankees when he retired Rizutto and fanned Atley Donald for two outs, but Johnny Strum spoiled Higbe's escape with a single to score Keller and Dickey and increase the Yankees lead 3–0.

With two outs in the bottom of the fourth, Atley Donald walked both Owen and second baseman Pete Coscarart. Wasdell atoned for his failure in Game 1 with a double to score Owen and Coscarart. Like yesterday's game, the Dodgers trailed the Yankees 3–2, but his time, the Dodgers would rally. With Wasdell on second, Pete Reiser came up and hit a two-run home run off of Yankee reliever Marv Breuer to put the Dodgers ahead 4–3.

Dodger relievers Larry French, Johnny Allen, and Hugh Casey held the Yankees in check over the next four innings. Hugh Casey was still on the mound in the bottom of the ninth as the Dodgers clung to a 4–3 lead. Owen caught 128 games for the Dodgers in 1941 and knew Casey's repertoire consisted of two curve balls. The first curve ball was an overhand curve, or drop curve, which dropped down over the plate. His second curve ball was the three-quarter curve. This pitch would slide off to the left hand side of the plate. Casey relied primarily on the three-quarter curve ball, but soon hitters were timing that particular pitch and just before the Series began, Casey switched to the overhand curve ball and again became an effective pitcher.

Casey was using the overhand curve ball in the top of the ninth when John Sturm grounded out to Coscarart at second base for the first out.

Next, Red Rolfe bounced back to Hugh Casey, who fielded the ball and threw to Dolph Camilli at first base for the second out.

Tommy Henrich, "Old Reliable," stepped into the batter's box. Hugh Casey got two quick strikes on Henrich, but Henrich hung in there and worked Casey to a full count. On Casey's sixth pitch, he switched to the three-quarter curve ball. Henrich initially thought Casey's pitch was a strike. When he realized that the pitch was a curve ball, he tried to stop his swing, but couldn't. Old newsreels of the fifth game of the 1941 World Series show that Henrich was fooled on the pitch that he called the best curve ball he'd ever seen in his life. Mickey Owen was locked into thinking that Casey would throw his overhand curve ball. He didn't realize that the pitch was the three-quarter curve ball until it arrived at the plate. Owen made a desperate attempt to catch the ball, but unfortunately, it was a low inside pitch that hit the bottom of Owen's mitt and rolled to the backstop. Home plate umpire Larry Goets lifted up his hand to indicate that Henrich had struck out, but then Henrich turned around to see what had transpired. When he realized the ball had rolled to the backstop, Henrich, who was never fond of Durocher after the Dodger manager once said that he, Henrich, could not run, sprinted towards first. The Yankees were still alive. Many people have commented that Durocher should have gone to the mound to relax Hugh Casey after the passed ball allowed Henrich to reach first, but, right before the Series began, Commissioner Kenesaw Mountain Landis informed both teams of the new rules that stated no big meetings could take place on the pitcher's mound. Only two players other than the manager and pitcher could go to the mound. A manager could make one visit to the mound as opposed to multiple visits. It was speculated that these new rules were designed to move the game along and restrict Leo Durocher, who was known for using such tactics to delay the game.[18]

Instead, Durocher went on to say that Owen could not retire Henrich at first because the police had crowded home plate after Casey fanned Henrich for strike three. Owen never blamed anyone as he realized that Henrich would have been safe on the play regardless of whether the police had not crowded the plate. After order was restored, Joe DiMaggio came up and singled to left field. Casey got two strikes on the next batter, Charlie Keller, and the Dodgers were again one strike away from tying the Series.

Keller took Hugh Casey's third pitch and doubled off the right field wall to score Henrich and DiMaggio. Casey then walked Bill Dickey, and Joe Gordon finally ended the Yankee ninth with a double to score Keller and Dickey. Four runs had crossed the plate after the passed ball by Mickey Owen. Johnny Murphy came in and retired the Dodgers in order. The Yankees won the game 7–4.

Mickey Owen: Took full responsibility for his passed ball in the 1941 Fall Classic, and felt bad not only himself, but for his teammates as well. However, Owen remained in the game and became a successful scout and manager in the winter leagues. (Photograph courtesy of the National Baseball Hall of Fame Library, Cooperstown, N.Y.)

Owen spoke to reporters after his passed ball in Game 4. "Sure it was my fault. The ball was a low curve that broke down. It hit the edge of my glove and glanced off, but I should have had him out anyway. I gave it the best I had, I don't mind being the goat, but I'm sorry for what I've cost the other fellows."[19]

Ebbets Field gave Mickey Owen a standing ovation at the start of the game. Owen never forgot the token of appreciation from the ebullient fans at Ebbets Field, but the sportswriters were not forgiving.[20] The next day, the *New York Herald Tribune* wrote that Owen had entered the list of the classic "Goats" along with Fred Merkle and Fred Snodgrass.[21] Joe Trimble of the *New York Daily News* wrote that some of the fans at Ebbets Field got into the act by calling Owen a "bum" along with cries of, "Hey Owen, you're lousy!" and, "Which side are you playing on?"[22]

In the top of the second, in Game 5, Joe Gordon's RBI single gave the Yankees a 2–0 lead. After the Dodgers scratched for a run in the third, Earl "Tiny" Bonham retired 20 of the next 22 batters. The Yankees scored their final run of the Series in the fifth on a home run by Henrich. The Yankees held on to win the game 3–1 and become world champions.

Owen's error did not cost the Dodgers the World Series. Yes, if he had fielded the ball in Game 4, the World Series would have been even at two games.

But Reese's base-running blunder in Game 1 was just as important as the Dodgers' missed opportunity on Owen's error in Game 4. If the Dodgers had won the first game, then the Series still would have been tied at two games apiece.

Plus, Hugh Casey could not get anybody out after the ball skipped past Owen. Keller, who was also down to his last strike, doubled in Game 4 and gave the Yankees another chance. (Hugh Casey would end his life ten years later over a marriage dispute.)

Though the Dodgers were down three games to one in the World Series, it was not impossible to come back and win the World Series as the 1925 Pirates, 1958 Yankees, 1968 Tigers, 1979 Pirates, and 1985 Royals proved possible. There is just too much speculation on what might have been. The bottom line is that the 1941 World Series was dominated by good pitching. As the old adage goes, "Good pitching stops good hitting." The irony was that Owen set a major league record that year of not committing an error in over 509 chances.[23]

Owen would play for three more seasons with the Dodgers before joining the Navy in 1944. After the war, he made a decision he would later regret. The Dodgers did not tend Owen a contract, so he signed with the

Mexican League, only to be let go after one year. Owen had to wait until 1949 to apply for reinstatement.[24]

In 1949, the Dodgers reinstated Owen, then promptly sold him to the Cubs. After three seasons, the Cubs parted with Owen and he went on to play with the Kansas City Blues of the American Association. After a stint with Piedmont in Norfolk, Virginia, in 1953, Owen went to Puerto Rico during the winter of 1954 and managed the Caguas Criollos team. He even inserted himself as a catcher and helped the team win the Caribbean Series championship.[25] Owen's experience in Puerto Rico led him back to the major leagues where he joined the Red Sox that same year and remained with the team as a coach for the next two seasons. Owen continued to play winter ball, serving as a player-manager first in Venezuela from 1954 to 1955 and then in Puerto Rico during the 1955-56 season. Finally, Owen managed in Mayaguez from 1956 to 1958. More importantly, Owen was pleased to help develop the careers of Hank Aaron, Brooks Lawrence, and Maury Wills. After he left the Red Sox, Owen scouted for the Baltimore Orioles and managed the Yankees' Double A team in Norfolk, Virginia.

Owen would run for and be elected as sheriff of Greene County in southwest Missouri in 1964. He held that job for many years.[26] In the mid 1970s Owen ran for office again, this time for lieutenant governor of Missouri, but his campaign was unsuccessful.

Over the years, Mickey Owen and Tommy Henrich would bump into each other at various card shows. Both men were attending a baseball card show in the 1970s when Owen began to recount the events of Game 4 of the 1941 Series. Henrich was impressed as Owen recounted every detail of their famous rendezvous, noting that Owen did not alter any information to save himself from any potential embarrassment and took full responsibility for the passed ball.[27]

Mickey Owen has lived nearly sixty years since his muff in 1941, but now has Alzheimer's disease. Mickey Owen's son, Charlie, was very instrumental in providing information on the passed ball in Game 4 of the 1941 Series. Mickey Owen has regaled Charlie with this play a thousand times. Charlie said that his father felt he should have caught Casey's pitch that day. It was just one of those days when Owen forgot that Casey could employ his three-quarter curve. More importantly, Owen has said when a ballplayer experiences a bad day, he has to go on and play the next day.

Hopefully, when Owen passes away people in the sporting world will have the decency to treat Owen much more kindly than it did Fred Snodgrass when he died. Mickey Owen is a true testament that life goes on.

CHAPTER 4

Ralph Branca

Victory has a thousand fathers, and defeat is an orphan.
— John F. Kennedy

The next two chapters in this book are about two men who were good pitchers when their careers began. Each pitcher won twenty games and appeared in the World Series. However, both men share another dubious distinction: their teams blew a double digit lead in the standings, and when the hitting stopped for both teams, their adversary made a run at the pennant. To make matters worse, the winning team was an old time rival. It is also startling that on an early October day, a three-run home run would make heroes out of two men who had ordinary baseball careers and brand two other men scapegoats for losing the pennant. Still, to this day, some fans have not forgiven either of them.

Ralph Branca — a gentleman of class and dignity. Ralph Branca has endured the unfair and unwarranted reminder of his fifteen minutes of fame for half a century.

Baseball fans who never saw either of the former New York teams know Branca's name through old news reels, or former Giants announcer Russ Hodges' famous call, "The Giants win the pennant! The Giants win the pennant! The Giants win the Pennant!"

Branca has lived through reminders of his playoff loss with candor, and he has been philosophical about the pitch he made to Bobby Thomson. Richard Nixon, John F. Kennedy's contemporary, said it best in regards to setbacks in life. On the day of his resignation the 37th president of the United States uttered, "The greatness comes not when things always go good for you, but the greatness comes when you're really tested — when you take some knocks, some disappointments — when sadness comes.

"Because only when you've been in the deepest valley, can you ever know how magnificent it is to be on the highest mountain. Always give our best — never get discouraged — never be petty. Always remember, others may hate you, but those that hate you don't win unless you hate them — and then you destroy yourself."[1]

Branca has never let his playoff loss destroy him, as another pitcher would nearly forty years later.

In 1997, Branca spoke on the fiftieth anniversary of Jackie Robinson's breakthrough as the first African-American to play organized baseball in the modern era. He recounted the problems that Jackie endured when he joined the Dodgers— the taunts, the jeers, and the fact that some of Jackie's own teammates did not want to play with him. Branca probably understood Jackie's situation not only as a witness, but because some baseball fans throughout the generations still press him for an explanation concerning his pitch during the last playoff game in 1951.

America had gone through a tremendous change by the time of Branca's story. World War II ended in 1945; that year, the world entered the Nuclear Age when two atomic bombs were dropped on Hiroshima and Nagasaki. The baby boom generation was in its fifth year. The Cold War became intensified by the Korean conflict which started in 1950. President Harry S Truman did what many Americans thought was an act of treason eight months later when he fired General Douglas MacArthur, who at the time was leading the United Nations forces in South Korea against the Communists in North Korea who were backed by China.

Baseball itself had undergone a significant change as it entered its fourth year of integration. At long last, baseball had truly become all America's pastime.

Ralph Theodore Joseph Branca was the fifteenth out of seventeen children, born on January 6, 1926, in Mount Vernon, New York, to John and Katherine Branca.[2] While growing up in Mount Vernon, Branca rooted for the Giants and starred as a pitcher for A.B. Davis High School. At age sixteen, he was given a tryout with Giants, but it was postponed due to rain. Branca tried out for the Yankees, but the team bypassed him because of his age and slight build.

The Yankees informed Branca they would keep in touch with him, but they did not. Finally, Branca had a tryout with the Brooklyn Dodgers, who liked him and made good on their word, signing him right out of high school at age seventeen.[3]

Branca pitched for Olean of the Pony League during the summer. When he arrived home from Olean, he was offered a basketball scholarship at New York University. Branca attended NYU for two seasons during the off season and even played a few games for the NYU basketball team.

But fate had other plans. World War II had taken away many of the game's best players, and major league teams were strapped for replacements. So on June 12, 1944, Branca made his debut with the Dodgers.

His first year was unspectacular, and after 21 appearances with an 0–2 record, Branca was sent to the Montreal Royals, the Dodgers' top farm team in the International League. The following year, Branca began the season for St. Paul in the American Association, but was recalled by the Dodgers and finished the season with a 5–6 record.[4]

In the 1946 season, Branca was injured. It was one of many injuries and bad breaks that he would endure throughout his career. The injury prohibited Branca from tossing the ball for two weeks. Despite Branca's ailment, Dodger coach Charlie Dressen wanted him to pitch batting practice. Branca refused on account of his arm injury. This defiance cost Branca, as he was relegated to the bench and from then on would only pitch in mop-up games. When he returned to the rotation in mid–September, Branca won his last three starts.[5] The Dodgers and Cardinals finished the season tied for first place, so both teams squared off in a best two out of three playoff for the National League pennant. Branca pitched the first playoff game against the Cardinals which the Dodgers lost 4–2 the Cardinals went on to win the pennant.

In 1947, at the age of 21, Branca appeared in 43 games, pitched 280 innings, won 21 games, and sported a 2.67 ERA.[6] Branca's contribution led the Brooklyn Dodgers to the World Series against the New York Yankees.

The Brooklyn Dodgers fought valiantly to win the Series. Dodger outfielder Cookie Lavagetto's pinch-hit single, which broke up Yankee pitcher Bill Bevins' no-hitter in Game 4 along with another Dodger outfielder, Al Gionfriddo, who robbed Yankee great Joe DiMaggio of a three-run home run in Game 6 (which Branca won), also stands out in that Fall Classic of 1947.[7] DiMaggio, who rarely displayed any emotion on the field, kicked the dirt after Gionfriddo made that catch. Despite these Dodger highlights, the Yankees prevailed as New York won the seventh game 5–2 and were world champions.

The next year Branca was 12–5 by the All-Star break, but he was hurt when a teammate playing in the clubhouse threw a bat that hit Branca in the shin.

Branca continued to pitch when he should have rested his leg. This injury had immediate consequences as Branca tailed off and finished the season with a 14–9 record.[8]

The Boston Braves won the National League pennant that year, but lost the World Series to the Cleveland Indians. In 1949, Branca returned to his old form and carried a 10–1 record by July, but ill fortune followed Branca again. This time, he hurt his arm and finished with a 13–5 record.

The Yankees and Dodgers were back in the Series that year. Unfortunately for Brooklyn, the story was the same, and the Yankees won the World Series in five games. In 1950, Branca was converted to a starter and reliever. This was the only year that Branca had a losing season at 7–9.

Later that year, after trailing the Philadelphia Phillies by 9 games in early September, the Dodgers made one last charge to win the pennant. On the last day of season, the Dodgers trailed the Phillies by one game.[9] A win would force a playoff which the Dodgers were confident they could win. After nine innings, the Dodgers and Phillies were tied at 1–1. In the bottom of the ninth, outfielder Cal Abrams walked. Shortstop Pee Wee Reese followed Abrams with a single. With runners on first and second and no outs, Duke Snider, the great Dodger center fielder, came up and lined the ball into center field. Dodger third base coach Milt Stock sent Abrams home. Phillies center fielder Richie Ashburn did not have a strong throwing arm, but quickly fielded the ball, and made an accurate throw to nail Abrams by a mile.

If Milt Stock had held up Abrams, the Dodgers might have won the game, for two batters later, Gil Hodges hit a fly ball that would have scored Abrams from third base. Instead, Hodges' fly ball became the third out. In the top of the tenth, Dick Sisler hit an opposite field three-run home run off of Don Newcombe to win the game 4–1 and give Philadelphia the pennant. If Dodger fans thought 1950 was hard to take, then the next year must have been unbearable.

Ralph Branca began the 1951 season as a reliever, but before long he was back in the starting rotation. Once again we return to the New York Giants back in the Polo Grounds. By 1951, Leo Durocher, the New York Giants manager, had refashioned the team that was once known for its power into a team that scratched and clawed its way to a run.

Three years earlier fans on both teams were shocked as Brooklyn Dodger president Branch Rickey traded managers with Giants owner Horace Stoneham. Leo Durocher, then the Dodgers' manager, changed uniforms to manage the Giants. The Dodgers did not retain Mel Ott, the former Giant manager and Hall of Famer. Instead, Rickey hired Burt Shotton. After Branch Rickey was forced to leave the Brooklyn Dodgers in 1950, Walter O'Malley, the new Dodger president, replaced Shotton with Charles Dressen, who was once a protégé of Leo Durocher.

The Durocher and Dressen rivalry that dated back to the nineteenth century was the latest between the two clubs. The rivalry continued into the next century when Wilbert Robinson, who was once a teammate of John McGraw on the old Baltimore Orioles (New York Highlanders and Yankees) and later pitching coach for McGraw's Giants, became the manager of the Brooklyn Dodgers.[10] Robinson's Dodgers won two pennants in 1916 and 1920 when McGraw's Giants were out of contention. In the early 1920s the Giants were back in the Series and won four pennants from 1921 to 1924.

In the early 1930s, a reporter queried Bill Terry, then the Giants' manager, regarding the Dodgers' chances of winning the pennant that year. Terry responded, "Was Brooklyn still in the league?"

Brooklyn was in the league and beat the Giants twice during the last days of the 1934 season as New York lost the pennant to the eventual World Series champs St. Louis Cardinals and their famous "Gas House Gang." The second baseman on that Cardinal team was none other than Leo Durocher.

The New York Giants, once dominant at the beginning of the twentieth century, began to experience some lean years after the team's last pennant in 1938. Meanwhile, the Dodgers, who hadn't won a pennant in 21 years, were in the World Series against the Yankees in 1941. After the 1941 World Series, which the Dodgers lost, baseball also lost, as many of its players enlisted in World War II. After the war, the players returned, and so did the rivalry between the Dodgers and Giants.

When Charles Dressen became the Dodger manager in 1951, he was obsessed with beating his former boss, Leo Durocher. This obsession would haunt the Dodgers in early October.

The season started on April 18, with the Dodgers losing to the Phillies 4–2 and the Giants defeating the Braves 5–0 at Braves Field in Boston. This would be the last time the Giants led the Dodgers until that fateful day at the Polo Grounds six months later, for New York then lost the second game to the Braves, and proceeded to lose two 3-game series to the Dodgers and Phillies. The carnage continued as the Giants dropped four more games, the first two to the Braves and the latter two games to the Dodgers at Ebbets Field, which added up to eleven straight losses. New York finally defeated the Dodgers in the rubber game of the series to stop their losing streak. By the end of April, the Giants record stood at 2–12. More importantly, though, they trailed the Braves by 7½ games.[11]

On the other hand, the Dodgers started their season by winning 8 out of 12 games in April, and although Brooklyn trailed both the Braves and Cardinals by two games, both teams could not maintain the top spot as the Dodgers took over first place on May 13. Also in May, Branca was summoned back to the pitching rotation from the bullpen to replace an injured Erv Palica. These moves proved fortuitous as the Dodgers went 17–9 in May and led the Cubs by 2½ games.

The Giants won 10 out of 13 games during the first two weeks in May to get out of the cellar. Though New York revisited the cellar two days later, help was on the way. On May 25, the Giants brought up twenty-year-old Willie Mays, who at the time was batting .477 in Minneapolis, the Giants' top farm team, to play in center field.[12] Mays would go on to win the Rookie of the Year in 1951. Mays' arrival allowed Leo Durocher to move Bobby Thomson to his former position in left field and finally to third base. Dorucher also convinced Thomson to change his batting stance, which helped Thomson immensely as his batting average rose by seventy points.

The day after Mays arrived, the Giants defeated the Phillies 2–0 to reach the .500 mark at 19–19.[13] More importantly, New York finished the month at 18–9 in fourth place, 8½ games behind the Dodgers.

Brooklyn did not rest on its first place laurels, as the team acquired Andy Pafko from the Chicago Cubs on June 16.

Carl Erskine[14] was kind enough to share his memories about the 1951 baseball season. Erskine reminded me that the Dodgers, who won the pennant in 1949, then lost the pennant in 1950, began the 1951 season strong, but had a problem in left field, and needed a leftfielder. The Dodgers were playing the Cubs in Chicago when Brooklyn made a four for four trade. All four players—catcher Bruce Edwards, pitcher Joe Hatten, infielder Eddie Miksis, and outfielder Gene Hermanski — walked from the Dodgers dugout to the Cubs dugout. And the Cubs players—catcher Rube Walker, pitcher Johnny Schimtz, infielder Wayne Terwilliger, and outfielder Andy Pafko— in turn walked from their dugout and were now members of the Brooklyn Dodgers. No money was involved; it was just a four for four trade, and Pafko helped the Dodgers club after he came over from the Cubs.[15]

This became evident as Brooklyn began to separate itself from the rest of the National League, and on June 21, Preacher Roe defeated the Reds 6–4 for his tenth win in a row.[16] Don Newcombe joined Roe with 11 wins and made the All Star squad along with Branca, who chipped in with five wins. Despite dropping a doubleheader to the Pirates three days later, Brooklyn rebounded in the next series by taking 2 out of 3 from the Giants at the Polo Grounds. The Dodgers swept a twin bill from the Giants on July 4 at Ebbets Field, then won the next day to complete a three game sweep and lead the Giants by 7½ games.

By the All-Star break the Dodgers (50–26) led the Giants (43–36), who briefly moved into second place in mid–June before solely occupying the position in July, leading by 8½ games.

Brooklyn's lead reflected the strength of their pitching: Don Newcombe, 12–4; Preacher Roe, 13–2; Carl Erskine, 8–8; and Ralph Branca rounded off the staff at 7–2. Jackie Robinson, Roy Campanella, Pee Wee Reese, and Carl Furillo led the offense by batting over .300.

The Giants also possessed pitching aces of their own. Sal Maglie and Larry Jansen each went 12–4, and Ed Hearn chipped in with a 7–4 record. The trio of .300 batsmen Alvin Dark, Don Mueller, and Monte Irvin were also assets to the team.

Though Brooklyn sported a comfortable lead, ominous signs appeared within the Dodger pitching staff as Branca, Newcombe, and Palica were dealing with arm problems.[17]

After the All-Star Break, the Dodgers lost 6 out of 9 games, but maintained their 8½ game lead over the Giants who lost 5 out of 8 games and briefly fell into third place. Brooklyn then went on a ten game winning streak, but the Dodgers only managed to increase their lead by one to 9½ games, for the Giants ended July on a high note by winning 9 out of 11 games to recapture second place.

On August 1, Branca was knocked out after surrendering four runs in the bottom of the fourth in a 12–9 loss to the Pirates, but he was back on the mound in an extra inning affair two days later.[18] Unfortunately, his return was inauspicious for in the bottom of the fourteenth, with the Dodgers holding a 4–3 lead, the Reds tied the score and had a man on second when Branca threw a wild pitch that sent the runner to third. Willie Ramsdell came up with the count 2–0 and tried a suicide squeeze, but the ball got by Campanella to give the Reds a 5–4 win.[19]

On August 5, following a 7–3 loss to the Reds that ended Newcombe's nine game wining streak the night before, Branca was on the mound again. This time he went all the way, allowing 5 hits in a complete game 2–0 as Brooklyn swept a twin bill over the Reds.[20]

Meanwhile, in early August, the Giants split their next six games, and headed back to the Polo Grounds for an all-important three game series with the Dodgers. Brooklyn swept the series to increase their lead to 12½ games. After the game, with both teams in their respective clubhouses that were separated by a brick wall, Dressen could be heard saying, "The Giants were through, they will never bother us again." The Dodger players joined in the chorus and began yelling, "The Giants are dead, the Giants are dead."[21] It looked like Dressen's boast was true, because the next day, on August 11, Branca threw a six hitter and defeated the Braves 8–1. Although Brooklyn lost the second game of a doubleheader, the Giants also lost to the Phillies, which left New York 13½ games behind the Dodgers.

But the jeering by the Dodgers on August 10 awoke the sleeping Giants. New York swept three games from the Phillies and went on to sweep three from Brooklyn at Ebbets Field. New York took six more games from the

Phillies, Reds, and Cardinals before finally sweeping two doubleheaders from the Cubs on August 26 and 27 to give the team a sixteen game winning streak, the team's longest in thirty-five years.

As for Brooklyn, they lost 10 out of the next 18 games after August 11. To compound matters, the Dodgers were rained out twice in August and would have to make up these games later in the season.

One moment of levity happened during the fierce battle for the pennant: Music Depreciation Night. Any fan who brought an instrument into Ebbets Field saw the game for free. Although many fans played horribly that day, the music was joyful or cacophonous to the Dodgers' ears as they beat the Braves 7–6.[22]

Despite the win, the Dodgers struggled offensively, and as the Dodger hitting began to wane, Dressen relied more on his pitchers. Then Brooklyn suffered a setback when relief pitcher Clyde King, who sported a 13–4 record by August, came down with tendonitis and was virtually an ineffective pitcher. He won only one more game for the rest of the season.[23] For Branca, despite some off days when he was not sharp, he was a dependable arm as he did relieve and start games.

On August 24, Branca hurled a three-hitter and shut out the Cubs 1–0.[24] He was even better three days later in a game against the Pirates. In the top of the third, Pittsburgh was still searching for its first hit when starter Mel Queen hit Branca's offering into right field. But Queen lollygagged down to first base and Carl Furillo, who was known as the "Reading Rifle" and possessed one of the best arms in baseball, threw out Queen at first. From there on not a single Pirate registered a base hit until the top of the ninth when Pete Castiglione led off and lined a 1–1 pitch over Pee Wee Reese to break up Branca's no hitter. Although George Metkovich reached Branca for another single, Branca retired the next two batters and fanned Gus Bell for the final out. The Dodgers won the game 5–0.[25]

Despite Branca and the rest of the Dodgers' pitching staff, by the end of August, the team's once invincible lead was down to five games.

On August 28, Southpaw Howard Pollet shut out the Giants 2–0 to end New York's sixteen game winning streak. The Dodgers took advantage and won their game over the Reds 3–1.[26]

Both teams won on August 29. The next day, a Giant loss coupled with a Dodger win put Brooklyn at seven games.

The Giants entered the final month of the season by sweeping a two game series from the Dodgers to reduce Brooklyn's lead again to five games. The highlight of the two game set was Don Mueller, who homered three times on September 1 in an 8–1 win and hit two more home runs the next day as the Giants pounded the Dodgers 11–2.[27]

The Dodgers still hung in there as Branca beat the Phillies on September 5.[28] This would be his last win of the season, for Branca's next start on September 9 would turn out to haunt the Dodgers. Brooklyn again squared off with New York in a two game series.

The Dodgers whipped the Giants 9–0 in the previous day's game, so New York knew they had to win or else they would again trail the Dodgers by 7½ games. Branca gave up a two-run home run to Monte Irvin in the fourth. Sal ("The Barber") Maglie, whose pitches were so close to a batter it was thought that the batter was getting a shave, was stingy that day as he carried a shutout into the eighth, but the Dodgers had a rally going when Snider doubled. Next, Robinson stepped up to the plate, and tripled to score Snider and cut the Giants lead in half, 2–1. New York moved the infield in to cut off the tying run. Up came Andy Pafko who hit the ball down the line at third base. Bobby Thomson made a backhand catch and noticed that Robinson had veered off from third and was now trapped. Thomson tagged Robinson and threw to Whitey Lockman at first to get Pafko for the double play. The Giants held on and won the game 2–1 for Maglie's 20th win and cut the lead back to 5½ games.[29]

New York played great baseball over the next week, winning 6 out of 8 games to trim Brooklyn's lead to three games. On the other hand, the Dodgers lead eroded as they lost 4 out of 8 games and now had to look over their shoulder as New York kept on winning.

However, New York stumbled, as the Giants lost a key game to the Reds 3–1 on September 20. The Dodgers took advantage of New York's loss and defeated the Cards 4–3 to lead the Giants by 4½ games with seven left to play.[30] Despite the loss to Cincinnati, New York went out and swept the Phillies and Reds for a five game winning streak to trail the Dodgers 1 game. Brooklyn lost 4 out of 6 games, this time to the Phillies and Braves.

The Giants were idle on September 27 and 28. Brooklyn had to play two different teams in two cities in two days. With the season winding down, every game became crucial; however, one game stands out that could have altered the 1951 season. It is not to say that the pennant was lost on this one game alone. It does demonstrate how a few turns of events could have changed baseball history.

On September 27, the Dodgers led the Braves 3–0 until the sixth when the Braves rallied to tie the game at 3–3.

In the bottom of the eighth, Braves leftfielder Bob Addis singled. Up came center fielder Sam Jethroe who also singled to move Addis to third. The Dodgers then moved the infield in to prevent the winning run from scoring. With the infield drawn in, Braves first baseman Earl Torgeson hit a ground ball to Jackie Robinson. Addis raced home, but Robinson fielded the ball and made a perfect throw to Dodger catcher Roy Campanella at home plate.

But home plate umpire Frank Dascoli called Addis safe. The Dodgers became incensed and vehemently protested the call. Soon Dascoli had enough of the Dodgers' harangue and threw out Campanella and everybody else on the Dodger bench.[31] On the bench was a player named Bill Sherman, who was just called up by the Dodgers in early September. Sherman became a footnote in baseball history as the only man ever to be thrown out of a game without ever playing in one. When the shouting was over, the Braves won the game 4–3. As for the Dodgers, they still insist that Dascoli blew the call that gave the winning run to the Braves. Nevertheless, Brooklyn now led New York by only half a game.

The Dodgers lost the next day to the Phillies in Shibe Park 4–3, and were now tied for first place with the Giants as Brooklyn again let a 3–0 lead slip away.

On September 29, the Giants beat the Braves in Boston as Brooklyn rebounded from yesterday's loss. Newcombe would not lose the pennant for a second year in a row and beat the Phillies 5–0.

On September 30, the last day of the season, in Boston, Larry Jansen pitched the Giants to a 3–2 victory to ensure New York at least a tie for the National League pennant. Baseball's famous playoff game almost did not happen.

At Shibe Park, the Phillies knocked out starter Preacher Roe for four runs in the second. Branca came in and pitched two innings, but the Phillies scored two more runs, as Philadelphia raced to a 6–0 lead.

The Dodgers, still smarting from their defeat by the Phillies a year ago, struck back with two runs in the second and three in the third to trail Philadelphia 6–5. Brooklyn tied the game in the top of the fifth, but the Phillies answered with two more runs in the bottom of the fifth to take an 8–6 lead. Carl Erskine came out of the bull pen and restored order by tossing two shutout innings. The Dodgers took advantage of Erskine's stability on the mound and reached Phillies reliever Kal Drewes for two runs to again tie the game at 8–8.

In the bottom of the twelfth, the Phillies had the bases loaded with two outs when first baseman Eddie Waitkus hit a line drive near second base. It looked like a sure hit to win the game and end the Dodgers' season until Jackie Robinson dove and caught the ball in mid-air for the final out. To this day, Robin Roberts, the great Philadelphia Phillies pitcher, claims that Robinson trapped the ball, but Erskine and the Dodgers still insist that Robinson made the catch.

A great ball player capped off a great defensive statement by making a great offensive statement. In the top of the fourteenth, Robinson homered off of Robin Roberts. Dodger reliever Bud Podbielan came in and shut down the Phillies as the Dodgers held on and won the game 9–8 to tie the Giants for the National League pennant.[32]

Although the Dodgers went 25–22 since August 11 (3 games over .500 with a 13½ game lead), the Giants won enough games to prevent the Dodgers from winning the pennant, as New York won 37 of their final 44 games, including their last 12 out of 13, to clinch a tie. So for the second time in the National League, a best two out of three playoff would decide the pennant. Although the next three games were part of the National League playoffs, each statistic would be counted as part of the regular season.

In Game One on October 1, 1951, Ralph Branca opposed Jim Hearn of the New York Giants. Andy Pafko homered to give the Dodgers their only run in the bottom of the second. In the top of the fourth, Don Mueller flied out to deep center field for the first out. The next batter, Monte Irvin, received a free pass to first base when Branca struck him on the arm. Whitey Lockman followed Irvin with a fly out to center field where Snider hauled it in for the second out. Bobby Thomson stepped up to the plate and put the Giants in front for good with a two-run home run off of Branca. The Giants would score no more as Branca got out of fourth still trailing by one run.

In the top of the eighth, Monte Irvin upped the Giants lead with a home run. Hearn held on and defeated the Dodgers 3–1.[33]

After the Dodgers lost the first playoff game, Dressen was making up his mind about who to put in to pitch: Carl Erskine or Clem Labine. Erskine had pitched during the last weekend of the season when the Dodgers lost to the Phillies 4–3. He also had pitched two innings during the last game of the season when Brooklyn rallied to the beat the Phillies on the last day of the season, so Dressen chose a fresh arm in Clem Labine.[34] Dressen would not be so judicious forty-eight hours later.

Game 2 was played the next day at the Polo Grounds. Sheldon Jones started for the Giants against Clem Labine for the Dodgers. The Giants, in their home ballpark, could clinch the pennant today.

The Dodgers shook off yesterday's loss with a 13 hit attack. In the top of the first, Jackie Robinson homered with a man on to give Brooklyn an early 2–0 lead.

The Giants put men on through the first four innings, but New York came up empty every time. George Spencer replaced Jones in the third inning and promptly gave up a home run to Gil Hodges in the fifth and surrendered three more runs in the sixth to increase Brooklyn's lead 6–0.

After a forty-one minute rain delay, Al Corwin became the third pitcher for the Giants in the top of the seventh. The change did little to

stop the Dodger attack as Andy Pafko and catcher Rube Walker, substituting for the injured Roy Campanella, each hit a home run in the seventh
and ninth innings. Clem Labine gave up six hits and shut out the Giants.
Brooklyn won the game 10–0.[35]

Scene: Polo Grounds IV

The horseshoe-shaped ballpark that many Giants fans fondly remember did not exist when we last left the Polo Grounds. On April 14, 1911,
two days after the Giants season opener, a mysterious fire burned down
the wooden left field grandstands and left field bleachers. Despite the copi-
ous amounts of water that were poured on the Polo Grounds, only the
center and right field bleachers remained. No one was ever charged with
the deed. For two months, the Giants played their home games at Hilltop
Park, home of the New York Highlanders.[36]

When the Polo Grounds re-opened on June 28, the stadium was a
steel and concrete edifice that seated 34,000 patrons.[37] The upper and lower
decks ended near the right and left field foul poles. The Roman Coliseum
frescoes gave the Polo Grounds a look of grandeur which was reminiscent
of the stadiums of the day such as Philadelphia's palatial Shibe Park. The
Giants would share the Polo Grounds with the recently renamed Yankees
(Highlanders), and when the Yankees lost their lease in 1913, the Giants
returned the favor and allowed the Yankees to use their home. For the next
ten seasons, fans at the Polo Grounds witnessed the Yankees' ascent to
greatness as the team finished third in 1919 and 1920 and won the pennant
in 1921 and 1922.

Coincidentally, the Giants also won the pennant in 1921 and 1922.
Thus, the entire World Series was played at the Polo Grounds in which
the Giants won them both. The Yankees' rise to success coincided with that
of Babe Ruth, whose home runs helped the Yankees draw more fans than
the Giants. The Giants were fed up with Ruth's drawing power and evicted
the Yankees during the 1922 off season. But the Bronx Bombers were not
homeless as the Yankees opened their own stadium in April of 1923.

The Polo Grounds was remodeled once again. During the winter of
1922, the double deck grandstands, all concrete, were extended all the way
to the bleachers, giving the Polo Grounds its famous horseshoe shape.
Seating capacity increased to 50,000.[38]

The Roman Coliseum frescoes were removed to make way for the new
structure. Even with these new improvements, the Polo Grounds remained
one of the friendliest ballparks for hitting home runs as the left field foul

line stood at 279 feet and the right field foul stood at 257. However, if you were not a pull hitter, the Polo Grounds would favor a pitcher as the vast outfield held up home runs and base hits and the center field stood at 500 feet before being moved to 483 during the early 1950s. But there was a downside to these improvements. The upper deck left field overhang stood out by 21 feet in contrast to the lower deck, which meant home runs hit to the upper deck were easier to reach as opposed to the lower deck.

Also during the early 1920s, a five-foot-high memorial was dedicated to Eddie Grant, who played for the Philadelphia Nationals, Cincinnati Reds, and New York Giants and was killed in World War I.[39] The memorial was situated in center field in front of the clubhouse and administrative offices that were constructed right after the bleachers were built. The last improvements to the Polo Grounds were the lights that were installed in 1940.[40] The left field fence was 17 feet before rising a foot to 18 feet in left center; the left field fences sloped from 16 to 14 and finally ended at 12 feet all the way to the bleachers in center field. The bleachers were separated by a 4-foot wall with a 4-inch screen until it was met with two backdrops which stood 20 feet by 17 feet. The center field clubhouse was constructed in the middle of each backdrop. From there the fences went back to 4 feet until they were met by the right field fence at 11 feet before finally rounding out at 12 feet from right center to right field.[41] Like Ebbets Field, other tenants inhabited the Polo Grounds such as the New York Black Cubans of the Negro League (1935–1950). Football was also played there as the New York Football Giants (1925–1955) and the New York Titans (later Jets) took the field during football season (1960–1963). Boxing legends Joe Louis, Rocky Marciano, Sugar Ray Robinson, and Floyd Patterson were victorious at the Polo Grounds during their heydays.[42]

The pitchers for this third contest were Sal Maglie for the New York Giants against Don Newcombe for the Brooklyn Dodgers. This game has been described as one of the best playoff games ever.

Many baseball fans already know the outcome, but for those who don't, 34,320 spectators filled the Polo Grounds on an overcast day to witness baseball history.[43]

In the top of the first, Maglie walked both Pee Wee Reese and Duke Snider. With two men on and one out, Jackie Robinson singled between third and shortstop. Pee Wee Reese raced home with the Dodgers' first run. Maglie settled down after that and retired the Dodgers without yielding any more runs that inning.

The Giants tried to respond in the bottom of the second. After Lockman singled, up came Thomson, who also singled, but ran past first with his head down and arrived at second when he noticed that Lockman was on the bag.

Thomson, now caught in a rundown, tried to get back to first base but to no avail and was tagged out. The rally was over as Newcombe escaped without yielding a run that inning. In the bottom of the fifth, Thomson doubled, but Newcombe again escaped without allowing a run. Finally, the Giants scored on Newcombe in the bottom of the seventh as Irvin doubled. Next, Lockman came up and sacrificed Irvin to third.

Thomson followed with a long fly to center field; Irvin tagged up and scored to even game at 1–1. In the top of the eighth, after Furillo grounded out, the Dodgers got to Maglie who gave up singles to Pee Wee Reese and Snider. With runners on first and third, Maglie bounced a curve ball that got past Giants catcher Wes Westrum. Reese scored and the Dodgers reclaimed the lead 2–1. With Snider on third, Maglie intentionally walked Robinson to face Andy Pafko. Pafko then hit a ball towards third to Thomson, who tried to backhand the ball. The ball bounced off the heel of Thomson's glove for a single. Snider came home and the Dodgers increased their lead 3–1 as Robinson went to second.

Billy Cox came up and lined a one-hopper to third, another chance for Thomson; this time the ball bounced off of his shoulder and into right field. Robinson scored and the Dodgers now led 4–1. But that was all the scoring for the Brooklyn Dodgers. The Giants did not score in the bottom of the eighth and in the top of the ninth, Larry Jansen relieved Maglie and retired the Dodgers without yielding a run.

It looked like Brooklyn would deny the Giants their Hollywood ending as Newcombe went out to pitch the bottom of the ninth with Brooklyn still ahead 4–1.

The Dodgers needed just three outs to win the pennant, but Newcombe had pitched nearly three hundred innings in 1951 and all those pitches began to take a toll on his arm. Two innings earlier, Newcombe admitted to Jackie Robinson that he was tired. Robinson coaxed Newcombe into pitching for two more innings. Newcombe's fatigue became apparent as Alvin Dark opened the bottom of the ninth with a single to right field. Gil Hodges chose to hold Dark at first. It is not known if Dark was planning to steal, but Hodges holding Dark on the bag left a hole between first and second. With a three run lead, Dressen should have moved Hodges to play behind Dark. This tactical error became apparent when Don Mueller followed with a base hit that eluded Gil Hodges' outstretched glove by a few inches, which could have been a potential double play ball, or definitely a force-out, if Hodges was playing at his normal position. Instead Dark raced to third. With Dark on third, up came Monte Irvin, who could not advance Mueller as Newcombe momentarily stymied the Giants rally. Irvin popped up to Gil Hodges for the first out. Had Hodges been positioned at his normal position and made the double play, the Dodgers would have retired the Giants and won the pennant. If Hodges had not turned a double play, there would be two outs and a man on base.

But there was only one out and Whitey Lockman kept the rally going with a double to left field. Alvin Dark trotted home to cut the Dodgers lead in half at 4–2.

As Mueller was running towards third base, he twisted his ankle. The game was held up as he was carted off the field on a stretcher. Clint Hartung went in to substitute for Mueller.

After the Giants scored their second run, the Dodgers had two men warming up in the bullpen: Carl Erskine and Ralph Branca. Dressen had asked Clyde Sukeforth, the bullpen coach, who was throwing in the bullpen. Erskine threw an overhand curve that had to be low to be good, so he threw the ball low and Sukeforth said, over the phone, that Erskine had bounced a curve. Dressen said, "Let me have Branca."[44] Erskine said over the years that the best pitch he threw throughout his entire career was the one he tossed in the bullpen on that afternoon of October 3rd. Erskine went on to say that no one ever asked Dressen, but Erskine speculated that since Campanella was hurt, Rube Walker, the back-up catcher, could hit the ball, and was a good catcher, but was slow of foot. Dressen was afraid that Walker might not be able to block one of Erskine's low curves in the dirt.[45]

Branca had pitched relief during the last game of the season, and threw 133 pitches over eight innings in the first playoff game on Monday.[46] Now he was pitching on one day's rest. Branca, who had warmed up before in the fifth and seventh innings when Newcombe allowed doubles to Thomson and Irvin, walked to the pitching mound from the bullpen and greeted Newcombe before the big right-hander headed back to the clubhouse in center field. When Branca arrived on the mound to greet Newcombe, both men patted each other, and exchanged a few pleasantries. Next, Branca conferred with Reese, Robinson, Walker, and Dressen.

The next batter up was Bobby Thomson. Thomson was in his sixth season for the Giants. He had a break-out year in 1949 when he batted .309 with 193 base hits, 27 home runs, and 109 RBIs. This year, Thomson's average was at .292 and with 152 base hits, 31 home runs, and 100 RBIs.[47]

Thomson hit a home run off Branca in the first playoff game at Ebbets Field, his fifth off Branca in 1951. But Thomson also had made two bad plays at third that day. Although Thomson's sacrifice fly scored the Giants' first run, Thomson looked like he would be the scapegoat that day. A young Willie Mays was on deck.

Durocher walked up to Thomson and said, "If you're ever going to hit one, hit one now."[48] Thomson went up to the plate.

Ralph Branca: Surrendered one of the most famous home runs in baseball history, and yet Branca has triumphed over his defeat with aplomb and grace. Today Branca's contributions have helped many retired ballplayers, winning him respect from many in the baseball and sports communities. (Photograph courtesy of the National Baseball Hall of Fame Library, Cooperstown, N.Y.)

Thomson dug in and Branca's first pitch to him was a high strike on the inside corner. Branca's next pitch was also high and inside, but Thomson swung and on the crack of the bat, the ball sailed 315 feet into the lower deck of the left field stands. Giants announcer Russ Hodges began screaming, "The Giants win pennant! The Giants win the pennant! The Giants win the pennant!" Thomson began leaping as he headed toward first. Giants infielder Eddie Stanky grabbed Durocher, jumped on his back, and happily tackled the Giants manager to the ground as Thomson kept leaping around the bases.

When he finally arrived at home, Thomson took one final leap and triumphantly jumped on home plate. There, he was met by his delirious teammates who picked him up and carried him off the field like a conquering hero. As for the Dodgers, they slowly walked to the center field clubhouse in shock and in disbelief that the game, as well as the pennant, was lost. The final standings in the National League for 1951 stood at 98–59 for the Giants and 97–60 for the Dodgers. The next day, on page 73 of the *Daily News*, the byline, written in bold words, read, "THOMSON THE HERO, BRANCA THE GOAT IN BIG PLAYOFF."[49] Joe Trimble wrote, "Ralph Branca, the poor man who threw the worst pitch in the history of Brooklyn baseball, sat down on a small set of steps, with his head in his hands." Branca's pitch to Thomson was high and inside — it was not a bad pitch. The first pitch that Thomson took for strike one according to Carl Erskine and the rest of the Dodgers was a terrible pitch.

After the Giants defeated the Dodgers in the playoffs, Durocher's men lost the World Series to the Yankees in six games. Years later, Branca spoke about his fateful pitch to Thomson: "I'll never forget watching it [the ball] head out toward left field. I thought it was just a long fly at first. I thought it was the second out ... but then I saw he'd pulled it more than I thought he had. I knew then it was going to hit the fence and that the score would be tied. But I kept praying that it wouldn't go in. And right up to the last second I didn't think it would. I can still see Pafko right up against the wall, saying, 'Sink, sink, don't go over.' But it did and all I could do was stuff my glove in my pocket and head for the clubhouse."[50]

The next year Branca wanted to come back from the playoff game loss and prove to everyone that he was not affected by Thomson's home run. Unfortunately, Branca hurt his back in spring training as he was trying to sit down when the chair fell from under him, hitting a coke bottle.[51] The trainer did not think Branca needed any adjustments to his arm so his condition was undiagnosed, and Branca had a disappointing 4–2 record that year.

In 1953, Branca received the adjustment that he should have had the year before when he found out that his pelvis was tilted, but it was too late. Though Branca regained the strength in his arm, he was not the same pitcher he was when he was 21. Branca won 68 games from 1947 to 1951 as a starter and reliever while only losing 47. Branca also pitched in over 1000 innings during that period — an average of 256 innings per year. On July 10, 1953, he was sold to the Detroit Tigers.[52] A year later, Branca appeared in five games for the New York Yankees, going 1–0 with 9 hits and 7 strike-outs. The Yankees won 103 games, but failed to win the pennant as Cleveland won 111 games that year. He came back for one more stint with the Dodgers in 1956. In his final game, Branca gave up one hit, walked two, and struck out two men. In twelve seasons Branca finished with an 88–68 record, a 3.79 ERA, and 71 complete games.

After his retirement from baseball, Branca went into the insurance business with Security Mutual Life. Branca took a five-year course and eventually became a certified insurance underwriter.[53] Throughout the sixties and seventies, Ralph Branca and Bobby Thomson made many appearances at Old Timers' games and other events to re-create their famous day on October 3, 1951. In the mid-eighties, Ralph Branca became the first president of the Baseball Assistance Team (B.A.T.S.), an organization that provides help to retired baseball players, umpires, and their families.[54]

In 1991, I saw in the paper that Ralph Branca, Bobby Thomson, and Mel Allen would be appearing in a card show at Madison Square Garden and I felt compelled to meet these men that I had watched on television many times. Upon arriving at Madison Square Garden, I wondered what I should say to Branca and Thomson. As I walked up to the table, there sat Thomson and Branca, graciously receiving autograph seekers. Baseball fans young and old who never saw either man play ball nevertheless wanted to converse with baseball history personified in these two men.

Now it was my turn to get an autograph. I was still amazed that I was meeting Thomson and Branca, who were now in their sixties. Thomson noticed my amazement and broke the ice, "Hey, where you been? I have been waiting for you." I looked around and I knew that Thomson had beckoned me to come to the table. I spoke to Thomson first. "You hit the home run," I said. "Yes," Thomson replied with a chuckle, "But you must have not been born yet." Thomson was right. I was born 17 years after his home run won the pennant for the New York Giants.

After a couple of more questions to Thomson, I gave him the book *Dynasty,* written by Peter Golenbock, to sign. The book chronicled the Yankees during their fifteen years of baseball dominance: I couldn't find the book *Bums,* also written by Golenbock, which chronicled the history of the Brooklyn Dodgers. But since Mel Allen would be there, I decided to bring *Dynasty* since all three men — Branca, Thomson and Allen — appeared in the book. After Thomson signed my book, I went over and met Ralph Branca. "So you threw the pitch," I said. "Yea, I threw the pitch," Branca replied. His voice reflected a man who has answered this question a million times, but one who knows that life goes on even after a devastating loss.

I remembered reading in *Bums* how Branca recounted to Golenbock that he was a good pitcher when his career began. Based on this information, I thought for a second before asking another question.

"You won 21 ball games when you were 21 years old," I said. Branca's face brightened. "Yeah, I did. I did win 21 ball games." He replied, "Sit down." Branca seemed to appreciate my comment, as a knowledgeable baseball fan who knew his record — a young man who never saw the New York Giants or the Brooklyn Dodgers play baseball, but a baseball fan who had the decency to take the time and read about Branca's entire career. Ralph Branca won more than he lost. When one looks at his record it is clear that he was a good pitcher. Branca explained to me how Dressen made bad decisions by overusing the Dodgers pitching staff, which inevitably led to sore arms. In short, Dressen used only five starters down the stretch and wore a couple of his pitchers out.

Branca is correct with this assessment. In a game on September 12 against the Reds, Don Newcombe gave up three runs to Cincinnati and was knocked out in the first inning. Newcombe reported that he had a sore arm the next day, but Dressen pitched him in his next start on September 17, which Newcombe also lost.[55] In all, Newcombe would lose 3 out of his last 5 starts. Branca also told me how passionate the fans in Brooklyn were, especially when it came to rooting for their Dodgers in Ebbets Field. And he drew the exact dimensions of Brooklyn fabled ballpark — 393 feet toward center field, 351 toward left center and 315 down the right field line. I sat there like a child on Santa Claus' lap as I hung on every word that Branca said. After our conversation, I left feeling one word about Branca: class.

Mel Allen was next. Allen, known as "The Voice of the Yankees," broadcast Yankee games for four decades. We talked about how Phil Rizzuto, whom Mel had watched play baseball and whom I had a chance to listen to growing up as a baseball fan, should be in the Hall of Fame. Rizzuto made the hallowed sanctum in 1994. After our conversation, Allen signed my book.

Before the 2000 Subway Series, Branca attended an inter-league game in 1998 with his son-in-law Bobby Valentine, the manager of the New York

Mets. The Mets were playing the New York Yankees at Shea Stadium. Inter-league baseball, which started the year before, allowed a new generation of New York fans to experience the feeling of a Subway Series. Though it was not October, the games counted in the standings.

In the top of the eighth, Mets reliever Mel Rojas gave up a three-run home run to Yankee rightfielder Paul O'Neill. Many people jumped on Bobby Valentine for allowing Rojas, who had been ineffective in his pre-vious relief appearance, to pitch to O'Neill. O'Neill's home run enabled the Yankees to win the game 8–4, and the new rivalry in New York City must have reminded Branca of the rivalry that he had participated in years ago. Branca came to Rojas' defense, saying that Rojas threw a pitch and you have to give O'Neill credit for hitting a home run.

Branca is a hero for the things he has done on and off the field. Since B.A.T.S. was founded in 1986, Branca, along with Carl Erskine, has raised millions of dollars in grants to help retired ball players. Some of these men have been afflicted with alcohol and drug problems. Other recipients include former Negro League players and widows of former baseball play-ers whose houses might have been foreclosed on if it were not for the selfless-ness of one man whom some people might only know for the home run that was hit by Bobby Thomson. Finally, Branca is a hero for the dignity he has displayed after his fateful pitch in 1951. Joe DiMaggio, who became a legend one month after he retired following the World Series that year, was treated as a hero until he died in 1999. Ever since Thomson's home run, Branca has exhibited the same class that was attributed to DiMaggio.

Branca said it best: "A person commits a crime, and he gets pardoned. I've never been pardoned; then again Nixon was pardoned."[56]

If society can forgive a criminal, then why can't it forgive a ball player? Those who still want to hold Branca responsible for losing the pennant can be described one way: narrow-minded.

Looking back on the 1951 season, manager Charles Dressen deserves some of the blame. Dressen was so keen on beating his former boss that some of his actions cost the Dodgers the pennant. Though it doesn't show up in the box score, Dressen had the Dodgers yell at the Giants. Both club-houses were only separated by a brick wall. After the Dodgers bellowed, "The Giants are dead, the Giants are dead," the Giants had an added incen-tive to beat the Dodgers.

Out of the five pitchers that Dressen used during the last five weeks of the season, Clem Labine did not make a start during the last nine days of the season. On September 25th, Bud Podbielan relieved Branca after he was knocked out in the first inning in a 6–3 loss to the Braves.[57] Podbielan came in and threw eight shutout innings. Podbielan also won the last game of the season in relief and always had success against the Giants, but did not make an appearance in any of the playoff games. Branca started 27 games and made 13 relief appearances in 1951.

If Dressen had inserted Labine or Podbielan, the Dodger pitching staff would not have been tired and overused during those crucial five weeks left in the season. And with a few more Dodger wins, Branca wouldn't have had to pitch the final playoff game.

Recently, the *Wall Street Journal* unearthed information that Leo Dorucher and the Giants stole the signs from the Brooklyn Dodgers during the 1951 season.[58] This theft was done using a powerful telescope that was positioned in center field. Giants catcher Sal Yvars would see the signs and then relay them back to the bullpen. From there the bullpen would relay the signs to the batter. The hitting that seemed powerful in the first half disappeared in the second half of the season as both Snider and Furillo were mired in batting slumps.

Finally, the potential double play that could have occurred if Hodges was playing in his proper position at first base might have changed things. If Hodges had not turned a double play, he certainly could have made the force-out and Thomson's home run would have tied the game at 4–4.

With this evidence, it is obvious that Branca cannot be blamed for losing the pennant for the Dodgers, yet baseball fans still pin the loss of the pennant on Branca because he was on the mound when the winning run was scored. The only run charged to Branca was Thomson's home run. Branca was not responsible for the other four runs. Simply put, the 1951 Dodgers lost the pennant as a team.

The New York Giants would win one more pennant in 1954. In that World Series, the Giants swept the Cleveland Indians in four games. The Series was highlighted by Willie Mays' over-the-shoulder catch in Game 1.

The Brooklyn Dodgers would win four more pennants and the World Series in 1955. Game 7 of the 1955 Series would always be known as the sweetest for all Brooklyn fans, as starter Johnny Podres, first baseman Gil Hodges, and leftfielder Sandy Amoros all single-handedly helped give Brooklyn its first and only championship. The Dodgers won the pennant the next year but lost the 1956 Series to the Yanks. Highlights of this Series include Don Larsen's perfect game in the fifth contest. The New York Giants and Brooklyn Dodgers ceased to exist after September 29, 1957.

CHAPTER 5

Mike Torrez

The next five stories differ from the previous four. Baseball fans were able to watch these five contests unfold due to the media, which had increased ten times since the playoff game in 1951.

Television: a wonderful medium. The ability to see a live event or even a tape-delayed program can leave a lasting impact on our lives, shape our culture, and greatly influence our opinions. Though it has recently been criticized for some of its content, television still remains a powerfully influential medium, even with the advent of the Internet.

Americans celebrated as a nation in triumph when Neil Armstrong walked on the moon. And we as a nation came together in tragedy when our other American heroes— seven brave Americans— perished aboard the space shuttle *Challenger*.

Television has the same impact in baseball. The 1951 Giant-Dodger playoff was the first televised game coast to coast. In 1950, 9 percent of American households owned a television. By 1960, 87 percent of American households owned a television.[1] That year Americans witnessed the first televised presidential debate between John F. Kennedy, then a Massachusetts senator, and Richard M. Nixon, then the vice president. Those who heard the debate on the radio thought Nixon won, while those who viewed the debate on television thought Kennedy won. But it was not about the issues; rather it was Nixon's televised appearance, his five o'clock shadow and perspiration, that made a negative impact on the viewers.

Today, one can hardly walk into a house, or an apartment, without seeing a television. When the post season arrives in baseball, every hit, play, pitch, and strike becomes magnified by the use of television, for the images are burned into every viewer's memory. As Dodger broadcaster Vin Scully said during the 1986 World Series, "If a picture says a thousand words, we [watching television] have seen a million words."[2]

Baseball, as did America, transformed itself again during the next 27 years leading up to our next story. During the late 1940s and 1950s highways were constructed all over America. Baseball fans abandoned the inner cities for life in the suburbs. Soon baseball began broadcasting its games coast to coast; now, fans could view the games from their homes on television and were hesitant to travel into the cities to the stadiums. This mass exodus had a profound impact on the game as attendance plummeted.

Ultimately, a losing team could not survive financially, and baseball experienced a geographical shift as the Boston Braves transferred the franchise to Milwaukee. The Braves would move to Georgia 12 years later and become the Atlanta Braves. The following year the St. Louis Browns moved and resurfaced as the Baltimore Orioles. In 1955 the Philadelphia Athletics moved to Kansas City, and like the Braves, the team would be moved to California a decade later to become the Oakland Athletics. New York also experienced the changing times in 1958, as both National League teams migrated to California and were re-born as the San Francisco Giants and Los Angeles Dodgers. The nation's capital was not spared as the Washington Senators moved to Minneapolis and were re-named the Minnesota Twins. As the 1960s ushered in a new era of space technology, baseball expanded as a new Washington Senators team was created. A decade later, the Senators moved to the Lone Star State to become the Texas Rangers.

The American League finally arrived on the West Coast in the beginning of the decade. The Los Angeles Angels team made its debut in 1961. They would become the California Angels, and then the Anaheim Angels.

Ebbets Field, the Polo Grounds, and Sportsman's Park would be demolished. It was during this decade that America witnessed Camelot, only to see John F. Kennedy assassinated in his prime. Minorities finally were treated as first class citizens with the passage of the Civil Rights Bill. This bill allowed black, white, and Hispanic players to eat and lodge in the same hotels together, which was a far cry from when minority ball players lived in separate facilities even after baseball was integrated in 1947.

As the 1960s bought change in America, baseball was also affected by this change. In 1966, the ballplayers revamped the Players Association. Though it was founded 20 years before, the Players Association was ineffective regarding the players' salaries and pension benefits. The improved Players Association, led by Marvin Miller, raised the ball players' salaries and improved their pensions.[3]

The end of the decade brought surprises, as baseball became an international sport with the addition of the Montreal Expos. For the first time baseball would be divided into divisions and league championships would decide the pennant. Men would walk on the moon and the Mets would win the World Series in only their eighth season — a giant leap considering their inept play at the beginning of the decade.

Out of all the years during the sixties, 1968, like 1941, left its mark on baseball as well as America. In the beginning of 1968, the Tet Offensive convinced many Americans that the United States was losing the Vietnam War. On March 31, President Lyndon B. Johnson announced that he would not seek re-election.

In the next two months, assassins took the lives of Dr. Martin Luther King, Jr., and Senator Robert F. Kennedy. Rioting occurred at the Democratic convention in August. But some good news did happen. The crew of the USS *Pueblo*, which was captured earlier in the year, returned home safe.

In baseball, it was the year of the pitcher. Denny McLain of the Detroit Tigers went 31–9 in 1968; no one has won 30 games since. Bob Gibson of the St. Louis Cardinals went 22–9, pitched 28 complete games, and had an amazing 1.12 ERA. Don Drysdale of the Los Angeles Dodgers set a major league record of 55⅔ scoreless innings.

With the 1970s, baseball fans bade farewell to most of the old ball-parks, as Forbes Field, Crosley Field, and Shibe Park faded into memory. In only one year of existence, the Seattle Pilots would become the Milwaukee Brewers. Baseball would return to Seattle in 1977 when the Mariners and Toronto Blue Jays joined the American League.

Also in the 1970s, baseball would have different rules for each league. The American League adopted the designated hitter to bat for the pitcher. The National League did not adopt this rule. Thus, for the first time, the leagues would have two different rules in regards to the pitcher. The National League has said the designated hitter rule changes the strategy of the game. By putting the designated hitter in the game, a manager can prolong offense in an inning. In the National League, such a situation might require putting in a pinch hitter and taking out a pitcher. Also, for over a century, baseball had lived without the use of a designated hitter, but the rule was here to stay for the meantime.

The reserve clause, which bound a player to a team unless he was released or traded, was challenged by Curt Flood. Flood's case went all the way to the Supreme Court. The Supreme Court went against Curt Flood in 1972 by a 5–3 decision. However, three years later, an arbitrator named Peter Sietz would rule that two players, Dave McNally and Andy Messersmith, were free to sign by their own will. This decision put an end to the reserve clause.[4]

Our next story takes place in 1978. It was a memorable year for Yankee fans, but for Red Sox fans 1978 would be a disappointing season, though it was nothing compared to what would happen eight years later.

With the Giants and Dodgers firmly established in California, their rivalry went with them. However, baseball's East Coast rivalry was still alive between the New York Yankees and the Boston Red Sox, which has lasted nearly a century now. The rivalry began at the end of the 1904 season, when the defending World Champion Boston Red Sox [Pilgrims] led the New York Yankees [Highlanders] by a half game with two to play. New York needed to win the doubleheader to claim its first pennant.

Forty-one game winner Jack Chesbro, of New York, squared off against Bill Dineen, of Boston, who pitched 36 complete games that year. Chesbro and Dineen both were tough and up to the task. Both men yielded only two runs through eight innings.

In the bottom of the ninth, Lou Criger singled, made it to second on Dineen's sacrifice, then advanced to third on Albert Selbach's groundout. Fred Parent was at bat when Chesbro unloaded a wild pitch that sailed over catcher John Kleinow's head. Criger scored the winning run and Dineen held on to win his 37th complete game 3–2 as Boston won their second straight pennant.[5]

As mentioned in Chapter 1, New York Giants manager John McGraw and owner John T. Brush refused to play in the Fall Classic. However, that did not stop Boston as the Pilgrims (Red Sox), who appeared in the first World Series in 1903 with the Pittsburgh Pirates, had won five of them by 1918. Then in 1920 Red Sox owner Harry Frazee sold most of his star players to the Yankees. The most notable of these transactions was a 24-year-old pitcher named Babe Ruth, who was purchased by Yankees owner Jacob Ruppert for $100,000. Ruppert loaned Frazee, also a theatre owner, $300,000 to keep his play *No, No, Nannette* afloat.[6] Ruth, who possessed a great arm, also possessed a great bat and was converted to play right field when he became a Yankee.

But after Ruth and several other Red Sox joined New York, the Yankees, once dormant in the American League, became a dominant force. As for Boston, the Red Sox would not appear in a World Series for another 38 years. Meanwhile, the Yankees appeared in the World Series seven times during the mid–1920s and early 1930s, winning the championship four times. By the time Babe Ruth played in his last World Series in 1932, New York had the luster and prestige in baseball that once belonged to the Red Sox.

The Boston Red Sox slowly began to rebuild the franchise with its new owner Tom Yawkey, who bought the team in 1933.[7] Yawkey spent money refurbishing Fenway Park and the team by purchasing pitchers Lefty Grove and Jimmie Foxx from the Philadelphia A's. Second baseman Bobby Doer arrived in 1937. These improvements led the Red Sox to a second place finish the following year. In 1939, Ted Williams, a skinny leftfielder, arrived from San Diego, California, to play in Fenway Park. Williams went on to play for the Red Sox and became one of the greatest hitters in the game.[8]

After 1932, the Yankees had not appeared in a World Series for four years. That all changed when Joe DiMaggio, a rookie center fielder from San Francisco, California, came to the Yankees. DiMaggio, along with Lou Gehrig, who had been with Babe Ruth during the Roaring Twenties, led the Yankees to four straight championships from 1936 to 1939.

The Yankees won three pennants and two World Series from 1941 to 1943. Many baseball players had enlisted in the armed services during World War II and the Red Sox were hit the hardest by these enlistments. The team floundered. After World War II ended, most baseball stars had returned to the game and the Red Sox were ready.

In 1946, Rudy York joined a talented Red Sox team already stocked with players such as Williams, Dom DiMaggio (younger brother of Joe), and Johnny Pesky. Pitchers Denny Galehouse, Tex Hughson, and Boo Ferris led Boston to its first pennant since 1918. Their opponent, the St. Louis Cardinals, defeated the Red Sox in seven games. The deciding run was scored by Enos Slaughter, who raced home from first base after Harry Walker's base hit into center field, in a feat forever lauded as "Slaughter's Dash." The Yankees rebounded and won the World Series in 1947. The next year Boston would finish in a tie with the Cleveland Indians on the last day of the season, but Cleveland would defeat Boston in the American League's first playoff game 8–3.

In 1949, the Red Sox suffered even more hardship as they led the New York Yankees in the final weekend of the season by one game with two left to play. Then the Yankees took the final two games of the season to win the pennant by a single game. From 1948 to 1949, the Red Sox won 192 games, but had nothing to show for it. As for the Yankees, the team, under new manager Casey Stengel, won five straight championships from 1949 to 1953, and continued to dominate during the 1950s. The team won eight pennants and five World Series. The Yankees did not stop there; they won five straight pennants and two more World Series until the early 1960s. From 1921 to 1964, the Yankees had won 29 pennants and 20 World Series titles. During that time the Red Sox had only appeared in only one World Series and lost. The team did not fare well during the 1950s and early 1960s. Ted Williams retired in 1960; his replacement was Carl Yastrzemski, who, ironically, grew up in Long Island, New York, and whose father wanted his son to play for the Yankees. Instead, Yastrzemski replaced Ted Williams in left field.

The first six years of the 1960s did not bode well for the Red Sox, who failed to play .500 ball. Then in 1967, manager Dick Williams (no relation to Ted) arrived and instilled a new confidence in the team. This confidence propelled Boston to a tight race for the American League pennant. Four teams vied for a chance to play in the World Series.

Despite the loss of slugger Tony Conigliaro in August of that year, the Red Sox outlasted the Twins, White Sox, and Indians to win the pennant. Boston's pennant run was called "The Impossible Dream." But just as they did in 1946, the Red Sox lost the World Series to the St. Louis Cardinals in seven games, including three of those contests to Cardinals ace Bob Gibson.

By this time the Yankees had slipped into the second division finishing ninth in 1965 and dead last in 1966. In 1969, baseball was split into four divisions and the Yankees and Red Sox both were paired into the American League Eastern Division.

Both teams made a run at the Eastern Division title in the early seventies; however, both the Red Sox and Yankees failed to win the division by a few games.

In 1975, the addition of new players such as Fred Lynn, who that season won the rookie of the year and the MVP, and Jim Rice led the Boston Red Sox to the Eastern Division crown. In the LCS the Red Sox defeated the Oakland A's in three straight games to win the pennant. Boston faced the Cincinnati Reds in what some baseball fans have called the greatest World Series ever.

After five games, the Cincinnati Reds led the Red Sox three games to two. The Sox needed to win Game 6 to prolong the series. The Reds were leading the Red Sox 6–3 in the eighth when the Red Sox had a rally going with two men on. Then Boston pinch-hitter Bernie Carbo stepped up and tied the game with a home run at 6–6.

Brilliant plays by both teams in the ninth, tenth, and eleventh innings kept the score tied at 6–6. In the bottom of the twelfth, Boston catcher Carlton Fisk hit a long line drive that hit the foul pole for a home run. Boston won the game 7–6, but lost the series to the Reds 4–3 the next night.

For the Yankees, it took twelve years to rebound since their last pennant win in 1964. The comeback started in 1973 when the Yankees were sold to a shipping magnate from Cleveland, Ohio, named George M. Steinbrenner, III.[9] Slowly, the Yankees began to rebuild a winning team. In 1974, they almost made the post season for the first time in a decade, but lost a doubleheader to the Red Sox and their first Eastern Division championship.[10] It was one of a few times that the Boston exacted revenge on the Yankees since the sale of Babe Ruth.

Through trades that brought the Yankees Sparky Lyle, Lou Piniella, Graig Nettles, Willie Randolph, Chris Chambliss, and Mickey Rivers, and with the addition of free agent Catfish Hunter, the Yankees were back in the series when Chambliss led off the bottom of the ninth of Game 5 of the 1976 ALCS with a home run to beat the Kansas City Royals 7–6. That would be the highlight for the Yankees that year as the Cincinnati Reds swept four games from New York to win the World Series. As for the Red Sox, they finished third that year.

The next year, the Yankees went all the way and won the World Series in six games. The winning pitcher in the sixth game was Mike Torrez.

Michael Augustine Torrez was one of eight children born to John and Mary Torrez on August 28, 1946, in Topeka, Kansas.[11] Torrez grew up in a poor Mexican section of Topeka; since the neighborhood was populated by Mexicans, Torrez rarely encountered any prejudice.

Torrez had the makings to be in the major leagues. When he was 12, he participated in and won a pitching contest given by the Cincinnati Reds, whose top farm team was located in Topeka. Jim Maloney, the Reds' star pitcher, held a tryout for the youngsters in the area. After Torrez won the tryout, Maloney took the young pitcher under his wing and helped him improve his delivery. Topeka High School did not have a baseball program, but that did not stop Torrez. His years of playing sandlot ball paid off when at age 18 he was signed by Branch Rickey to play in the Cardinals organization for $20,000. Torrez would be the last person Rickey would sign to a major league contract; the man who broke the color barrier with the signing of Jackie Robinson would die a year later on December 9, 1965.

Torrez worked his way through the Cardinals organization, first playing for Raleigh in the Carolina League, then for the Tulsa Oilers (now the Drillers) in Double A ball, and finally for the Arkansas Travelers in Triple A. The nomadic career of Mike Torrez began when he appeared in a few games during the 1967-1968 seasons, the years the Cardinals were in the World Series. In Torrez's first full season in 1969, he appeared in 24 games with a respectable 10–4 record and a 3.59 ERA.[12]

His sophomore season was not as successful. He went 8–10 with a 4.22 ERA. The next season, after nine games and a 1–2 record, Torrez was traded to the Montreal Expos for righthander Bob Reynolds.[13]

His first year with Montreal was curtailed due to an arm injury. Torrez bounced back in 1972 with a 16–12 record; overall he would go 40–32 with the Expos over the next three years.

Torrez became a member of the Baltimore Orioles in 1975 when he and Ken Singleton were traded for Dave McNally and Rich Collins and a minor leaguer.[14] It was a trade that the Expos would later regret as Torrez went 20–9 and led the league in winning percentage with .690 that year, and Singleton went on to have a successful career playing for the Orioles in two World Series.

Despite his success as an Oriole, Torrez was involved in a seven player deal which sent him and Don Baylor to the Oakland A's in exchange for Reggie Jackson and Ken Holtzman.[15] The change in scenery did not stop Torrez, who won 16 games for the A's and threw 43⅓ scoreless innings, breaking the record held by Hall-of-Famer Jim "Catfish" Hunter. But these scoreless innings were not enough to keep Torrez an Oakland A as Torrez moved again on April 27, 1977. This time he was traded to the Yankees for Doc Ellis and two minor leaguers, Larry Murray and Marty Perez.[16] The acquisition proved fruitful to New York as Torrez helped the Yankees with 14 wins (including six straight complete games victories) en route to the Eastern Division crown.[17] In the fifth and deciding game of the LCS, the Kansas City Royals knocked starter Ron Guidry out after three innings. The Yankees were trailing the Royals by three runs when Torrez came in on only one day's rest and threw 5⅓ scoreless innings. The Yankees rallied and won the game and the pennant 5–3.

In the World Series against the Los Angeles Dodgers, Torrez threw two complete victories. His second complete game, which included three home runs from Reggie Jackson, clinched the Series for the Yankees. And it was Torrez who made the final put-out when he caught Lee Lacy's pop-up to end the 1977 World Series.

Over the off season, the Yankees offered Torrez a five year, $1.5 million contract. The Yankees declined to offer Torrez more money, for the organization feared that Torrez, at age 32, would be a high risk. Instead the Yankees spent $2.6 million and signed reliever Rich (Goose) Gossage for six years. Torrez opted for free agency and signed a six year, $2.7 million deal with arch rival Boston Red Sox.[18] It was his fifth team in five years. Boston also added second baseman Jerry Remy from the California Angels in exchange for Don Aase and righthander Dennis Eckersley from the Cleveland Indians for Rick Wise.[19]

Torrez and Eckersley joined the pitching staff that was led by Luis Tiant and Bill Lee. Sluggers Fred Lynn, Jim Rice, Carlton Fisk, and Carl Yastrzemski, who at age 39, still continued to produce at the plate. The Boston Red Sox finished 1½ games in second place tied with Baltimore in 1977. Boston's manager, Don Zimmer, was confident that his 1978 Red Sox could win the American League Eastern Division and possibly the pennant.

The World Champion Yankees also made a move to defend their championship. In addition to signing Gossage, New York signed free agent power-hitting first baseman Jim Spencer.[20] The Yankees pitching staff included Guidry, Ed Figueroa, Andy Messersmith, Don Gullet, and Jim

(Catfish) Hunter. Hunter, though plagued with arm trouble, gutted out the season and managed to win 17 games in 1977. Finally, they added Cy Young Award winner Sparky Lyle. The left hand reliever was on the mound when the Yankees won the pennant from the Royals the year before, but Lyle wondered about his role on the Yankees now that Gossage was on the team.

Sluggers Chambliss, Nettles, Piniella, catcher Thurman Munson, and Jackson provided the offense for the team. Both teams were evenly matched at the end of the season, but the Yankees would have a tough time getting there.

New York started off the season badly as the Yankees lost their first game on April 7 when the newly acquired Goose Gossage gave up a home run to Richie Zisk in the bottom of the ninth to give the Texas Rangers a 2–1 victory.[21] Despite the loss, Ron Guidry gave a solid performance. It was a portent of things to come for the Yankee southpaw.

Boston too started the season on a sour note, losing the first game 6–5 to the Chicago White Sox. The next day, Mike Torrez, Boston's new acquisition, started the second game of the season against the White Sox with a no-decision, giving up four runs and leaving the game in the sixth tied at 4–4. The White Sox scored two runs in the ninth to edge the Red Sox 6–5 for the second day in a row before finally winning the rubber game 5–0.[22]

The Yankees won their first game on April 9 as Ed Figueroa pitched a gem and downed the Rangers 7–1. But the Yankees received some bad news days later: Don Gullet, another pitcher who joined the Yankees via free agency, was sidelined with a shoulder injury on April 18. Jim Beattie, recalled from Tacoma, replaced Gullet in the Yankee rotation.[23]

New York and Boston both finished the month above .500. Each team trailed the Detroit Tigers, who got off to great start, but began to fade from the top of the standings. In May, it looked like the Yankees were back on track, but New York's pitching staff was further damaged as Hunter and Andy Messersmith went on the disabled list.

The hitting was good enough to offset the pitching woes of the Yankees as New York went 19–8 in May. But Boston went 23–7 during that month and moved into a first place tie with Detroit in mid–May before finally taking over for good on May 23.[24]

The Yankees began to fall behind Boston; New York lost 9 out of 12 games during the first two weeks in June. Yet, even when the Yankees won a few games that month, it was a Pyrrhic victory as the team received more bad news when they lost shortstop Bucky Dent to a pulled hamstring. Second baseman Willie Randolph and center fielder Mickey Rivers also were injured and joined Dent on the disabled list. The Yankees managed to stay in the pennant race largely due to Guidry, who was the only bright spot during the first two months of the Yankee season. In June, Guidry ran his unbeaten streak to 12 games and an astounding 1.45 ERA. Also, Guidry was now the stopper to Yankee losing streaks as each win followed a Yankee loss.[25] One of Guidry's gems occurred on June 17. The Angels had beaten the Yankees the night before 10–7 to leave New York seven games in back of the Red Sox. Guidry took the mound that night and after Bobby Grich led off the game with a double, Guidry was in complete command of the game, striking out Angel after Angel. Guidry set a precedent that evening which remains to this day. As the game wore on, the strikeouts piled up, and when Guidry had two strikes on a batter, the fans would begin to cheer for Guidry to get that third strike. Guidry did not disappoint the fans that night; he fanned 18 Angels en route to a 4–0 masterpiece.[26]

Along with Guidry's winning streak, Gossage was starting to save ball games.

But New York returned to its losing ways the next afternoon as Ron Fairly of the Angels blasted a home run to edge the Yankees 3–2.[27] The next night the Yankees headed to Fenway Park to play Boston in a three game series. This was the first time that both teams had faced each other in 1978. It was Boston who seized the opportunity and won the first game. With the score tied at 4–4 in the eighth, the Red Sox exploded for six runs off of Gossage and Sparky Lyle to win the game 10–4. In the second game, New York turned the tables on Boston and won by the same score.[28]

It was Torrez's first start against his former team, and it was an inauspicious one at that. The big blow occurred in the top of the seventh, when shortstop Fred ("The Chicken") Stanley, substituting for the injured Bucky Dent, deposited a Mike Torrez slider into the screen over the left field wall to turn a 4–3 deficit into a 7–4 lead. The Yankees added three more runs to turn out the lights on the Red Sox.

But the celebration was short lived. The next night, Boston whipped the Yankees 9–2. The loss dropped New York into third place and dropped Jim Beattie back to the minors.[29]

Despite splitting a two game series the next week, both teams were headed in different directions as the Yankees finished the last days in June by losing a doubleheader to the Brewers to end the month by going 14–15. Boston went 18–7 in June and led the Yankees by nine full games.[30,31]

However, more was yet to come. In July, the Yankees again went to Boston for a short two game series. New York lost the first game at Fenway Park as Eckersley defeated the Yankees 8–5. It was Eckersley's third win against the Yankees in the last two weeks. Rain postponed the next day's game on

July 4, which gave the wounded Yankees a reprieve. This game would be made up in September.

But the brief interlude did not help the Yankees as New York won only 2 out of their next 10 games. By July 20, the Yankees record stood at 48–42 while Boston's record was at 62–28, a full fourteen games in front of New York.

Carl Yastrzemski had commented that the 1978 Red Sox had the best pitching and hitting that he had ever seen. At this point in the season, Yastrzemski was right. Dennis Eckersley was 11–2, Bill Lee was 10–3, Mike Torrez was 12–4, and Luis Tiant chipped in with a 7–2 record. The Boston outfield comprised Yastrzemski, Lynn, and Rice who batted over .300.[32]

The only Yankee who batted over .300 was Lou Piniella. His average stood at .303 followed by Munson's .295, Chambliss' .289 and Jackson's .262. The only Yankee starter in double figures was Ron Guidry whose record stood at 13–1. Ed Figueroa was second at 8–7, followed by reliever Sparky Lyle who stood at 6–1.[33]

There was more drama in store for New York. On July 17, the Yankees were playing the Royals when Reggie Jackson, whose relations with Yankees manager Billy Martin had always been strained, ignored Martin's orders. The score was tied 5–5 in the tenth. Jackson was at bat with Munson on first, when Martin instructed Dick Howser, the third base coach, to flash the bunt sign to Jackson. On the mound was Al Hrabosky, known as "The Mad Hungarian," who would stand on the mound and psych himself up before facing a batter. Hrabosky threw a fastball by Jackson, so Martin took off the bunt sign. Jackson didn't move. Howser called time, went to see Jackson, and told him that Martin had taken off the bunt sign, but Jackson remained adamant, tried to bunt, and struck out. Jackson contended that he was trying to move the runners which was why he ignored the bunt sign. Whatever the slugger's reasons, Martin was livid. To make matters worse, the Yankees lost the game 9–7. After the loss to the Royals, Martin suspended Jackson for five games for his insubordination.[34]

A week later, the Yankees actually started to turn their season around with a modest five game winning streak. However, peace and tranquillity still eluded the Yankees.

On July 23, after Reggie Jackson's five game suspension had expired, the Yankee slugger returned to the lineup. Coincidentally, New York's five game winning streak occurred during Jackson's absence. After the Yankees defeated the Chicago White Sox 3–1, Martin, still miffed over Jackson's defiance a week earlier, uttered these famous words, "The two of them deserve each other. One's a born liar [Jackson] the other is [Steinbrenner] convicted."[35] Martin was referring to George Steinbrenner, who was convicted in 1974 for illegally giving money to former President Richard Nixon's 1972 re-election campaign.

Martin, in tears, thanked his coaches and his players and resigned as manager of the Yankees the next day. After Martin's resignation, Hall of Fame pitcher Bob Lemon became the new manager of Yankees. Under Lemon's quiet stewardship, the Yankees began their comeback. New York won 12 out of their next 14 games and by the end of July, the Yankees had cut the Red Sox lead to 6½ games. After the All-Star Break in mid–July, Boston had lost 8 out of 10 games.

On August 1, Pete Rose's hitting streak ended at 44 games. The Yankees, on the other hand, opened the month of August with an 8–1 win over the Rangers. The next night, Boston arrived in New York for a crucial two-game series at Yankee Stadium. The Red Sox responded to the Yankees charge with an assault of their own. In the first game Boston spotted the Yankees five runs by the third, but the Red Sox rallied and tied the game in the eighth. Both teams scored three more runs, and the game went into extra innings, but was called due to the one o'clock curfew with the score still tied at 8–8.

Boston won the suspended game the next day by scoring two runs in the seventeenth inning. Then the Red Sox won the rain-shortened second game 8–1 to push their lead back to 8½ games.[36]

Many in the baseball world thought the Yankees had suffered a major blow and that the Eastern Division race was over, especially the next night when New York lost to the Orioles 2–1. However, the Red Sox gave the Yankees some hope by losing to the Brewers 5–1, to keep New York's faint Eastern Division hopes alive.

The Yankees picked themselves up with a six game winning streak, but the streak only shaved a game off the Red Sox's lead to trail Boston by 7½ games. This mini–winning streak seemed to put New York back on the right track, but then disaster struck. On August 12, the Yankees were playing Baltimore in Memorial Stadium when the lights went out three times. The blackouts angered the Yankees, who felt that the delays cost the team a win.[37]

The Red Sox had an easy night, sweeping a doubleheader from the Milwaukee Brewers. The next night, the Yankees seemed to hit rock bottom. After six innings, the Orioles led the Yankees 3–0, then New York struck for five runs in the top of the seventh to take a 5–3 lead. This time, the elements conspired against the Yankees as it rained profusely. The field became so unplayable that the Orioles could not bat in the bottom of the seventh. The rules mandated that the score revert back to the last completed inning which gave Baltimore a 3–0 win.[38] The loss pushed the

Yankees back to 9 games, for in Milwaukee, Torrez went 10 innings and won his fourteenth game 4–3.

Torrez won his next start on August 18, as he gave up three hits and defeated the A's 6–3 to push his record to 15–6.[39] Jim Rice supplied the offense as he went 4 for 5 and hit his thirtieth home run. But this would be Torrez's last win for six weeks until he won his sixteenth game; his next start would make baseball history. Torrez's problem mirrored those of his teammates in late August, and as if on cue, the Red Sox experienced the same problems that plagued the Yankees earlier in the season.

On August 26 Jerry Remy was injured when he was hit by a pitch that left him with a damaged wrist. Four days later, rightfielder Dwight Evans was beaned in the back of the head by Seattle pitcher Mike Parrott, causing Evans to miss a few games. When Evans returned to the lineup, he became a liability, dropping four balls in right field in one week. Lynn, Fisk, and shortstop Butch Hobson joined Evans on the disabled list. As for Hobson, who had a strong bat, he was playing with a bad elbow which caused him to make a league-leading 43 errors at third base. It became so bad that Hobson asked out of the lineup; he feared he was hurting the team with his defense.[40] First baseman George Scott, known as "the Boomer," was in a batting slump. The pitching was no better as Lee fared even worse than Torrez. He lost seven games, feuded with manager Don Zimmer, once calling him a gerbil, was taken out of the rotation, and was replaced by Jim Wright.[41]

New York — given up for dead on July 20, August 3, and on August 13 — won 12 out of the next 15 games and lost no ground to the Red Sox in August as they trailed Boston by 6½ games on August 31. Despite their injuries, the Red Sox put together a winning month by going 20–9.

One of the main reasons for the Yankees' success was Catfish Hunter. Through the use of arm manipulation, Hunter won six games in August to stabilize the pitching staff.

September 1 was another matter as the Seattle Mariners defeated Hunter 3–0, but the lead remained the same as the Red Sox lost that day to the A's 5–1. Mike Torrez sported a 25–9 lifetime record in September, but on the 2nd of September, Torrez's pitching longevity could not help him as the A's defeated Torrez 4–3, and along with New York's 6–2 win over the Mariners, reduced Boston's lead to 5½ games.[42]

Both teams won on the next day. On September 4, New York split a doubleheader with the Tigers as Boston lost again to the A's to shave off another half game to lead the Yankees by five games.[43]

The Red Sox could not stop the bleeding as they lost the next night to the Orioles 4–1. In that game, Orioles starter Jim Palmer defeated a Boston rookie named Bobby Sprowl, who took the loss, giving up three runs in the game. The Red Sox did not help matters by committing three errors that night. Meanwhile, the Yankees triumphed over the Tigers 4–2 to trim Boston's lead to four games.[44]

The following night veterans Luis Tiant (37) and Yastrzemski (39) helped Boston slow down their losing streak as Yastrzemski homered and Tiant shut out the Orioles 2–0. The lead remained the same as Yankees kept pace by defeating the Tigers 8–2.[45]

New York marched into Fenway Park on September 7 for an all-important four game series. The Yankees knew that if they won 3 out of 4 games, New York would only trail the Red Sox by two games. Boston knew that if they split with the Yankees there would be no damage as the Red Sox would still retain their four game lead.

Some have called the four game series between the Red Sox and Yankees "The Boston Massacre." The Red Sox simply collapsed. In the first game of the series Hunter opposed Torrez; this was the make-up game originally scheduled on July 4. At that time the Yankees were losing and the Red Sox were winning. Now, both teams were experiencing a reversal of fortune. The Yankees won the game 15–3, scoring most of their runs in the first four innings.

Yankee rookie pitcher Jim Beattie, who was sent back to the minors in mid–June, opposed Boston's Jim Wright in the second game. The Yankees continued the onslaught as they pummeled the Red Sox 13–2. This time New York scored eight runs in the first two innings. The Red Sox made matters worse by making seven errors in the game. Hoping for a split that would have given the Red Sox an emotional and psychological lift, Boston had its fire-baller, Dennis Eckersley, on the mound. But not even Eckersley, who had beaten the Yankees thrice in 1978, could save the Red Sox that day, as Guidry tossed his seventh shutout of the season and blanked Boston on two hits as the Yankees won the game 7–0. In the final game of the series, played on September 10, Ed Figueroa beat Bobby Sprowl and Boston lost 7–4 to complete an unlikely four game sweep at Fenway Park. The win moved New York into a first place tie for the Eastern Division with the Red Sox.[46]

For the Yankees, they had done what no one expected. New York not only swept the Red Sox in four games, something they had not done since 1949, but also embarrassed Boston in their own ballpark. It seemed as if the Yankees batted at will against the Red Sox. New York outscored Boston 42–9, outhit them 67–21, and outplayed them as the Yankees committed five errors as opposed to twelve by the Red Sox.

A week later at the stadium, the Yankees took 2 out of 3 from the Red

Sox. In the first game Guidry again pitched a two hit shutout, his eighth of the season as the Yankees defeated the Red Sox 4–0. In the second game, Hunter opposed Torrez again. Unlike the previous week's game, that day's contest only yielded five runs. The Red Sox drew first blood on Jim Rice's two-run home run in the top of the first.

The Yankees cut the lead in half in the bottom of the inning and tied the score at 2–2 on Jackson's home run in the bottom of the fifth. In the bottom of the ninth, Rivers tripled over Yastrzemski who played a shallow left field. After Torrez retired Randolph, Munson stepped up to the plate and drove the ball into right field. Rice dove and caught the ball, but his momentum carried him into the right center field. Rivers scored easily from third and the Yankees won the game 3–2.

The Red Sox won the rubber game of the series, defeating the Yankees 7–3. Dennis Eckersley returned to his dominating form; he won for the fourth time in five meetings against New York. First baseman Scott finally ended his 0–33 slump with a double to right field.[47]

The Yankees now led the Red Sox by 2½ games with 14 left in the season. Then, New York lost its edge as the Yankees lost 3 out of their next 4 games. Boston, on the other hand, refused to die and took advantage of the Yankees' mini–losing streak by winning 4 out of 6 games. On September 23, a Yankee loss to the Indians left the Red Sox one game behind New York with seven games left in the season.[48]

On September 30, Ed Figueroa fulfilled his lifelong ambition of becoming the first native-born Puerto Rican to win 20 games. John Candelaria, a fellow Puerto Rican born and raised in New York City, had accomplished this feat in 1977. Figueroa's win enabled the Yankees to clinch a tie for the Eastern Division as New York won its sixth game in a row.

But when the Yankees went for the clincher the next day, they lost the game when Indians southpaw Rick Waits, whom the Yankees twice defeated on May 24 and July 26, exacted some revenge as he whipped the Yankees 9–2 to drop New York into a first place tie.

Over in Boston, Luis Tiant pitched his last game in a Red Sox uniform and blanked Toronto Blue Jays 5–0. In the Red Sox's dugout, Mike Torrez was seen rooting for the Cleveland Indians by donning an Indians jacket and cap. On the Boston scoreboard, the message read, "Thank you, Rick Waits." The win by the Red Sox capped off a week that saw Boston win their last eight games to tie the Yankees for the Eastern Division.[49]

The 163rd game of the season was played October 2. As in the other playoff games to decide a championship, each statistic incurred would affect the player's average.

For Bob Lemon it was like going back in time. He was on the

Cleveland pitching staff when the Indians won the first American League playoff game 8–3 against the Red Sox in 1948.

Ron Guidry, who sported a 24–3 record with a 1.74 ERA, was chosen to start for the Yankees, but Guidry was not at full strength since he was pitching on three days' rest. On the other hand, Mike Torrez, who sported a 16–12 record with a 3.96 ERA, had started off the season strong, winning fifteen games by August 15 before beginning another streak, losing six games with two no decisions. However, in his last start, Torrez pitched brilliantly, as he tossed a 1–0 shutout against the Detroit Tigers.[50]

This was a fitting end to the regular season. Torrez and Guidry each pitched during the first week of the baseball season for their respective teams; now they would pitch the last game of the season in 1978.

Torrez was the toast of the pitching world after his performance in the 1977 post-season which included his win in the ALCS and two games in the World Series. Guidry was now the toast of the baseball world in 1978 as he was regularly mentioned as a Cy Young and MVP candidate.

The Yankees and Red Sox were both tied at 99–63; each team knew the winner of this playoff game would get a lift into ALCS and possibly the World Series. The bright sun pervaded Fenway Park as 32,925 participants watched Mike Torrez throw eight warm-up pitches before the start of the game.[51] Fenway Park gave the Red Sox an ovation when Mickey Rivers stepped into the batter's box to begin this historic playoff game. Torrez walked Rivers, who promptly stole second, but Torrez prevented any more damage as he struck out Munson, then induced Piniella to ground out to Brohamer at third base, and then retired Jackson who hit a fly ball that, for a moment, looked like it would bounce off the Green Monster, but the wind blowing in from left field kept the ball in Fenway Park. Yastrzemski settled under it and caught the ball on the warning track for the third out.

Guidry retired the side in the bottom of the first, and Torrez did the same in the top of the second. In the bottom of the second, the fans in Fenway Park rose and gave a standing ovation when Yastrzemski came to the plate. Yastrzemski responded to the cheers by hitting Guidry's second pitch down the right field line. The ball hooked around the foul pole and gave the Red Sox a 1–0 lead. Guidry retired the next three batters to get out of the second inning still trailing by one run.

Yet, Guidry struggled this day as Scott led off the bottom of the third with a double that Rivers could not come up with in center field. Next, Brohamer sacrificed Scott to third, but the Sox did not capitalize with Scott at third. Rick Burleson grounded out to Nettles at third, who looked Scott back to the bag, and threw to Chambliss to complete the force-out. Guidry got out of the inning when Remy flied out to Roy White in right field.

Mike Torrez

Mike Torrez: Durable right-hander who played on both sides of the Red Sox–Yankee rivalry. Although Torrez was not involved in the final outcome of the 1978 A.L. East playoff game, fans remember him for yielding a home run to Bucky Dent. (Photograph courtesy of the National Baseball Hall of Fame Library, Cooperstown, N.Y.)

Meanwhile, Mike Torrez was cruising through the Yankee lineup. He only gave up two hits: a double to Rivers in the third and a single to Piniella in the fourth. As for Guidry, he ran into more trouble in the bottom of the sixth, when Burleson led off with a double. Next, Remy came up and sacrificed Burleson over to third. This time the Red Sox capitalized on their scoring opportunity.

Jim Rice, the eventual 1978 MVP, stepped up to the plate and fought off a Guidry inside fastball that jammed him, but muscled the ball into center field to score Burleson and increase the Boston lead 2–0.

Yastrzemski came to the plate and Guidry was careful with the venerable leftfielder, getting Yastrzemski on a groundout to Chambliss at first. But Guidry could not put out the fire when he walked Fisk. With runners on first and second and two outs, up came Fred Lynn. Lou Piniella, playing in right field, knew that Guidry was pitching on three days' rest and was not as dominating as he had been during the season. The Red Sox were pulling Guidry's pitches. Fred Lynn battled Guidry to a full count and on the pay-off pitch, Lynn connected and hit the ball to deep right field. Piniella, running on the crack of the bat, caught up with the ball on the warning track and made a basket catch that saved two runs.

In the top of the seventh, Torrez was still mowing down the Yankees as he got Nettles on a fly out to Rice in right field for the first out. Then the tide began to turn against the Red Sox when Chambliss singled between third and short and Roy White followed with a single up the middle. With two men on and one out, Lemon sent up first baseman Jim Spencer to pinch-hit for Brian Doyle.

Torrez spoiled this move when he induced Spencer to fly out to Yastrzemski in left field. Although the Yankees still had two men on base, there were now two outs. The odds seemed to favor the Red Sox as Russell Earl ("Bucky") Dent stepped up to the plate. This matchup did not even cause much of a stir. Though he possessed a good glove, Dent was never known to be a Bronx Bomber.

Dent was in his sixth year in baseball. He began his career with the Chicago White Sox; his best season was in 1975 when he batted .264 with 159 hits, 3 home runs and 58 RBIs. Dent, injured in June, managed to play in 123 games with 92 hits, 4 home runs and 40 RBIs to his name in 1978.[52] Torrez had retired Dent twice today, on a fly out to right field and on a fly out in the infield. Second baseman Willie Randolph was injured with a pulled hamstring and after Spencer batted for Brian Doyle, Lemon didn't have a lot of men on the bench he could pinch-hit for Dent.

Scene: Fenway Park

Like the Polo Grounds, Fenway Park underwent a massive makeover. However, unlike the old horseshoe stadium, Fenway Park still stands today in its ninth decade of baseball. The Green Monster was not the first distinctive feature in the grand old ballpark. That honor belonged to Duffy's Cliff—a 10-foot incline that stood in front of the left field wall when the park was constructed in 1912.[53]

The cliff was named after leftfielder Duffy Lewis, who was one of a handful of players who adroitly patrolled the incline in left field. After Fenway Park was constructed, Taylor sold the Red Sox to Harry Frazee, who in turn sold the club to Bob Quinn in 1923.[54] Boston's franchise suffered in more ways than anyone could possibly imagine. After Ruth was sold to the Yankees, the Red Sox began to slip from top of the league. Besides the second place finishes, three years later fire felled the left field bleachers along the foul line. The charred debris was removed, but the bleachers were not restored. Thus, ballplayers were able to haul in a fly ball that had wandered behind the third base line.[55]

Fenway Park would receive a new lease on life when Thomas Yawkey, a 30-year-old millionaire, purchased the team February 25, 1933, and began making improvements to the ballpark over the off season.[56] Refurbishing

Fenway Park would not come without a price. The ballpark suffered a setback when, for the second time, fire ravaged Fenway Park in January 1934. The park burned down, destroying most of the construction that was underway.

But Fenway bounced back when the wooden grandstands were replaced by steel and concrete just in time for the Red Sox's home opener on April 17 of that year.

Other noticeable changes included the leveling of Duffy's Cliff, which was replaced by a 37-foot wall in left field.[57] Built into the left field wall was a manually operated scoreboard which still exists to this day. Later a 23-foot screen would be placed above the wall to shield the stores along Landsdowne Street. Two years after Fenway Park was rebuilt, a 36-foot ladder was placed atop the wall to retrieve the baseballs that were hit into the net during batting practice.

In 1940, the Red Sox constructed the bullpen in right field, which shortened the distance to hit a home run by 23 feet. The bullpen was called Williamsburg, named after Ted Williams, who had joined the team a year before. It was speculated that shortening the distance would benefit Williams' home run production. Ironically, with the new bullpen, Williams' home run production dropped by eight.[58]

Sky boxes were added during the forties, along with lights in 1947. Also that year, the Red Sox took down the advertisements in left field and painted the whole wall green, thus creating the Green Monster. It has been a fixture of the ballpark ever since. Along with Wrigley Field, Fenway still uses a hand-operated scoreboard although an electronic scoreboard was installed in 1976.

Football became a part of Fenway when the Boston Redskins occupied the park from 1933 to 1936 until the team moved to Washington. The Boston Yanks followed the Redskins and became tenants from 1944 to 1948. Eventually, the Boston Yanks transferred the franchise to New York, Dallas, and Baltimore to become the Colts, before finally settling in Indianapolis. The third professional team was the Boston Patriots, who used the ballpark from 1963 to 1968 before moving to Foxboro, a suburb outside of Boston, and becoming the New England Patriots.[59]

When Tiger Stadium was demolished in 1999, Wrigley Field and Fenway Park were the only stadiums that remained from the early twentieth century. Fenway Park reminds many fans of Ebbets Field. Like Brooklyn's fabled ballpark, seating capacity is slightly above 34,000. The right and left field foul lines are close — 315 above the Green Monster in left and 302 down the right field line. The deepest part is in center field at 420 feet. This separates Fenway Park from many of today's ballparks as the fences are less than 400 feet, allowing for an easy home run. Besides the Green Monster, the left center fence to center field stands at 18 feet, then slopes to five feet from the center field bullpen to the rest of the park from right center to right field.[60]

Torrez's first pitch to Dent was low for a ball. He took the next pitch for a strike and then fouled the third pitch off of his ankle. Gene Monahan, the Yankee trainer, came out to apply the ethyl fluoride to Dent's ankle to give him some temporary relief. What was also noticeable was that a few innings earlier, the wind that blew in from left field and held Jackson's fly ball in the first inning had switched directions. Now the wind blew out to left field.

After Dent received ethyl fluoride, the Yankee batboy brought Dent a new bat from his teammate Mickey Rivers. The count was 1–2 as Dent went back in the batter's box; he crouched over the plate, choking up on the bat as he usually did. Dent waved the bat across the plate as many batters do to keep the adrenaline going. Torrez, on the other hand, did not throw the ball around to keep loose during the four minutes since Dent's foul ball.

Torrez's fourth pitch to Dent was waist high, right in the middle of the strike zone. Dent connected and the ball headed towards the Green Monster. At first, Yastrzemski thought he had a chance to catch what looked like a routine fly ball, but then realized that he had no chance to make the put out, so he stopped a few feet short of the Green Monster and decided to play the carom, something Yastrzemski did better than anybody who ever wore the Red Sox uniform.

Suddenly, the ball cleared the Green Monster and landed in the net. Yastrzemski, reminiscent of Joe DiMaggio's disappointment in the 1941 World Series after Gionfriddo robbed him of a home run, fell to his knees. The score was now 3–2 in favor of the Yankees.

The Yankee bench came alive; as for Fenway Park, it became lifeless as Dent rounded the bases. Still, Torrez did not settle down and he walked Rivers. Thurman Munson was the next batter, but he would not face Torrez, who had thrice fanned him that afternoon. Zimmer immediately went to the mound and replaced Torrez with Bob Stanley. As he walked off the mound, Fenway Park gave Torrez a standing ovation, but they would not forget his pitch to Bucky Dent.

Stanley, who sported a 15–2 record and 2.60 ERA, seemed like a good choice to stop the Yankees, but Stanley had pitched on Saturday when he tossed a complete game and shut out the Blue Jays on three hits in a 3–0 win, so Stanley entered the game on only one day's rest.[61]

Back to the top of the seventh, Rivers immediately tested Stanley who threw twice to Scott at first to keep Rivers on the bag. Then Rivers timed

Stanley perfectly and took off for second base. Munson swung and missed, but Rivers slid safely into second, despite a good throw from Carlton Fisk. Munson then hit a double that landed between Yastrzemski, and Lynn Rivers easily scored from second. New York now led 4–2.

Stanley retired Piniella on a fly out to Rice in right field. Mercifully, the top of the seventh inning came to an end for the Red Sox. New York had doubled Boston's run production with one swing from an unlikely source of Yankee power and speed and timely hitting. Yet, the New Englanders would not back down.

The Red Sox again had a threat going in the bottom of the seventh. After Guidry fanned Hobson for the first out, Scott came up and reached Guidry for a single. Lemon went to the mound, removed Guidry, and replaced him with Goose Gossage.

Gossage struck out pinch hitter Bob Bailey for the second out, then Burleson was at the plate when Gossage threw a wild pitch that sent Scott to second base. Again, the Red Sox stranded Scott in scoring position as Burleson grounded out to Dent to end the inning.

In the top of the eighth, Jackson hit a long home run off of Stanley to deep center field to make the score 5–2. Andy Hassler and Dick Drago came in and kept the Red Sox deficit at three runs.

The Red Sox, who had battled back after the Yankees took over first place in mid–September to force a one-game playoff, were not about to back down now. Jerry Remy led off the bottom of the eighth with a double. Rice came up and flied out to Piniella in right field. With one out Yastrzemski came up and lined the ball into center field to score Remy from second.

Boston trimmed the Yankees' lead to 5–3, and Fenway Park was alive again. The next batter, Carlton Fisk, battled Gossage pitch after pitch, until Fisk finally won the battle with a hit to center field. With runners on first and second, Lynn kept the rally going with an opposite hit to left field to score Yastrzemski. The score was now 5–4 in favor of New York. Fenway Park was on its feet, cheering wildly for their Red Sox, but Gossage put out the fire as he got Hobson to fly out to Piniella in right field and then struck out Scott to retire the side.

The Yankees went down in the top of ninth without scoring another run. With New York still clinging to a 5–4 lead, Zimmer sent up pinch hitter Dwight Evans to bat for Bob Bailey in the bottom of the ninth.

Again, the fans in Fenway Park stood and cheered as their Red Sox took their last turn at bat. Gossage got Evans on a fly out to Gary Thomasson, who replaced Roy White in left field, for the first out. Gossage then walked Burleson on four pitches. Up came Jerry Remy who lined Gossage's first pitch for a hit. As the ball headed toward right field, Lou Piniella, who momentarily lost the ball in the sun, pretended he saw the ball, sticking both arms out as if he were about to make the catch. Suddenly, Piniella saw the ball land in front of him, and stuck out his glove and caught it on one bounce like a hockey goalie.

It was the play of the game. Piniella's acting held up Burleson, who had to stop at second. Piniella's second heads-up play in the game would not show up in the box score, but it was crucial.

Piniella was still shielding his face with his glove when Rice came up to bat. Gossage fired low and outside, but Rice managed to hit the ball off of the end of the bat and the ball again headed toward right field. The crowd rose to its feet. This time, Piniella saw the ball and caught it a few feet in front of the warning track for the second out.

Burleson went to third on Rice's fly ball. Two outs, runners on first and third. The next batter: Carl Yastrzemski.

As a baseball fan, one could not ask for a better match-up. The veteran Yastrzemski against the young reliever Goose Gossage. Yastrzemski, the heart and soul of Boston, had carried the mantle of the Red Sox for nearly two decades. He had the unenviable task of replacing baseball's greatest hitter, Ted Williams, in left field after Williams retired in 1960, and endured six losing seasons with the Red Sox during the early and mid 1960s.

Yastrzemski watched as Boston experienced 11 winning seasons that included the 1967 and 1975 World Series, both of which the Red Sox lost. Though Yastrzemski was older than Gossage, this match was even. The veteran Red Sox had taken Guidry's fastball and parked it into the right field seats for a home run, then singled off of Gossage in the last inning to bring his Red Sox back in the game.

For Gossage, it was the moment of truth. He had signed his big contract during the off season and the Yankees brought him to the team for these types of situations. However, Gossage was not dominating anyone on October 2 as he did a month before on September 3, when in that game, the Yankees led the Seattle Mariners 4–0. Then, the Mariners loaded the bases in the top of the ninth. When Gossage came in he retired the side on eleven pitches.[62] No matter how hard Gossage threw today, the Red Sox hit him with relish, scoring two runs off of him to make the game a contest and a season again at 5–4.

Manager Bob Lemon and catcher Munson came out to the mound to talk to Gossage. After a few minutes, home plate umpire Don Denkinger went out to the mound and broke up the discussion. Gossage's first pitch to Yastrzemski was low for a ball. Gossage's next pitch was a fastball high and tight. Yastrzemski took a vicious cut and popped up to Nettles. The

Yankee third baseman back-pedaled into foul territory and caught the ball for the third out to give the Yankees the Eastern Division crown. The New Yorkers swarmed out of the visitors' dugout and celebrated in front of a Fenway Park that had to contend with another frustrating year without winning the World Series.

After reality had set in a few minutes later, dejected Red Sox players remained in the dugout as the Yankees celebrated the Eastern Division Championship in the visitors' clubhouse.

The final standings stood at 100–63 for the Yankees and 99–64 for the Red Sox. As in the previous chapters, playoffs do not exist unless one team goes on a winning streak, and the other team suffers a losing streak: which is what happened. After trailing the Red Sox by 14 games in mid–July, the Yankees won 51 out of their last 72 ball games to tie the Red Sox for the Eastern Division. More importantly, from August 30 to September 16, Boston won only 3 out of 17 games. During that time, the Yankees moved into first place. Overall the Red Sox only won 37 out of 72 games after July 20, only two games above .500 ball.

But Boston pulled itself together and staged a comeback of its own. After trailing the Yankees by 2½ games in mid–September, the Red Sox won 12 out of 14 games to force the one game playoff.

Like the 1951 Dodgers, one game could have prevented a playoff. In hindsight, it is easy to point out the past and wonder which one of the 63 games the Red Sox could have won to clinch the Eastern Division. During this writer's research, many sportswriters have focused on the last game that occurred during the four game series between the Yankees and the Red Sox in early September that could have given the division to the Red Sox. Keep in mind, however, there is no certainty that Boston would have won this contest, but after the loss, many people would have liked to have this game back. On the morning of the fourth game of the four game series during that September weekend in Boston, Yastrzemski went to see Don Zimmer in his office and implored Zimmer to start Bill Lee, now in the bullpen, over Bobby Sprowl, who was ineffective in his last start against the Orioles.[63] Lee had a lifetime record of 12–5 against the Yankees. Also, Luis Tiant volunteered to start this game, but would have pitched on three days' rest. But as Guidry proved in the one day playoff, you might not be sharp, but with a little help, you can win on three days' rest.

Boston needed to win this game to avoid a sweep by New York that would leave both teams tied in first place. Zimmer insisted on using Bobby Sprowl, saying the now infamous words, "The kid [Sprowl] has got ice water in his veins."

In the first inning Sprowl surrendered two walks to Rivers and

Randolph. Though Munson hit into a double play, Jackson kept the inning alive when he singled Rivers home for the first Yankee run. Sprowl gave up two more walks to Piniella and Chambliss. Zimmer had had enough and removed Sprowl from the game.

As for Sprowl, he never won a game in the major leagues and the Red Sox traded him to the Montreal Expos the following spring. Bob Stanley came in to relieve Sprowl. He gave up a hit to Nettles which netted the Yankees two more runs.

The Yankees added four more runs and led the Red Sox 7–4 in the ninth. In the bottom of the ninth, the Red Sox finally had a chance to tie the game. With two outs, Boston had runners on first and second, but third baseman Jack Brohamer hit a fly ball deep to left field to Roy White who caught the ball on the warning track for the final out.

Don Zimmer should be given credit for trying to do something to inject some life into the slumping Red Sox. Bill Lee, for his part, had lost seven games, but the debate will go on regarding Zimmer's decision to start Sprowl instead of Lee. In retrospect, Bobby Sprowl's loss was no different from the other 62 defeats that Boston suffered in 1978. After the game, Torrez spoke with reporters: "It was a fastball inside. And perhaps I didn't get it in as far as I needed to. But it wasn't that bad a pitch. He hit it and I thought for sure it was a fly ball. Pudge [Carlton Fisk] told me the same thing. But the ball kept sailing and went over the wall. I was shocked. But there was noting I could do about it."[64]

Larry Whiteside's column in the next day's *Boston Globe* could not have been more prophetic. He wrote, "In a few days Mike Torrez will forget about his 16–13 record this year. But he'll have to live with his gopher pitch to Dent that turned the playoff game around. And there are people who'll make sure he won't forget what happened."[65] Torrez went on to pitch for the Red Sox for five more seasons, but he did not escape the occasional jeering by the Fenway fans whenever he warmed up in the bullpen. It became so bad that he was even booed in the parking lot.[66]

Torrez was traded to the New York Mets in 1983. A year later he finished his career with the Oakland A's.

Torrez went on to work as an executive for Contract Furnishing Systems Ltd., a company that supplies office furniture. He now works for a promotional logo company. Torrez, now a grandfather, is content with his life.[67]

Like Ralph Branca before him, Mike Torrez was a good pitcher. From 1972 to 1979 Torrez won 109 games and lost 92. Except for 1973 and 1980, Torrez always posted double figure wins, including a 10–3 record during the strike-shortened season of 1981. He would end his career with 185 wins and 160 losses and a 3.79 ERA. The only downside to Torrez's career was missing the plate. This wild streak led to devastating consequences in 1984, when Torrez hit Dickey Thon of the Astros, all but ending a once bright future. Nevertheless, Torrez was a good pitcher.

Like the Dodgers-Giants playoff run, did one team have an advantage over another team? A rumor that still continues to this day holds that Mike Torrez has said that Mickey Rivers confessed to him that he loaned Bucky Dent a corked bat to hit his famous home run. But Rivers jokingly denied the charge.[68]

The mystery only adds to this now legendary game that vaulted the Yankees into the post season. The Yankees defeated the Royals for the third straight year in the LCS and won with their second straight World Series against the Los Angeles Dodgers.

Like 30 years before, the Red Sox would win over 190 games in two seasons, but they would have nothing to show for it.

Torrez, like Branca before him, would participate in a reenactment of his famous pitch eleven years later at Bucky Dent's baseball school in Delray Beach, Florida. Torrez again faced Dent on the mound. He threw a few pitches before Dent hit a home run over the makeshift Green Monster.[69] Sadly, Torrez has never been invited back to Fenway Park.

In 1998, at a Yankees old-times' game, Mike Torrez's introduction ended as the man who gave up Bucky Dent's home run. Torrez responded, "They still have to bring that up?" But at the 2000 Yankees old-timers' game, Torrez's introduction ended without any reference regarding his home run pitch to Bucky Dent.

Torrez did not lose the 1978 season for the Red Sox, but fans do not let him forget that pitch. In truth, the Red Sox lost the Eastern Division collectively. Although Dent's home run put the Yankees in front 3–2, over-all, Torrez was charged for four runs in that game. The final Yankee run that made the difference in the game was a home run by Reggie Jackson who hit it off of reliever Bob Stanley.

Today, some Red Sox fans blurt out "Bucky Bleeping Dent" when Mike Torrez's name is mentioned. Though his pitch to Dent was a bad one, Torrez must be given his due for sporting a 60–54 record in his five years with the Red Sox. Torrez, like Branca, has been forthright about that game. He admitted that he was in his groove, but after Bucky Dent fouled the ball off of his foot, he did not loosen up by throwing the ball around which led to serving up an easy pitch to Dent. As for Dent, he was a major lea-guer, and you don't make the major leagues unless you are good. Torrez deserves credit for having the guts to face the fans.

Although his battle with the fans might not be as gallant as some other players in this book, Torrez has taken a lot of heat for a game he would not have had to pitch if the Red Sox had not blown a fourteen-game lead in the standings.

In 1979 the Yankees and Red Sox did not contend for the pennant. Torrez would again finish at 16–13. Bill Lee, who always spoke his mind, making friends and enemies alike, went to the Montreal Expos where he would play sixteen games. Tiant would sign on as a free agent with the Yankees. Boston got a little revenge as Yastrzemski collected his 3,000th hit against the Yankees. That year the Red Sox managed to win 91 games and finish in third place.

Jim Rice and Fred Lynn both repeated as offensive threats as each man hit over .300, belted 39 home runs, and drove in over a hundred runs. But it was Rice who won the MVP, his second in two years.

New York would not go to the World Series the next year. Nineteen seventy-nine turned into a house of horrors for the Yankees. Days after the 1978 World Series, Bob Lemon's favorite son, Jerry, was killed in a car crash. Lemon was not the same manager when he reported to spring training in 1979. He was fired by Steinbrenner and replaced by none other than Billy Martin. In June, Goose Gossage broke his thumb when he got into a fight with backup catcher and DH Cliff Johnson. Mickey Rivers was injured and soon he was traded to the Texas Rangers for Oscar Gamble. There, Rivers would join Sparky Lyle, who had been traded to the Rangers during the off season. Three days later, the Yankees lost team captain Thurman Munson as he crashed his airplane while doing touch and go landings.

The Yankees would play the Royals again in the championship series in 1980, but this time the Royals finally beat the Yankees by sweeping them in three games. Game 3 would be capped off with George Brett's upper deck home run off Gossage.

The next year it would be the Dodgers who finally avenged their World Series defeats by finally beating the Yankees in the Fall Classic. It was the third time in five years that both teams played in a World Series.

CHAPTER 6

Tom Niedenfuer

How can the same thing happen to the same guy twice?
— Bruce Willis in *Die Hard 2*

The Dodgers remained a contender following their triumph in the 1981 World Series, but Los Angeles did not make the post season the next year. Their old rivals, the Giants, beat the Dodgers 5–3 on a three run home run by Joe Morgan, to knock Los Angeles out of the pennant race on the next to last day of the season.[1] Los Angeles rebounded to win the Western Division in 1983, and faced the Phillies in the NLCS for the third time in six years. This time, it was the Phillies who triumphed over the Dodgers in four games.[2] Los Angeles did not contend for the division as they finished at 79–83 and fell to fourth place the following year.

The beginning of 1985 looked like a holdover from the previous year as the Dodgers played below .500 for the first two months with a record of 23–24. What kept Los Angeles in the race was their pitching: as starters, Orel Hershiser with a record of 19–3 and a 2.03 ERA; Fernando Valenzuela, the ace of the staff, 17–10 with a 2.45 ERA; Bob Welch, 14–4 and a 2.31 ERA; and Jerry Reuss, 14–10 and a 2.92 ERA. The Dodgers began to turn their season around when Pedro Guerrero, an outfielder out of his normal position at third base, made 23 errors before returning to his normal position in left field.[3] The reacquaintance with left field helped Guerrero, as the Dodger slugger clubbed 15 home runs to set a Dodger record in the month of June. The Dodgers went on to win 15 out of 25 in June and 20 out of 27 in July to lead the Western Division by the All-Star Break. The Dodgers picked up Enos Cabell and Bill Madlock in the second half of the season and held off the Cincinnati Reds and won the Western Division with a 95–67 record for the fifth time in nine seasons.[4] A rejuvenated Pedro Guerrero led the offense as he batted .320, had 33 home runs, 87 RBIs, and 156 hits. Mike Marshall batted .293 with 95 RBIs, 28 home runs, and 152 hits, followed by Mike Scioscia batting .296 with 53 RBIs and 127 hits. The bullpen was supported by Ken Howell and Tom Niedenfuer.

Thomas Edward Niedenfuer was born on August 13, 1959, in St. Louis Park, Minnesota, to James and Rodonna Niedenfuer. By the time he was pitching in high school, Tom resided in Redmond, Washington, a suburb of Seattle.

In his junior year at Redmond High, Tom threw a no-hitter. He also led his division in strikeouts, and had the fewest walks. As a senior, Tom was spectacular on the mound as he again led his division in strikeouts and fewest walks per inning and sported a 10–0 record and 0.89 ERA.[5] He was drafted by the Dodgers at age 17, but Niedenfuer did not become a Dodger. Instead, he opted to pitch for Washington State University, where as a Cougar, in his sophomore season, Tom started eight and relieved ten games for a pitching staff that was saddled with injuries. In Tom's junior year, his last with the Cougars, he became the ace of the staff. Though he finished with a 6–4 record in 12 contests, he threw three complete games, winning them all. Tom went on to win the 1980 Buck Bailey Award as the Cougars' top pitcher, and was one of two pitchers named to the All-Northern Division team.

Eligible for the draft that year, Niedenfuer was not selected by any of the then 26 major league clubs. However, as a free agent signee, Niedenfuer became a member of the Dodgers.[6] He began his career with the San Antonio Missions in AA ball for the Texas League in 1981 where he went 13–3 with a 1.80 ERA. After the baseball strike ended, the Dodgers made a run at the pennant, and pitching became paramount for the Dodgers. Niedenfuer impressed Los Angeles Vice President Al Campanis, who selected Niedenfuer to be part of team's roster.[7] When he arrived at the Dodgers, Niedenfuer reminded Los Angeles of another big, tall, hard-throwing reliever, Goose Gossage. But Niedenfuer, a 6'5", 225 pound frame with long and bushy brown hair, was given the name "Buff" for Buffalo by his teammates. And Niedenfuer was a buffer. In 17 games Niedenfuer had a 3–1 record with two saves. Later in the post season, including divisional play, League Championship Series, and the World Series, Niedenfuer threw a sparkling 5⅔ scoreless innings as the Dodgers won the World Series.

Niedenfuer began the 1982 season in Albuquerque of the Pacific Coast League, the Dodgers Triple A affiliate. Soon he was back in the big leagues where he appeared in 55 games and sported a 3–4 record with 9 saves.[8]

The next year Niedenfuer was even better. That season "Buff" pitched in 66 games, carried an 8–3 record, 11 saves, and a 1.90 ERA.[9] Injuries forced Niedenfuer to the bench in 1984; despite these ailments, which included kidney problems, he managed to save 11 games, the most by a

Dodger reliever that year. When Ken Howell, a hard-throwing left handed reliever, joined the bullpen, Niedenfuer's days appeared to be numbered.[10] Los Angeles was thankful they kept the big burly righthander, for Steve Howe, the Dodgers' number one reliever, was suspended for the 1984 season due to his substance abuse problems and was released in July the following year after missing a game.[11] Niedenfuer stepped in and was joined by Howell. The two relievers saved 27 games for the Dodgers—the team's total number for the 1984 season.

Niedenfuer was a workhorse for the 1985 season. Appearing in 64 games, Niedenfuer struck out 102 batters in 106 innings, and saved 19 games with a 2.71 ERA.

However, in September, Niedenfuer and Howell began to show signs of fatigue as both men combined to go 1–7 with an ERA over six.[12]

Over in the Eastern Division, the New York Mets surprised everyone the year before by winning 90 games en route to a second place finish, and were legitimate contenders for the Division crown in 1985.

But that year, the St. Louis Cardinals, winners of the World Series three years before, were the surprise team in the National League East. Joaquin Andujar, the ace of the staff, went 21–12 with a 3.40 ERA. However, John Tudor made a name for himself as he went 21–8 with a 1.93 ERA, and pitched 14 complete games with 10 shutouts. He was followed by Danny Cox's 18–9 record, 2.88 ERA, and Bob Forsch at 9–6 with a 3.90 ERA.

St. Louis was led by batting champion Willie McGee's .353 average, 10 home runs, 82 RBIs and 216 hits. Second baseman Tommy Herr hit .302, 8 home runs, and 110 RBIs. Rookie leftfielder Vince Coleman batted .267, 1 home run, 170 hits, and 40 RBIs and stole 110 out of the team's 314 stolen bases. The Cardinals would not beat you with the long ball as the team only connected for 87 of them. A quarter of those round trippers were supplied by Jack Clark, who batted .281, with 22 home runs and 87 RBIs.

The only thing that could derail St. Louis' pennant hopes was the baseball strike. Unlike the stoppage in 1981 that crippled the baseball season for 50 days and generated negative publicity for both the players and owners, both sides resolved their differences over salary arbitration in two days.

At the season's end, the Cardinals and Mets fought down to the wire for the Eastern Division crown. New York came to St. Louis trailing by three games with six games to play. If New York swept the Cardinals, both teams would be tied for first place. However, if the Cardinals won any of the three contests, they would retain a two game lead with three games left in the season. The Mets won the first two games 1–0 and 5–2, but St. Louis won the third game 4–3 and won the division by three games.[13]

The best four out of seven games to decide the National League pennant began at Dodger Stadium on October 9.

In Game 1, John Tudor faced Fernando Valenzuela. The Dodgers and Cardinals each managed three hits through the first three innings, but produced no runs. Then in the bottom of the fourth after Enos Cabell struck out, Dodger third baseman Bill Madlock came to the plate and got around on Tudor's slider and drove it directly to Terry Pendleton at third. Pendleton booted the play for an error. Madlock wasted no time, capitalized on Pendleton's error, and swiped second base. He then came around and scored on Guerrero's bloop single to right field and the Dodgers took a 1–0 lead before Tudor retired both Mike Marshall and Scioscia to get out of the fourth inning with only a one run deficit.

The game remained the same until the bottom of the sixth when Madlock came up again with one out. And the results were nearly the same. This time Madlock connected off of Tudor and hit the ball to shortstop Ozzie Smith, known as "the Wizard of Oz" for his spectacular plays at shortstop. But Smith's wizardry failed him as the ball went right past his glove and into left field. However, Smith, recognized as the game's best shortstop, was not given an error. It was figured that if the Wizard could not make the play then it must be a hit. Yet, the die had been cast. Guerrero was walked intentionally, and Tudor retired Mike Marshall on a fly out. Scioscia singled to drive home Madlock as the Dodgers increased their lead to 2–0. Los Angeles scored two more runs and led 4–0 and knocked starter John Tudor out of the game.

Valenzuela held the Cardinals to five hits and no runs through the first six innings, but in the seventh the Cardinals got to Valenzuela. Pendleton made up for his error with a single to right. After Valenzuela retired catcher Darrell Porter on a groundout to first base, Terry Pendleton moved to second base. Smith singled, but Pendleton could not score. Manager Whitey Herzog sent up pinch-hitter Tito Landrum to bat for Daley, which paid off as Landrum singled to score Pendleton. With the score 4–1 and two men on, Lasorda went to the mound and replaced Valenzuela with Tom Niedenfuer, who induced the next batter, Vince Coleman, to hit into an inning-ending double play. That was all the scoring for St. Louis that day as Niedenfuer pitched 2⅔ innings of one hit shutout ball. The Dodgers held on and won the first game 4–1.

Game 2 pitted Orel Hershiser against Joaquin Andujar. The Dodgers won the next day with relative ease. After St. Louis touched starter Orel Hershiser for a run in the top of third, Los Angeles struck back with three runs in the bottom of the inning and two in the fourth, to knock the Cardinals' ace Joaquin Andujar out of the game. The Dodgers added three more runs as Hershiser pitched a complete game as the Dodgers won 8–2 and led in the Series 2–0.

Game 3 featured Danny Cox against Bob Welch. St. Louis was down but not out as the NLCS moved to Busch Stadium. The Cardinals had a mission — win two out of three to guarantee a return trip to Los Angeles for a sixth game and possibly extend the series to a seventh contest. St. Louis got off to a great start as leftfielder Vince Coleman singled off Bob Welch, then stole second to the delight of the Cardinal crowd. Next, batting champion McGee came up and walked. Now the Cardinals had two base stealing threats on base which seemed to unnerve Welch. He tried to pick Coleman off second, but the ball sailed into the outfield, allowing Coleman to race around and score, and St. Louis led 1–0. The Cardinals pushed across another run and added two more runs in the second inning to take a 4–0 lead. The Dodgers could only cut the lead in half. Behind a gutsy performance from Danny Cox, St. Louis won the game 4–2 and was now back in the Series.

But the Cardinals' triumph did not last long. Just before the start of the fourth game, Vince Coleman's ankle was caught under the automatic tarpaulin. Coleman's injuries at first were thought to be innocuous, but it was later learned that Coleman would not play for the rest of the post season.

John Tudor and Jerry Reuss pitched Game 4, which tied the Series.[14] Coleman's loss was a setback; nevertheless, yesterday's win by the Cardinals lifted St. Louis' spirits. This attitude was reflected as the Cardinals exploded for nine runs in the bottom of the second inning. Dodgers starter southpaw Jerry Reuss took an early shower as opposed to John Tudor, who pitched seven strong innings without much of a sweat and gave up only one run as the Cardinals won 12–2 to even the Series at two games apiece.

Fernando Valenzuela faced Ken Forsch in Game 5. In the previous sixteen League Championship Series, the winner of the fifth contest won the pennant. Now it would take a fourth win to advance to the World Series. Though today's winner would not claim the pennant, it would give that team an emotional edge and take it a game closer to the World Series.

Ken Forsch retired the Dodgers in the top of the first, yielding one hit, but was helped when Guerrero hit into a double play. Valenzuela was the money pitcher any manager would want in a game. He came to the Dodgers five years before from Mexico. Although Valenzuela's first full season was interrupted by the baseball strike, he won the Cy Young and Rookie of the Year awards. In 1985, Valenzuela was the most dominant pitcher in the game. But in the bottom of the first, Valenzuela walked

Smith and McGee. Up came second baseman Tommy Herr who wasted no time on St. Louis' scoring opportunity and doubled to left field. Smith and McGee, running on the crack of the bat, scored to give the Cardinals an early 2–0 lead. With Herr on second, Valenzuela was mindful of St. Louis' speed, so the screwball specialist tried to pick Herr off second and threw the ball into center field. The Cardinals had Valenzuela on the ropes when the Dodger ace received a break. Clark lined out to Madlock at third. Valenzuela regrouped and fanned Cesar Cedeno and retired Tito Landrum on a fly out to center. From there, Valenzuela did not yield another run through eight innings.

Forsch had given up one hit through the first three innings, but in the bottom of the fourth, Ken Landreaux singled. Forsch retired Guerrero on a fly out to center field, but Bill Madlock came up and reminded the Cardinals that he was still the hot hitter when he lined Forsch's fast ball over the left field wall to even the game at 2–2. Now the Dodgers had the momentum, but did not score any more runs that inning despite a walk to Mike Marshall and Porter's interference allowing Scioscia to reach first. Whitey Herzog replaced Forsch with Ken Daley, who induced Cabell to hit into a double play. The game moved to the bottom of the ninth with both teams still tied at 2–2. Niedenfuer replaced Valenzuela on the mound. It was Niedenfuer's first relief appearance since he pitched in Game 1. Niedenfuer retired Willie McGee; then with one out, Osborne Earl Smith, Jr., stepped up to the plate. The light hitting shortstop batted from the left hand side to face the right handed Niedenfuer; this matchup did not cause any concern to Lasorda or Niedenfuer. Smith only had eight home runs that year, and none of them were left handed. Like Dent before him, Smith seemed like an easy out. Even longtime Cardinals announcer Jack Buck mentioned that Smith was not the long ball threat, until Niedenfuer came low and inside. Smith connected and on the crack of the bat the ball sailed down the line for a home run. Jack Buck, reminiscent of Russ Hodges, exclaimed, "Smith corks one down the line — it may gooooo! Go crazy folks, go crazy! The Cardinals have won the game on a home run by the wizard! Go crazy."[15] Smith's home run shocked all of Busch Stadium, but not Tom Lasorda, who reminded everyone that Mel Ott and Joe Morgan were small men who hit 779 home runs between them.

Orel Hershiser and Joaquin Andujar faced off in Game 6 on October 16, 1985.[16] The sixth contest began rather oddly. Traditionally, both teams stand along the foul lines during player introductions. However, Whitey Herzog felt that the Cardinals' introduction in Game 1 was sufficient and his team remained in the dugout. John McGraw would have been proud. The Cardinals would not come out onto the field until they took their turn at bat. When they did, Hershiser retired St. Louis in the first without yielding a run.

The bottom of the first was no different as the game was delayed for eight minutes. Andujar tried to throw and was uncomfortable on the mound, so the grounds crew added more sand to it to give what Andujar thought was needed. Perhaps Andujar was onto something, for he surrendered a double to lead-off batter Mariano Duncan. Next, Landreaux came up and nearly took Andujar over the wall, but the ball died on the warning track for a long out. After Guerrero flied out for the second out, Madlock came up and singled to score Duncan and Los Angeles took a 1–0 lead. The Dodgers added another run in the second to lead 2–0.

In the top of the third, Andujar helped his own cause with a double to left field. McGee made a productive move as his groundout allowed Andujar to take third base. Andujar then scored on Herr's single to cut the Dodger lead in half 2–1.

Los Angeles scored two more runs on Guerrero's sacrifice fly and Madlock's home run, his third of the NLCS.

With a 4–1 lead, Hershiser was cruising through the Cardinal lineup. Then in the top of the seventh, Darrel Porter, nicknamed Clark Kent because the spectacles he wore reminded many of Superman's alter-ego, led off with a single. Jerry Reuss and Tom Niedenfuer began to throw in the bullpen when Tito Landrum followed Porter with a single which brought Steve Bruan to pinch hit for Andujar as the tying run. Though Bruan grounded out, Porter and Landrum advanced one base to second and third. Willie McGee slapped a single to center to score Porter and Landrum. The Cardinals were back in the game trailing Los Angeles by 4–3.

Lasorda went to the mound and replaced Hershiser with Niedenfuer. Smith was the next batter, and with their last confrontation still fresh in everyone's memory, the pressure was on Niedenfuer. The Wizard bested the Dodgers' reliever again with a triple to score McGee to tie the game at 4–4. Lasorda walked Tommy Herr to set up a possible double play, but the pitcher's best friend was not needed as Niedenfuer fanned both Clark and Van Slyke to keep the game knotted at 4–4.

The game did not remain the same for long. Mike Marshall led off the bottom of the eighth with a towering home run as Los Angeles reclaimed the lead 5–4.

Niedenfuer fanned Cesar Cedeno, who pinch-hit for Todd Worrell to start the bottom of ninth for the first out. Reuss was joined by Ken Howell in the bullpen, but Ruess rarely made any relief appearances and Howell was ineffective, so Niedenfuer faced the next batter, Willie McGee, who promptly singled and then stole second. With the tying run in scoring position,

Lasorda, pitching coach Ron Perranaski, and the Dodger infielders conferred on the mound to decide what to do with the next batter, Ozzie Smith. The Wizard walked, which seemingly did not bother the Dodgers as Smith suddenly had Niedenfuer's number. Tommy Herr hit what looked like an inning-ending double play down the third base line, but the ball went into foul territory by inches.

Niedenfuer managed to retire Tommy Herr on a groundout to first, but Mc-Gee and Smith each advanced a base so the Cardinals now had men on second and third. Jack Clark stepped up to the plate. Clark began his career with the Giants in 1975, and became a full-time player in 1977. His best all around season came a year later when Clark batted .306 with 25 home runs, 181 hits, and 98 RBIs.[17]

Tom Niedenfuer: In 1985 Niedenfuer was a workhorse for the Los Angeles Dodgers, helping the team reach the post season. Then in the NLCS he yielded not one, but two devastating home runs. (Photograph courtesy of the National Baseball Hall of Fame Library, Cooperstown, N.Y.)

As Clark's career blossomed throughout the late seventies and early eighties, his numbers remained the same. But in 1984, he only played in 57 games, though he batted .320 with 11 home runs and 44 RBIs. The Giants decided to trade Clark over the off season for Dave LaPoint, David Green, Jose Uribe, and Gary Rajsich.

Scene: Dodger Stadium

Oh what the Flatbush Faithful must have been thinking when Dodger Stadium opened in Los Angeles, five years after their Beloved Bums from Brooklyn abandoned the borough. Nineteen fifty-three, the Braves' first year in Milwaukee, paid dividends as attendance rose from 281,000, in the franchise's previous year in Boston, to two million.[18] This immediate impact reverberated around the baseball world, especially in Brooklyn, where owner Walter O'Malley, who succeeded the legendary Branch Rickey, began looking for a new stadium for his celebrated Lords of Flatbush.

O'Malley concentrated his efforts at the adjoining avenues at Atlantic and Flatbush, which were also situated along the Long Island Railroad Terminal. O'Malley hoped the city of New York would extend Title 1 of the 1949 Federal Housing Act to assemble some parcels of land whereby the Dodgers would construct their stadium.[19] But Robert Moses, who single-handedly rebuilt New York State through his construction of beaches, highways, and roads, was chairman of Mayor Robert Wagner's Committee on Slum Clearance. In Moses' view, Title 1 could not be used to construct the Dodgers' new stadium.[20] It should also be noted that Moses, the master builder who constructed these roads and tunnels, saw the new stadium at the Atlantic and Flatbush as a threat. If constructed, many passengers would travel to the new stadium by the Long Island Railroad rather than on the highways and avoid the tolls, which would benefit Moses, who depended on such expenditures to maintain his influence in New York City and state politics.[21] Instead, Moses offered a new stadium at the site in Flushing Meadows, Queens.[22]

Meanwhile, the city of Los Angeles began a campaign to acquire a major league team. As reported in *Bums*, Kenneth Hahn, then a member of the Board of Supervisors, was sent to the 1956 World Series to lure a professional baseball team to California. Kahn met Walter O'Malley, who was having trouble securing a new stadium in New York and seemed interested in transplanting his franchise to Los Angeles. When O'Malley arrived in Los Angeles, he and Hahn flew by helicopter to where O'Malley had selected a site at the Chavez Ravine.[23]

The Ravine was purchased by the city of Los Angeles in 1951. The Chavez Ravine, a hilly 300 acre lot, was originally slated for public housing. However, instead of housing, the City Council decided that the Ravine should be used for some other form of public purpose. The Ravine was named after Julian Chavez, one of the first members of the Los Angeles City Council when it was formed in the mid-nineteenth century.[24]

In return for moving Los Angeles, the Dodgers would exchange Wrigley Field, a minor league stadium that O'Malley purchased from Cubs owner Phil Wrigley, for the Chavez Ravine, and their share of mineral oil revenues gleaned from the Ravine would fund the Dodgers' youth programs.[25] But some Los Angelinos were opposed to the Dodgers acquiring the Chavez Ravine and not long afterward, a referendum was held to decide if the

Dodgers should take over the Chavez Ravine. The referendum passed in favor of the Dodgers by 24,000 votes out of 660,000-plus cast.[26]

The Dodgers were not in the clear yet. Taxpayers filed suits in the Superior Court.[27] The suits were sustained by Judge Julius Praeger, who invalidated the Chavez Ravine contract with the Dodgers.[28] Praeger ruled that the City Council acted without authority to cede the mineral (oil) rights to the Dodgers for the team's youth programs, and that the contract did not justify the form of a "public purpose." But in January 1959, the California State Supreme Court overturned Judge Prager's decision, declaring that Praeger exceeded his authority.[29] Thus, the original agreement between the Dodgers and the Chavez Ravine was valid. After the California Supreme Court validated the Chavez Ravine contract, the litigants appealed to the United States Supreme Court.

Meanwhile, the Dodgers began the construction of their stadium on September 17, but the team was mindful that if the Supreme Court reversed the California Supreme Court's decision, all work would cease.[30] The problem was averted when the United States Supreme Court refused to hear the appeal in October, and the Dodgers had a green light to build their stadium.[31]

The Dodgers, who had been playing at the Los Angeles Coliseum since the team's arrival in 1958, won a championship in 1959. However, the Coliseum was hardly the place for baseball. The Coliseum, built for the 1932 Olympic Games, served as a home to college football. Two hundred thousand dollars was spent to add lights to illuminate the infield.[32] Dugouts were constructed and a 40-foot screen from the left field foul line to 140 feet to deter home runs was also constructed. It should be noted that home plate was only 250 feet from the left field foul line and many fans feared that Babe Ruth's then single season record of 60 home runs would fall in the Coliseum.

The first to take advantage of the new screen was Wally Moon, a left handed batter, who tattooed the screen with base hits called "Moon shots." What must have pleased O'Malley in the Coliseum was the fans; attendance soared above 90,000 during the 1959 Fall Classic, as the Dodgers defeated the Chicago White Sox. The Coliseum would not see another championship, as Los Angeles did not contend for the pennant in 1960 or 1961.

On April 10, 1962, Dodger Stadium opened. At a cost of $23 million, it was the first privately financed ballpark since Yankee Stadium was constructed in 1923. Since then, Coors Field, built in 1995, is the other stadium that holds this distinction.

Nicknamed the Taj Mahal of Baseball, Dodger Stadium is a six level edifice that provides the fans a comfortable setting to watch a baseball

game. In their first year in Dodger Stadium, Los Angelinos witnessed the
emergence of Sandy Koufax, who with Don Drysdale, both holdovers from
the Brooklyn days, formed a one-two punch in the pitching rotation. But
the Dodgers were denied another pennant for the second time in eleven
years by the Giants who defeated Los Angeles in another best two out of
three playoff. A year later, Dodger Stadium witnessed the team's World
Series victory as the Dodgers swept the Yankees in four straight games.
The final game was a 2–1 masterpiece by Koufax at the stadium. The Dodgers
would reclaim the World Series in 1965. That year Koufax, in Dodger Stadium, threw a perfect game against the Chicago Cubs on September 9.
One ignominious moment occurred in Dodger Stadium when Los Angeles was held scoreless for over 33⅓ innings during the Baltimore Orioles'
four game sweep in the 1966 World Series.

Following the retirement of Koufax in November that year, Don Drys-
dale tossed his sixth straight shutout on June 4, 1968, as he blanked the
Pirates 5–0 to set the then all time mark of 55⅔ scoreless innings. Orel
Hershiser would break the record with 56 scoreless innings in 1988. Los
Angeles would win the pennant in 1974, 1977, 1978, but lost to the Oakland A's and then in back to back losses to the Yankees. However, in 1978,
Dodger Stadium became the first ballpark to seat three million fans. Fer-
nandomania swept through Dodger Stadium when Fernando Valenzuela
arrived in 1981, which gave Mexican Americans a hometown hero. It was
Valenzuela who won the critical third game of the 1981 World Series at
Dodger Stadium after the Dodgers lost the first two contests to the Yankees in New York. The Dodgers won two more games in Los Angeles en
route to their fourth championship.

The right and left field foul lines extended to 330 feet. The Power
Alleys stood at 385 feet and center field was 395 feet away.

Since entering the game in the seventh inning in this place in 1985,
Niedenfuer had thrown 68 pitches, or two-thirds of an entire ball game.

As Tommy Lasorda was making up his mind on the next batter, he
was overheard in the dugout by Vin Scully, who, along with Joe Garagiola, was one of the announcers of the NBC television broadcast for the
NLCS. Scully reported on the air that Lasorda said, "Do I walk Clark to
get to that so and so [Andy Van Slyke]." Jack Clark stepped in the batter's
box when Scioscia called time out. After both men conferred on the mound,
Scioscia went behind the plate, Niedenfuer went back on the mound, and
Clark stepped into the batter's box. Niedenfuer wanted to throw a fastball
away; instead he unloaded a pitch right down the middle. Clark connected
and the ball soared 450 feet over the left field fence. As Pedro Guerrero
watched the ball sail into the left field bleachers, he slammed his glove

down in disgust as Clark did his best Babe Ruth imitation, trotting slowly around the bases.

Niedenfuer retired the next batter, that "so and so," Andy Van Slyke, on a pop-up to Scioscia in front of the on-deck circle. The Dodgers sat impassively in the dugout as Ken Daley took the mound in the bottom of the ninth and wasted no time as he fanned both Duncan and Cabell, and induced Pedro Guerrero to fly out to McGee for the final out. The Cardinals won the National League pennant.

Niedenfuer spoke to reporters after the game: "He did his job. I didn't do mine. How would you feel? It's like the other day, when Ozzie hit one. It's not the highlight of my career, if that is what you mean."[33]

Niedenfuer was not the sole person blamed for losing the pennant. The next day in the *Los Angeles Times* sports section Mike Downey wrote,[34] "He [Lasorda] should not have pitched to him. That is all there is to it. He should have walked Jack Clark, or hit Jack Clark in the ribs with a change-up, or offered Jack Clark several billion dollars to leave the bat on his shoulder. Anything but pitch to him."

Lasorda lamented, "Tough, God, tough — just breaks my heart. It's the easiest thing to say. I should have walked him [Clark]. But if he hit a deep fly to center field and caught it for the third out, not one guy would say I should have walked him.[35]

There is some validity to Lasorda's comment, for Niedenfuer fanned Clark in Clark's previous plate appearance. Though Van Slyke, a .091 hitter in the playoffs, was an easy out as opposed to Clark's .391, and Mariano Duncan was batting .077 before he got two hits in Game 6. Lasorda was damned if he did, and damned if he didn't. However, this time the manager seemed to take the blame for losing a playoff series.

A day after the NLCS ended, Niedenfuer received some words of encouragement while he was golfing the next day with a Hall-of-Famer. Dodgers legend Sandy Koufax informed the beleaguered pitcher that if it weren't for him, the Dodgers never would have gotten to the NLCS in the first place, and to look at the whole year, not just the playoffs.[36]

So Niedenfuer returned to the bullpen next year. But in 1986 he was booed throughout the season as he went 6–4 with 10 saves before he was sidelined in August with a hamstring injury. Many fans thought Clark's home run had a holdover effect regarding his short season, and he did yield nine home runs in forty plus innings. Niedenfuer chalked up his ineffectiveness to the 106 innings he threw in 1985 and getting off to a slow start this season.[37] In 1987 Niedenfuer was traded to the Baltimore Orioles for John Shelby and Brad Havens.[38] As an Oriole, Niedenfuer went 6–9 with 31 saves. In 1988, he saved 18 games, a significant number considering the

Orioles won only 54 contests that season. Signed by the Mariners as a free agent the next year, misfortune felled Niedenfuer during the last spring training game when he sustained a broken left wrist after he was hit by a line drive off the bat of Mike Gallego. Ironically, Niedenfuer ended his career in 1990 with the St. Louis Cardinals.[39]

Tom Niedenfuer has put his back-to-back blown saves behind him. In 1996 Niedenfuer appeared with his wife, actress Judy Landers, whom Niedenfuer married in 1987, in the *Huggabug Club,* a children's video titled *You Can't Win 'Em All.* Judy and her sister, actress Audrey Landers, started the *Huggabug Club* in the early 1990s and it received the prestigious Parents' Choice award. Today the Niedenfuers live with their two daughters, Lindsey and Kristy, in Sarasota, Florida.[40]

Tom Niedenfuer should be applauded for going back on the mound after Smith touched him for a home run in Game 5. He should also be applauded for taking over the closer's role twice when Steve Howe's recurring substance abuse problems could have put the Dodgers in a serious predicament. Throughout his Dodger career, Niedenfuer put up some good numbers. He went 36–28 with 64 saves with a 2.76 ERA.

After the Cardinals defeated the Dodgers, St. Louis lost the World Series to their cross-state rivals, the Kansas City Royals, in seven games. Two years later, the Cardinals made it to the World Series and again lost in seven games, this time to the Minnesota Twins. St. Louis managed to win the Central Division in 1996 and 2000, but lost the pennant to the Braves and the Mets. Since then, the Cardinals have not been back to the World Series.

CHAPTER 7

Donnie Moore

He couldn't get over it.
— Dave Pinter

The third playoff game between the New York Giants and Brooklyn Dodgers in 1951, immortalized by the phase the "Shot Heard Round the World," was memorable to those who viewed it on television or heard it on the radio. The phrase was borrowed from the first salvos that were fired at the start of the American Revolutionary War.

Not long afterward, the Constitution was written. The First Amendment to the Constitution, Freedom of Speech, Press and Assembly, has been adopted by all Americans who want to express their views. No matter how many times we as Americans might agree or disagree, the right to express one's opinion is guaranteed by law.

For instance, in the 1960s, Americans were divided over the Vietnam War. The Supreme Court upheld the right of students to wear black armbands as a demonstration of free speech. Recently, to the consternation of many Americans who fought or served in the armed forces, the burning of the American flag was also upheld by the Supreme Court as freedom of speech.

Baseball has experienced similar instances throughout its history. Besides the attacks on Merkle, Snodgrass, Branca, and others, baseball has always dealt with some unruly fans who choose to express themselves in words or deeds, be it jeering, the middle finger, signs, beer bottles or cans or other types of debris thrown onto the field.

In the beginning of the game, blue laws were supported by those who believed that such laws were needed to maintain order and prevent any immoral activities such as Sunday baseball.[1] Ballgames on Sunday were banned on a major league level in the Midwest until the 1880s and unofficially in the northeast until after World War I.[2]

Baseball, in an attempt to present the game in an orderly fashion, allowed women to be admitted to the game for free. The idea was that their husbands would behave with their wives in attendance. They did not.

In Game 7 of the 1934 World Series, the St. Louis Cardinals were leading the Detroit Tigers 9–0 when Joe [Ducky] Medwick slid hard into Tiger third baseman Marv Owen (no relation to Mickey Owen) who retaliated and kicked Medwick. A fight ensued. Tiger fans took umbrage and felt slighted by Medwick's perceived arrogance.

When Medwick took the outfield, he was heckled by the fans and showered with debris from the seats. Baseball commissioner Kenesaw Mountain Landis removed Owen, and especially Medwick, from the game for their own protection.

Jackie Robinson's arrival to the major leagues was not without struggle. Robinson received death threats in the mail, along with torrents of racial abuse, from fans throwing a black cat to being spiked by an opposing player, having baseballs constantly thrown at his head, or seeing a watermelon placed on the field.

Roger Maris was booed incessantly throughout the 1961 season during his assault on Babe Ruth's then record of 60 home runs. And when Henry Aaron led an assault on Ruth's all-time home run record during the 1973-1974 season, Aaron too received death threats, and racist hate mail, and had to enter and exit stadiums under tight security.

Sadly, this chapter illustrates what can happen to an athlete when the public constantly blames only one person for the team's loss of a pennant.

The Los Angeles Angels debuted in 1961 and owner Gene Autry, the famous singing cowboy, chose Bill Rigney to manage the Angels in the team's first year in the American League.[3]

The Angels finished their first season at Wrigley Field, the same minor league ballpark that the Dodgers exchanged to receive the Chavez Ravine (see Chapter 6), in eighth place at 70–91.[4] The next year, the Angels moved into Dodger Stadium, which also housed the Dodgers. Sharing the stadium with the Dodgers, the Angels, in only their second year in the league, were in a pennant race with the World Champion New York Yankees of Mickey Mantle, Roger Maris, Whitey Ford, Elston Howard, and Yogi Berra. But the Angels lost steam in September and wound up in third place with a remarkable 86–76 record.[5] Los Angeles did not enjoy its success for long as they fell into the second division in 1963. Over the next four years, the Angels played near or slightly above .500. In 1966, the Angels moved into their own ballpark in Anaheim, California.[6] The move also brought a new name: The California Angels. The new name did little to improve the

Angels' position in the standings as the team remained in the second division. In 1970, the Angels, in their second year in the new Western Division, won 86 games and finished a respectable third — the team's best since 1962. Unfortunately, the Angels returned to their losing ways despite the arrival of Nolan Ryan, who in 1973 struck out 383 batters, and threw four no-hitters between 1972 and 1975. The Angels averaged 74 wins during this period. As the 1970s came to a close, the Angels ended the decade on an upswing. In 1978, the Angels won 87 games and finished in a second place tie with the Texas Rangers.[7] The following year the Angels won one more game and the Western Division.

Although the Angels lost the LCS to the Baltimore Orioles, California was competitive in the first three games and with a little luck, the Angels could have won the pennant. In Game 1, with the score tied at 3–3, Orioles pinch hitter John Lowenstein hit an opposite field three-run home run in the bottom of the ninth to win the game 6–3. In Game 2 the Angels rallied from a 9–1 deficit and came within one hit of tying and possibly winning the game, but Brian Downing made the last out as the Orioles held on and won 9–8. In Game 3, the Angels scored two runs in the bottom of the ninth to win their only playoff game 4–3. The next night the Orioles, behind Scott McGregor, blanked the Angels 8–0 to win the pennant.

The Angels fell into sixth place in 1980 and failed to qualify for the post-season in the strike-shortened season of 1981.

In 1982 Gene Mauch became the manager and with newly acquired free-agent Reggie Jackson, who hit 39 home runs, and pitchers Tommy John and Geoff Zahn, the Angels won 93 ball games and the Western Division. California looked to win its first pennant after the Angels won the first two games from the Milwaukee Brewers in the LCS, but the Brewers would make LCS history by becoming the first team to rally from an 0–2 deficit and won three straight games and the pennant.

Losing the pennant was disappointing for Gene Mauch, for it was Mauch who managed the Philadelphia Phillies in 1964 when the team led the National League by 6½ games in the middle of September. Then Philadelphia proceeded to lose 10 out of their next 12 games during the final two weeks of the season, and ultimately lost the pennant to the St. Louis Cardinals on the last day of the season.

John McNamara managed the Angels in 1983-84. During those years California lost the division to the Chicago White Sox and the Kansas City Royals. In 1985, a retired Gene Mauch came back to manage the Angels, and with newly acquired reliever Donnie Moore, the Angels were back in the pennant race.[8]

Donnie Ray Moore was born February 13, 1954, in Lubbock, Texas, to Conaway and Willie Moore.[9] Tragedy first struck the Moore family when Ronnie Moore, Donnie's older brother, died when Donnie was young.[10]

Many baseball fans remember Donnie Moore for one pitch, but in truth, as expected, Moore threw many pitches throughout his competitive life. This competitiveness began when Moore played Little and Pony League ball in his youth and continued to pursue his dream of making the major leagues at Monterey High, a predominately white school where Moore was the only African-American on the baseball team.[11] Because Moore chose Monterey High, he was labeled a renegade by his friends, by the mostly black and Hispanic students from nearby East Lubbock.[12] But Monterey High had one of the best baseball programs in Texas, and Moore knew that attending Monterey was a step to reaching the majors. At Monterey, Moore starred as a pitcher and played the outfield.

After leaving Monterey, Moore was drafted by the Red Sox as an outfielder in 1972. However, he chose to attend Ranger Junior College in Texas where Moore knew he would have a chance to pitch. It was at Ranger Junior College where Moore was named Most Valuable Player and Outstanding Pitcher as he led Ranger Junior College to the National Tournament Championship.

In January of the following year, Moore signed with the legendary Negro League player and manager John [Buck] O'Neil to the Chicago Cubs as a pitcher. Moore worked his way through the Cubs' minor league team in Midland, Texas, and was on the Cubs' roster during the last few weeks of the 1975 season. But Moore's stay in the major leagues was short lived, and over the next four years Moore went back and fourth between the Cubs and their minor league affiliate in Wichita of the American Association. During this time Moore became a reliever, but still, he toiled in the minor leagues. Days after the 1979 World Series, Moore was traded to the St. Louis Cardinals for infielder Mike Tyson.[13]

Moore would not stop there as he was sold to the Milwaukee Brewers in September of 1981, only to be returned to the St. Louis Cardinals two months later, before finally being shipped to the Atlanta Braves in February of 1982. The changes in address did little to help Moore, who still toiled in the minor leagues. That all changed when Moore went to the Braves. Moore progressed steadily and it was Richmond, the Braves' triple A farm team, where Moore finally found his niche as he mastered the forkball. His saved total rose from 6 games in 1983 to 16 games for the Braves in 1984.

Moore was also helped by Joe Torre, the Braves manager, who allowed Moore to pitch, including when the game was on the line. Torre's confidence in his reliever helped Moore, who finally found someone who believed in him.[14]

During the 1984 off season, Atlanta signed reliever Bruce Sutter and the Braves chose not to protect Moore. Fred Lynn departed the Angels that year and the team chose Donnie Moore as a compensation package for the loss of a free agent.[15] Today, ball clubs are awarded amateur draft choices as compensation for the loss of a free agent.[16]

For Moore it was a golden opportunity and he took advantage of his situation. In 65 appearances, including two innings in the All-Star Game, Moore saved 31 games for the Angels, a team record, and sported a 1.92 ERA.

At the end of the 1985 season, the Angels led the Western Division over the Kansas City Royals by seven games in early September, but California lost 3 out of 4 games to the Royals during last week of the season to fall one game short of the division championship.

After the 1985 season, Moore signed a three year contract that would pay him about $1 million per year and allowed Moore to purchase a nice home for his wife and three children, Demetria, Ronnie, and Donnie, Jr.[17] It also represented a sense of accomplishment for Moore, who spent years toiling in the major and minor leagues, and now at the age of 31 was one of the best relievers in baseball, while other players at age 31 had either given up or were released from their teams for their lack of productivity.

In 1986, the Angels took over first place in mid–May from the Texas Rangers and won the Western Division for the third time in seven years, posting a 92–70 record.[18] The 1986 California Angels could have been dubbed the senior league: Catcher Bob Boone was 38, second base was occupied by Rob Wilfong at 32 and Bobby Grich at 37, third baseman Doug DeCinces was 35, outfielders Ruppert Jones and Brian Downing were ages 31 and 35, and finally Reggie Jackson was 40 years old.[19] But these seniors were not over the hill as DeCinces and Downing each hit over 20 home runs and had over 90 RBIs. Jackson chipped in with 18 home runs and 58 RBIs.

But California did look to the future with 22-year-old rookie first baseman Wally Joyner who batted .290 with 22 home runs and 100 RBIs. Yet, the average age for the Angels stood at 31.8.

Mike Witt led the Angels staff at 18–10 and a 2.84 ERA and fanned over 200 batters. Kirk McCaskill was next at 17–10 with a 3.36 ERA, followed by the 41-year-old Don Sutton who chipped in 15–11 and a 3.74 ERA. John Candelaria rounded off the staff at 10–2 and a 2.55 ERA.

The year 1986 would be a tough one for Donnie Moore. Moore hurt his arm in spring training and his condition grew worse.[20] Throughout the season, Moore's shoulder, then his rib cage, caused him considerable pain. Still, Moore hung in there as he received cortisone shots to ease the pain. He would be out there any night if he was needed, because he always wanted the ball, wanted to help the team. Then as the end of the season wound down, Moore was bothered with migraine headaches.[21] Despite these ailments, Moore made 49 appearances and managed to save 21 games with a 2.97 ERA for the Angels.

Meanwhile, Boston was rebuilding itself.[22] In 1980 the Red Sox finished in sixth place at 83–77 and with one week left in the season, Don Zimmer was fired and replaced by Ralph Houk. Carlton Fisk was not offered a contract by the team after that season and signed on as a free agent with the Chicago White Sox. Fred Lynn and Rick Burleson were traded to the California Angels. In 1983, Boston bade farewell to Carl Yastrzemski, who hit over 452 home runs and had over 3,054 base hits.

However, as old favorites said good-bye to Fenway Park, new stars such as Wade Boggs, who joined the Red Sox a year before, helped to continue the Red Sox's glorious tradition, as he hit .349 in his rookie season.

In 1986, John McNamara, in his second year as manager, led the Red Sox to 95 wins en route to the Eastern Division title.[23] Wade Boggs batted .357 to lead the league and had 207 hits and 71 RBIs. The 1986 Red Sox were no spring chickens either as Jim Rice, age 33, batted .324 with 200 hits, 20 home runs, and 110 RBIs. Don Baylor, the DH at age 37, hit 31 home runs, with 94 RBIs. Rightfielder Dwight Evans, age 34, hit 26 home runs with 97 RBIs. Bill Buckner, age 36, and playing on a bad ankle, managed to hit 18 home runs with 102 RBIs. The Red Sox bench and pitching staff was under 30, which made for an average age of 28.0.

Roger Clemens, known as "the Rocket," led the staff and the American League with a 24–4 record and 2.48 ERA. He was followed by Dennis "Oil Can" Boyd at 16–10 and a 3.78 ERA followed by Bruce Hurst at 13–8 and a 2.99 ERA. Al Nipper rounded off the pitching staff at 10–12 but carried a 5.38 ERA.

All summer *Sports Illustrated* and other sportswriters kept bringing up the 1978 season, the year of the famous collapse.[24] But the Yankees got no closer than three games and Boston did not fold, for on September 28, the Red Sox defeated the Blue Jays to claim the Eastern Division.[25]

The American League Championship Series started on October 7, 1986, with the first two games held at Fenway Park. Boston was heavily favored to win this series, as opposed to the Angels, ⅗ of whose starting lineup was over the age of 30. Despite the age difference, the Angels won Game 1, as Mike Witt tossed a five-hitter and beat the Red Sox 8–1.[26] Roger Clemens, the Rocket, failed to lift off, and Clemens gave up four runs in the top of the second, and the Red Sox never recovered. In fairness to Clemens, he was hit in the arm during his last start of the regular season, which may have contributed to his ineffectiveness. In Game 2, the Red Sox made two errors, but they capitalized on three errors made by the Angels. Bruce Hurst went all the way as Boston won an ugly game 9–2.[27]

The scene shifted to Anaheim, California, for the next three games and for the next 72 hours, Californians would witness the thrill of victory and the crushing agony of defeat. In Game 3, with the score tied at 1–1 in the top of the seventh, Dick Schofield came up and hit a home run off of starter Oil Can Boyd to give the Angels a 2–1 lead.

Next, catcher Bob Boone singled and then outfielder Gary Pettis hit a home run to make the score 4–1. Angels starter John Candelaria had pitched seven strong innings so Mauch decided to take out Candelaria and replace him with Donnie Moore in the bottom of the eighth. Boston second baseman Marty Barrett reached Moore for a single. Up came Bill Buckner who flied out to center field, but Jim Rice doubled to put runners on second and third. Don Baylor, the designated hitter, was at the plate when Moore committed a balk, and Barrett scored to make the score 4–2 in favor of California. Moore got Don Baylor to pop out to Dick Schofield for the second out. However, Moore did not settle down as he walked rightfielder Dwight Evans and then gave up a hit to Boston catcher Rich Gedman. The Angels' lead shrank to 4–3 before Moore finally got out of the inning when he induced Tony Armas to fly out to Pettis in center field. The Angels tacked on another run in the bottom of the eighth to make the score 5–3. Moore retired both pinch hitter Mike Greenwell, batting for utility infielder Spike Owen, and Wade Boggs on fly outs, but he still could not put out the fire as Barrett singled to keep the inning alive. Bill Buckner again came to the plate to face Donnie Moore. This was a matchup of two men who would be ultimately vilified by baseball fans when the 1986 post season was over. This time it was Moore who won the battle as Buckner flied out to Downing to end the game. Moore got the save, but he struggled during his relief appearance.[28]

California, up two games to one in the ALCS, appeared to be in good shape; then the Angels suffered a major loss when first basemen Wally Joyner, who batted .455 through the first three games, was lost for the remainder of the Series due to a bacterial infection in his right knee. Could the Angels, like the Cardinals last year, prevail in the playoffs after losing a key player?

In Game 4, the Rocket, free from the ineffectiveness that had plagued him in Game 1, was back. Clemens took a 3–0 lead into the bottom of the ninth before running into trouble. Doug DeCinces led off the inning with a solo home run. But Clemens got into more hot water as both Dick Schofield and Bob Boone singled. McNamara then replaced Clemens with reliever Calvin Schiraldi. Up came Pettis who hit a fly ball to right field that looked like an easy out, but Jim Rice lost the ball in the lights. Schofield scored and Boston now led 3–2. Schiraldi struck out second baseman Bobby Grich and intentionally walked leftfielder Ruppert Jones to load the bases. The Red Sox came within one strike of tying the series, as Schiraldi had two strikes on Brian Downing, but like Moore in last night's game, Schiraldi did not settle down. He hit Downing on the leg to tie the game at 3–3. In the eleventh, with one out and two men on, Grich singled off of Schiraldi. Backup catcher Jerry Narron came around to score and the Angels won the game 4–3. Californians can vividly recall Bobby Grich jumping in the air and pumping his fist to celebrate his triumphant hit that gave the Angels the victory and put his team one win away from the World Series.[29]

Schiraldi had helped the Red Sox win the division, but he, like Moore, would experience many highs and lows in the 1986 playoffs, as his outing was a harbinger of things to come.

Like last year's championship series after four games, one team led the other with a three games to one edge in the playoffs. The Angels were so close to winning the pennant this time. In the 1979 ALCS, the Angels won only one game. Then in the 1982 ALCS, the Angels won two games, but failed to win the third game to advance to the World Series.

The Angels had won three games, but the rules now mandated that a team must win four games to advance to the World Series.

If California could win today's game they would stun the Red Sox in five games while beating Clemens in two of those contests.

Southpaw Bruce Hurst was Boston's last chance to stave off elimination.[30] The Red Sox scored in the second inning when Gedman, with a man on, hit a two run home run to give Boston an early 2–0 lead. In the bottom of the second, center fielder Tony Armas hurt his ankle when he crashed against the wall chasing a fly ball off the bat of DeCinces. Armas came up empty, but there was no damage as DeCinces did not score. The Angels countered in the bottom of the third when Boone hit a home run to cut the lead in half, 2–1.

Armas' ankle pain persisted and he came out of the game in the top of the fifth. Dave Henderson, also playing with a bad leg, replaced Armas in center field.[31]

In the bottom of the sixth, DeCinces doubled to right center. Grich came up to the plate. Hurst, who always threw the ball overhand, threw a changeup on the outside part of the plate, but the ball stayed up in the strike zone. Grich got out in front and made contact, and the ball immediately flew out to center field.

Henderson raced back to the fence, timed his leap, and got his glove on the ball, but as his free hand hit the wall, the ball deflected off his glove hand for a home run.

Henderson was playing hurt — and now the ball eluded his grasp for a home run. In short, he was having a bad day. The score was now 3–2 in favor of the Angels. The crowd went crazy sensing that the Angels were finally on their way to the World Series. In the next inning, the Red Sox had two men on with two outs when Henderson came up and Witt struck him out to preserve the lead, but Henderson was not done yet.

California scored two more runs to extend their lead to 5–2 and Mike Witt went out in the top of the ninth. Mounted policeman, security guards, and stadium attendants streamed onto the foul lines to prevent any fans from running onto the field. Bill Buckner opened the ninth with a single up the middle that barely got by Schofield.

Dave Stapleton, as he had always done in the late innings, replaced Buckner as a pinch runner at first. Up came Rice and the crowd hung on every pitch and grew louder when Witt struck out Rice for the first out. Don Baylor, who wore the Angels' halo and appeared in the 1979 and 1982 ALCS, came up and worked Witt to a full count. On the payoff pitch, Witt threw Baylor a curve ball up on the outside corner. Baylor extended his arms and connected. Suddenly, the Angels' cheers went to groans as the ball cleared the left center wall over a leaping Gary Pettis for a home run. California's lead shrank to 5–4.

Witt did not let Baylor's home run rattle him as he induced Evans to pop up to DeCinces at third base for the second out. The crowd again was cheering the Angels on to get the final out. But Mike Witt, who pitched fourteen complete games in 1986, would not be the one to get the final out. Witt was surprised to see Angels pitching coach Marcel Lachemann walk out to the mound to remove him from the game to the consternation of Boone and DeCinces.

Gary Lucas was summoned to retire Gedman and put his team into the World Series. In the meantime, plastic covering had been put up throughout the Angels locker rooms to prevent any champagne from wetting the lockers. Center fielder Gary Pettis was chosen as the Most Valuable Player of the ALCS. The California Highway patrol entered the Red Sox dugout to lead the Red Sox players to safety.[32]

Although Witt was confident he could get the last out, Mauch felt that Gedman, who had three hits off of Witt that day, would not do any damage to Lucas, who always handled Gedman when he faced him during the regular season and had struck him out the night before. Yet, Lucas' first pitch was an inside fastball that struck Gedman on his hand as the Boston catcher fell to the ground. Gedman trotted down to first as Mauch relieved Lucas with Donnie Moore.

Dave Henderson, who began his career with the Mariners in 1981, stepped up to the plate. His most productive season was in 1983, when he batted .269 with 17 home runs, 55 RBIs, and 130 hits. His average slipped in 1985, and although he drove in 68 runs, Henderson was expendable and traded to the Red Sox in August of 1986. But the change in scenery did little to help Henderson at the plate as he only batted .196 with one home run, and three RBIs. Nevertheless, this was the post season, where a player can shine on any given day.

Scene: Anaheim Stadium[33]

Today, the stadium called Edison International Field of Anaheim sounds more like an airport than a ballpark. But baseball is played there. The Angels did not traverse on the "Big A" when the team joined the league in 1961. That year, the then Los Angeles Angels played their home games at Wrigley Field, a minor league ballpark that seated 22,000, and like its major league namesake, vines draped the outfield walls of the ballpark. Construction began on Anaheim Stadium on August 31, 1964, and opened 20 months later on April 19, 1966, with seating capacity at 46,000. At a cost of $24 million, the stadium was nicknamed the "Big A" after a gigantic 230-foot letter "A" was positioned behind the fence in left field. The fences stood at 333 feet down the left and right field lines while center field stood at 406 feet; the fences from left to right stood at ten feet and were padded in 1981.

Like most new ballparks, within a year the All-Star game was held at Anaheim Stadium. The result was the same: the National League — as they did throughout most of the 1960s and 1970s — won the annual contest 2–1.

In 1979, Anaheim modernized the stadium which led to the removal of the big "A" to the parking lot, and augmented the seating capacity to 64,000. In the 1980s Anaheim Stadium witnessed two milestones: Reggie Jackson's 500th home run in 1984 and Don Sutton's 300th win in 1986.

Moore's first pitch to Henderson was a ball. His second was so perfectly placed on the outside corner that Henderson never bothered to swing for strike one. Henderson was late on Moore's third pitch — a fastball that exploded in Bob Boone's glove for strike two. Moore seemed to have good stuff on this day; each pitch looked like a laser when Moore delivered it to the plate. One "Moore" strike. Reggie Jackson and Gene Mauch were shown in the dugout and with the rest of the 64,223 Angels fans standing up, applauding, and waiting for what seem like the inevitable — the Angels' first trip to the World Series. The 25 season drought seemed like it was worth the wait. The 1979 and 1982 pennant losses were about to fade into memory. Moore's fourth pitch was a fastball in the dirt to even the count at 2–2. But Boone began to worry that Henderson was timing Moore's pitches, so he signaled for the forkball pitch, which Moore delivered and Henderson fouled back to the grandstands. So Moore went back to the fastball and Henderson fouled that one too, staying alive. More importantly, Boone's fears were well founded. Henderson was making contact, so Boone again signaled for the forkball.

Moore's seventh pitch, a forkball on the outside part of the plate, did not have the same bite as Moore's previous forkball that Henderson fouled to stay alive. This pitch stood up in the strike zone and Henderson got out in front and connected. The ball immediately jumped off of Henderson's bat, and seconds later, Downing watched helplessly as the ball cleared the left field fence for a two run home run and Boston took a 6–5 lead.

The replay shows Henderson leaping in the air and pirouetting like a ballet dancer after his home run cleared the wall. Henderson was nimble around the bases where he was met by his ecstatic Red Sox teammates who stormed out of the dugout.

Donnie Moore, who looked dazed after Henderson's home run, managed to pull himself together and retired pinch-hitter Ed Romero to get out of the top of the ninth. Although the Angels were dispirited, they did not go down quietly. In the bottom of the ninth, Boone reached base for the fourth time when he singled off of Bob Stanley who replaced Bruce Hurst in the bottom of the seventh. Mauch sent in Ruppert Jones to pinch run for Boone.

Next, Pettis came up and sacrificed Jones to second. Afterward, Joe Sambito replaced Stanley on the mound. The change did little as Rob Wilfong kept the rally going with a single to right field. Evans fielded the ball cleanly and made a beautiful throw to home, but Jones was even prettier as he slid around Gedman, stuck out his hand, and touched the corner of home plate to tie the game at 6–6. However, Wilfong stood camped at first, when he should have tried to take second after Evans threw home. If Wilfong had done so, he might have scored on the next play as Schofield reached Steve Crawford, Boston's fourth pitcher of the day, for a single. Instead Wilfong wound up on third. McNamara then gave an intentional pass to Downing to load the bases.

Doug DeCinces stepped up to the plate. DeCinces had doubled in the fourth and hit a fly ball that Henderson lost in the sun. More importantly, he was the right man for this situation. If DeCinces could get a hit, draw a walk, induce a balk, get a wild pitch, or hit a fly ball deep to the outfield to score Wilfong from third, Moore's earlier pitch would be forgotten. Crawford, a right hander fresh from the minors, stood nervously on the mound. DeCinces did the Red Sox a favor, for on Crawford's first pitch, DeCinces lofted a fly ball to shallow right field to Evans. Evans possessed one of the best arms in the game and he caught the ball for the second out, and Wilfong had to stay at third. California's pennant was still 90 feet away at third base. As for Crawford, his anxiety had not dissipated, which became evident as his first two pitches to the next batter, Bobby Grich, failed to touch the strike zone. Grich now had the count in his favor. With the count 2–0 Crawford's third offering nicked the outside corner for strike one — a questionable and generous gift considering the pitch looked like ball 3. Nevertheless, the count was 2–1 and Grich fouled the next pitch for strike two. Momentum swung back to Crawford as Grich popped up to Crawford to retire the Angels in the ninth.

After the Angels tied the score in the ninth, Mauch should have taken Moore out of the game. If Mauch had done so, Moore would not have had to deal with the weight of the pennant on his shoulders. Nevertheless, Mauch kept Moore, who in the tenth flirted with danger, but managed to survive the inning when he induced Rice to hit into a double play with men on first and third. In the bottom of the tenth, Gary Pettis came up and nearly won the pennant with a home run, but the ball died into Jim Rice's glove for a long out.

After that long fly out, the Angels went down in the bottom of the tenth. Moore was still on the mound in the top of the eleventh when he hit Baylor, yielded a single to Evans, and could not retire Gedman, whose bunt single loaded the bases.

Henderson came up again and hit a sacrifice fly deep to Pettis in center field to score Baylor from third. Boston reclaimed the lead 7–6 as cascades of boos rained down from the stands. Moore was clearly running out of gas, as Romero proved when he took Moore's last offering to deep left field. Brian Downing raced back, crashed into the wall, and made a spectacular catch to keep California's deficit at one run. Finally, Moore was taken out of the game, booed loudly as he departed the field, a portent of things to come.

Calvin Schiraldi came in and when Downing popped up to Stapleton in foul territory for the third out, the Red Sox proved what Yogi Berra said during the Mets' run at the Eastern Division in 1973: "It ain't over til it's over." Finally it was the Red Sox that turned the tables on another team during October, but by the end of the month, the Red Sox would disappoint their fans again.

Moore spoke with reporters after the game. "I really can't blame my arm. My pitch selection was bad. I was throwing fastballs and he [Henderson] was fouling them off, so I went with the split-finger, thought maybe I'd catch him off guard, but it was right in his swing. I really shouldn't

***Donnie Moore*:** In two seasons, Moore was the catalyst for the California Angels, saving over 50 games as the team vied for the post season. Needing just one more strike to reach the Fall Classic, Moore allowed a home run in Game 5 of the 1986 ALCS that began his downfall and untimely death. (Photograph courtesy of the National Baseball Hall of Fame Library, Cooperstown, N.Y.)

have thrown him an off-speed pitch, because that's the kind of bat speed he has. I should've stayed with the hard stuff."[34]

After Boston's improbable win in Game 5, the rest of the Series played at Fenway Park was anti-climactic. The Red Sox won the next two games with ease. The Red Sox won Game 6 when the Angels looked like they were going to come back from the heartbreaking loss in Game 5.

Red Sox starter Oil Can Boyd sprang a leak in the beginning of the game, but McCaskill could not hold a 2–0 lead. Boston, helped by the Angels' miscues, won the game 10–4.[35] John Candelaria was the Angels' last hope to avoid being the second team to blow a three to one game advantage in the championship series.

Clemens would be the beneficiary of poor defense as California made two costly errors in the early innings of Game 7. And Rice's three run homer in the fourth sealed the Angels' fate as the Red Sox beat the Angels 8–1 and won the pennant. To make matters worse, seven unearned runs had crossed the plate. Mauch's face said it all: frustration as he realized this post season might be his last chance to get to the World Series. Mauch could do nothing now.

As baseball fans, we might ask ourselves how a team could be so close and not win the pennant. When a team loses a series as California did, one automatically looks for a scapegoat to assuage the pain of the loss and disappointment, as if blaming Donnie Moore would somehow validate our faith in the team. The fans would feel okay to root for their team again because next year it would be a memory. Fans support a team with their hearts, and when their hearts are unexpectedly broken they lash out at the player like a scorned lover.

Forgetting what the player did before, the fans ask, "What have you done for me lately when it counts?" Didn't the game count before? Look it up in the record book. But today's game could lead to a championship and we can't forgive the player when he is not perfect on that day. Then should we punish ourselves when we, the fans, are not perfect and make a mistake? The reaction is emotional, not logical.

For Donnie Moore the game was a nightmare. As told by Doug DeCinces in the book *One Pitch Away* by Mike Sowell: "Donnie Moore received a cortisone injection the night before and he wasn't supposed to pitch. He was *not* supposed to pitch. So when we see this coming in, all the players on the team went, 'Oh, my gosh. What are we doing here?' Anybody who has had an injection, you know what you feel like the next day. It's extremely uncomfortable, and very sore to move the area. And you're extremely weak because of the medicine working on the muscles. It takes about forty-eight hours to recover.

"But Donnie was such a competitor. And sometimes, competitors like that aren't always intelligent, if you know what I mean. They're never not going to take the ball. It's that thinking, 'Hey sometimes you have to bite the bullet, just go out there, give it your best and whatever happens, happens.' But this was not the situation or time to do that. But there was nobody else, so in comes Donnie."[36]

Unlike the other newspapers after the ALCS ended, the *Los Angeles Times*, in its October 17th sports section, mentioned that Donnie Moore was saddled with a sore shoulder and received two cortisone injections in his right shoulder and right rib cage. The article went on to say that Moore should have been handled with care in the series.[37]

However, some fans were not as forgiving. After that pitch, baseball was no longer fun for Donnie Moore. Moore went to spring training and still he was in pain. He took more tests and tried acupuncture, but nothing had changed and the pain still lingered. He made only 14 appearances and was booed incessantly when he took the mound in 1987. If Moore had a bad outing, the jeering by the fans became much louder. Those jeers were accompanied by signs that insulted Moore to the point that he came home after a bad outing on the mound and cried.[38]

Moore's injury eventually forced him onto the disabled list. He became moody when he could not pitch. Moore, once a happy person, was now much more morose.[39] Moore wanted a trade and the Yankees were interested in him, but the reports on Moore's health discouraged any team from taking any chances on an injured reliever.[40]

The Angels had a chance to win the Western Division, but they had a terrible September and the team finished dead last. Moore could not convince the Angels that he was in pain. Mike Port, the Angels general manager, called Moore a malingerer, saying that he should be pitching. Mike Port, in *One Pitch Away*: "Instead of whining about hurting his rib cage, he should be out there earning his money. What do we pay him $1 million for?"[41] It is bad enough when the fans turn on you, but this coming from the general manager had to inflict even more psychological damage on Donnie Moore. Finally, it was discovered that Moore suffered from a bone spur the size of a dime at the base of his spine. Moore underwent a successful surgery, and although Port visited Moore in the hospital, the apology was too late, the damage was done — words can have an indelible impact on a player.

When Moore returned to the Angels in 1988, he was not the same pitcher as he was in 1985. The cortisone shots, the injuries, the boos, and the constant reminder from the media over that one pitch in the ALCS took their toll. Moore could not get anybody out.

Moreover, he kept blaming himself for the team's failure to advance to the World Series because of his forkball in Game 5. Moore did not help himself either by submerging his feelings. It was a noble thing for Moore not to burden anyone with his problems; however, the psychological toll could overwhelm anyone.

The final act of humiliation occurred on August 26, 1988, when Moore, on the disabled list with a broken finger, was activated by the Angels only to be released by the club that same day.[42]

There were some decent people in baseball who cared about Donnie Moore. In 1989, Bob Boone, his former teammate, now with the Kansas City Royals, recommended Moore to their top minor league team in Omaha, Nebraska.

But even in the minor leagues, Moore could not find tranquility. His new teammates mocked the beleaguered pitcher calling him "Million Dollars."[43] Plus, he was ineffective at Omaha, and after seven games, Moore went 1–2 in 12⅔ innings with a 6.39 ERA. He was released on June 12.[44]

Moore figured that his stint in Omaha had ended his chance to pitch again in the major leagues. But all was not lost. Dave Pinter, Moore's agent, had contacted Houston Astros general manager Bob Watson, who once played with the Astros and Yankees, about a job for Moore with the team. Watson informed Pinter that he was interested in Moore and he would try to sign him to their triple A affiliate as soon as a pitching position was available.

Still he was without baseball, and following a separation from his wife Tonya, Moore was virtually alone. To make matters worse, Moore faced financial problems and now had to sell his house that he had bought for his family four years earlier. Meanwhile, Pinter implored Donnie Moore to see a psychiatrist.[45] Moore told Pinter that he did not need to see a psychiatrist and that he could handle his problems. But on July 18, 1989, after a heated argument with Tonya, Donnie Moore shot his estranged wife with a .45 caliber handgun five times.[46] Three of the five bullets hit Tonya. The first bullet struck her in the neck and passed through the back of her spine. The second bullet landed below her chest and exited through her mid-section. The final bullet hit her in the chest and entered one of her lungs. The Moores' oldest child, 17-year-old Demetria, drove her mother to the hospital.

Miraculously, Tonya Moore survived the ordeal, as the bullets fired from Moore's gun did not hit any of her vital organs or spine. After Tonya was taken to the hospital, Donnie Moore ended his life.

Dave Pinter had this to say about Moore in the *Sporting News*: "Ever since he gave up the home run to Dave Henderson, he was never himself again. He blamed himself for the Angels not going to the World Series. He constantly talked about the Henderson home run. He couldn't get over it. I tried to get him to go to a psychiatrist, but he said, 'I don't need it. I'll get over it.' But he couldn't get over it. That home run killed him."[47]

When Brian Downing heard of Moore's death, he lashed out at the press for harping on the one pitch that occurred during the 1986 LCS. Downing reminded everyone that the Angels would not have won the Western Division if it were not for Donnie Moore's contributions through the season in 1986.

After Ralph Branca yielded his home run pitch to Bobby Thomson, a priest, who happened to be Branca's fiancée's cousin, informed Branca that God chose him because he would be strong enough to bear the cross. Branca would be a strong enough person to endure a devastating loss.[48] Moore was once quoted that he did not want to become another Ralph Branca.[49] The truth is that if he were a Ralph Branca, Donnie Moore would be alive today. Some might say Moore's life reminds them of a Shakespearean tragedy.

It is obvious that DeCinces' and Grich's failure to drive in the winning run from third base was just as critical as Moore's pitch to Henderson in the Angels' failure to win the pennant. Plus, the following two games where the Angels' miscues allowed the Red Sox to win the two remaining contests and advance to the World Series were important factors in the loss. Finally, Moore should have been taken out after the Angels tied the game in the ninth. Henderson scored the go ahead run in the eleventh inning when it was clear that Moore was without his best stuff that day. It is unfair to blame any individual for the negative result of the game when the efforts of so many determine the outcome.

Donnie Moore's death is a stark reminder of what this game means to everyone. To the ballplayer, baseball is a skill and an occupation that the average fan can only fantasize about. The fan might view baseball as an entertainment, a hobby, or even an obsession — an obsession that can lead a fan to taunt one player. Those taunts can take their toll like they did on Moore, causing him to take his life and leave three children without a father.

However, let us remember that Moore never gave up and kept pitching after Game 5 of the 1986 ALCS. With the fans and front office jeering him unmercifully during the following two years, he kept on. Though certainly not a perfect man, Moore was wrongly chosen to be the scapegoat as the Angels lost the pennant collectively to the Red Sox. But sadly, even after this tragedy, some baseball fans have yet to learn from Donnie Moore's death, as the experiences of other players demonstrate.

Since their Western Division title in 1986, the California Angels have not returned to the post season. The closest the Angels came to post season play was in 1995 when they lost a one game playoff 8–1 to the Seattle Mariners for the Western Division crown. The following year the California Angels became the Anaheim Angels.

CHAPTER 8

Bill Buckner

The Red Sox were in the World Series. Boston's triumph in the ALCS was one of the best comebacks in the post season. Surely, it was the "Impossible Dream" nearly twenty years later. In 1967, the Boston Red Sox outlasted the Chicago White Sox, Detroit Tigers, and Minnesota Twins to win the last pennant race in the American League before division play began. After winning the pennant, Boston looked like it would go all the way and win the world championship, but for Bill Buckner, this would be a painful series, literally and figuratively.

William Joseph (Bill) Buckner was born on December 14, 1949, to Leonard and Marie Buckner in Vallejo, California.[1] Buckner and his siblings, which included his brothers Bob and Jim and a sister Jan, grew up in Vallejo, where the Buckner children bided their time fishing or venturing in the woods. Their father, Leonard, loved baseball and taught his children the game. The Buckner clan played wiffle ball in the backyard. Leonard Buckner would never see his son play professional baseball; the elder Buckner lost his life after he was involved in a car accident. His death had a transforming effect on young Bill Buckner, as he drove himself to succeed in all facets of life, especially in sports. He played football and baseball at Napa High School, and was drafted by the Los Angeles Dodgers in the second round of the draft in June 1968. Upon graduating from high school, Buckner attended Southern California and Arizona State University.[2] Buckner set a high threshold for himself and when he fell below his expectations, he would become angry. Buckner was even given the name "Mad Dog" by his minor league manager and future Dodger skipper Tommy Lasorda.[3] Yet, these long hours paid off as he made his professional debut for Ogden in the Prairie League, and rose quickly through the minor leagues, sporting a .335 batting average for the Spokane Indians in the Pacific Coast League. Although Buckner had only a few at bats for the Dodgers in 1969 and 1970, he had high hopes for making the team the following year. Buckner went to the Dodgers' spring training camp that February, and though he batted .432, conflicting reports regarding his chances caused Buckner much anxiety. He could not sleep and dropped 12 pounds from his normal playing weight of 185.[4] His fears were put to rest as he made the team as the fifth outfielder. Buckner was in the lineup for good. There Buckner made a successful debut batting .277 in his rookie season.[5] In his sophomore year, Buckner was even better, as he batted .319 with 122 hits. His average slipped a bit in 1973, but Buckner rebounded a year later batting .314 with 182 hits to help lead the Dodgers to the World Series against the Oakland A's. Unfortunately for the Dodgers and every other baseball team in the early 1970s, Oakland dominated the Fall Classic, as the A's won their third championship in a row beating Los Angeles in five games.

By this time Buckner was playing in left field which allowed Steve Garvey, Buckner's teammate from his days in the minors, to play at first base. Garvey would become a mainstay at first for the Dodgers and would become part of an infield that would play together for the next eight seasons. After the Dodgers lost the World Series to the A's, Buckner, already established as one of the best hitters in the game, decided to take his game up a notch by using his speed. Buckner marveled at the way his teammate, second baseman Davey Lopes, used a quick slide whenever he stole a base. Buckner tried to copy Lopes' quick slide, but the move proved costly.[6]

The Dodgers and Giants squared off in a game at Dodger Stadium in April 1975. Buckner was on first when he took off for second base. As Buckner slid into second, his ankle got caught under the bag, and Buckner twisted his ankle as his body fell over second base. Buckner's injury led to an operation on his tendon and another operation to remove bone chips in his left ankle.

Though Buckner returned to the outfield, the injury robbed him of his mobility. Buckner should have let his ankle heal. He came back too soon and for the rest of his career Buckner, the warrior, played in pain. With Garvey firmly established at first, Buckner was the odd man out and during the 1976 off season, Buckner and his teammate, shortstop Ivan DeJesus, were involved in a five player deal and traded to the Chicago Cubs for Rick Monday and two minor leaguers.[7] Buckner did not want to leave the Dodgers, but the trade allowed the injured Buckner to play first base with the Cubs. In 1980, Buckner batted .324 to win the batting title, and he collected 201 hits in 1982.

Two years later, Buckner was traded again, this time to the Boston Red Sox for Dennis Eckersley and infielder Mike Brummley.[8] The uniform may have been different, but Buckner's level of consistency remained the same as he again collected 201 hits, 110 RBIs—his career best—and 46 doubles in 1985. He also set a new record for assists by a first baseman for the third time in his career.

In 1986, Buckner's contributions (see last chapter) helped the Red Sox win the pennant. But 1986 might have been 1976. As documented in *One Pitch Away*, ever since he twisted his ankle, Buckner's days began and ended as he soaked his ankles in a bucket of ice water for an hour.[9] If needed he would inject himself with painful cortisone shots to ease the sore, swollen muscles he bore throughout the years he played baseball. There were the numerous amounts of bandages that Buckner applied to his body as he prepared to play ball. Buckner's preparation reminded some baseball fans of another hero who retired when Buckner began his career: Mickey Mantle. Mantle also played in pain, but managed to pull himself together by applying reams of bandages around his body just to play ball.[10] The ALCS was no different, as Buckner applied an ice bag to his back to soothe a pulled muscle and bore another wound along his strained hamstring on his left leg. Finally, there were the ointments and acupuncture that he used—anything to get himself ready.[11]

To compound matters, in Game 7 of the ALCS against the Angels, Buckner injured his Achilles tendon as he ran towards first. While viewing a football game, Buckner saw the players on the gridiron wearing high top shoes, so he ordered black high top shoes that were designed to protect his injured tendon.[12] Buckner always played despite the pain and he was not going to miss his chance to play in the World Series.

The National League pennant was also decided on the same day hours earlier. Nineteen eighty-six was a special year for the New York Mets and their fans, but the season that ended spectacularly started off inauspiciously.[13]

In spring training during a run down exercise, center fielder Mookie Wilson was struck in the eye from a ball thrown by Rafael Santana, cutting him in the face and putting him on the disabled list for the first month of the season.

The injury seemed to be a bad omen as the Mets lost their first game of the season on April 14 to the Cardinals. After five games, New York's record stood at 2–3 and fickle Mets fans had already decided that the team was going to finish in second place for the third year in a row.

The Mets responded to the fans' complaints when they went to St. Louis and swept four games against the defending National League champions, all but knocking out the Cardinals from the Eastern Division crown in 1986.

The Cardinals were still recovering from the previous year's disappointing loss in the World Series to their cross-state rivals, the Kansas City

Royals. From there, the Mets went on a winning streak and took over sole possession of first place on April 23 for good.

By the end of June, Cardinals manager Whitey Herzog all but conceded the Eastern Division to the Mets. Herzog's prediction was correct and by the end of the summer, the *New York Daily News* ran a cartoon in the paper each day that featured manager Davey Johnson. Johnson was shown pulling a rabbit out of a Mets cap with the number of games left to clinch the division. The Mets' magic number eventually came to fruition.

The fourth New York team and the third National League team in the modern era, the Mets, as mentioned before, was enfranchised in 1962. The Mets lacked the rich and glorious history of the New York Giants (1883–1957) which included Mike "King" Kelly, of the "Slide, Kelly, Slide" fame, manager John McGraw, Christy Mathewson, Ross "Pep" Youngs, Rube Marquard, Met Ott, Carl Hubbell, Bill Terry, and Willie Mays. And they were not the beloved Bums, the Brooklyn Dodgers of Charles Ebbets, Wilbert Robinson, Van Lingo Mungo, the Boys of Summer (the members of the Dodgers who played between 1947 and 1957). Nor were they the mighty New York Yankees, who owned much of the baseball world from 1921 to 1964, winning 29 pennants and 20 world championships. They also were not the mini-dynasty from 1976 to 1981, which included four pennants and two championships.

But these Mets owned New York City in 1986. They were omnipresent as the team appeared on magazines, commercials, and MTV. They made a video, "Let's Go Mets," that was played throughout whole year. Met detractors complained about the numerous curtain calls after each Met home run or Met win. The team was labeled brash and arrogant, but the Mets would not back down. Third baseman Ray Knight fought with Dodgers pitcher Tom Niedenfuer and Reds outfielder Eric Davis. In truth, the Mets were a great team that year and they were not bragging; they could back it up.

The pitching staff was led by Dwight "Doc" Gooden.[14] Gooden was in his third year in the big leagues and finished the season at 17–6 with a 2.84 ERA. Bob Ojeda led the team in wins at 18–5 and had a 2.57 ERA. Sid Fernandez had a record of 16–6, a 3.52 ERA, and struck out over 200 batters. Ron Darling chipped in with a record of 15–6, and 2.81 ERA. Finally, Rick Aguilera rounded off the pitching staff with a 10–7 record and a 3.88 ERA along with Roddy McDowell and Jessie Orosco in the bullpen. Each saved more than 20 games.

The offense was powered by first baseman Keith Hernandez. The perennial Gold Glover batted .310 with 13 home runs, and 83 RBIs. Rightfielder Darryl Strawberry followed at .259, 27 home runs, and 93

RBIs. Second baseman Wally Backman hit .320 and 124 hits and 27 RBIs. Ray Knight hit .298, 11 home runs and 76 RBIs and catcher Gary "Kid" Carter hit .255 with 24 home runs and 105 RBIs.

The only time the Mets experienced any adversity during the season was the first weekend after the All-Star break when the Houston Astros swept the Mets in a three game series. The Mets would hear from the Astros again in October.

On September 4, the Mets went to Fenway Park to play the Red Sox in an exhibition game to benefit the Jimmy Fund. Before the game, the Mets and Red Sox players posed for pictures. At the same time, each position player was sizing up his counterpart for a possible World Series showdown. Fans on both teams wanted to forget the rest of the season and go straight to the World Series, but the rest of the season had to be completed and by the middle of September, the Mets needed one game to clinch the division. They went to Philadelphia to start the celebration with a win. But Phillies third baseman Mike Schmidt vowed that the Mets would not drink champagne in Veterans Stadium. The eventual 1986 MVP was right as Schmidt and the Phillies swept the Mets to put the champagne on hold.

But on September 17, the inevitable happened as Gooden beat the Cubs 5–4 at Shea Stadium. Fans ran onto the field to celebrate the Eastern Division with the Mets. Shea Stadium was a mess, but it had been 13 long years since the team played in a post-season game. Two weeks after the regular season ended, the Mets, with their 108 wins and 54 losses, faced the Houston Astros in the NLCS.

The Astros, then known as the Colt .45's, entered the National League with the Mets in 1962. Nineteen eighty-six was the second time that the Astros entered the post-season. Houston first went to the League Championship Series against the Philadelphia Phillies in 1980, losing the pennant to the Phillies in five thrilling games.

The Astros won the National League Western Division that year with a 96–66 record. Former Met Mike Scott was now the ace of the Astros and the Cy Young Award winner that year. He went 18–10 with a 2.22 ERA and a split-fingered fastball.[15] Some detractors claimed he scuffed the ball because Scott's pitches dropped down over the plate so abruptly. Whatever Scott did worked, for in the first playoff game, Scott struck out 14 Mets and won the game 1–0.

The lone run occurred when first baseman Glenn Davis homered off of Doc Gooden in the sixth inning.

Bob Ojeda pitched a complete game and the Mets won 5–1 to even the series at a game apiece. Both clubs split the next two games and then the Mets won the critical fifth game 2–1 in twelve innings. Game 6 of the NLCS was one of the most dramatic games in League Championship Series history. The Astros, behind southpaw Bob Knepper, took an early 3–0 lead and kept the Mets at bay for eight innings until the top of the ninth, when the Mets rallied with three runs to tie the game at 3–3.

The score remained the same until the top of the fourteenth when the Mets pushed across a run on two hits. The Astros knotted the game at 4–4 when outfielder Billy Hatcher homered off the foul pole in the bottom of the fourteenth. Hatcher's home run staved off elimination, but the Mets surged ahead with three runs in the top of the sixteenth. The Astros would not die as they fought back with two runs in the bottom of the inning. Houston had men on second and third with two outs when Jessie Orosco struck out Kevin Bass on a 3–2 slider to give the Mets the pennant.

So it was the Boston Red Sox against the New York Mets in the 1986 World Series. Thus the Red Sox became the first team to play all former and current New York teams in the World Series. Boston beat the New York Giants in 1912 and the Brooklyn Dodgers in 1916; however, this time the Red Sox were underdogs in the World Series.

After the Mets won the pennant, nothing else seemed to matter in New York City except for the World Series. It was like a coronation, as the Mets players became heroes in the city even before a pitch had been thrown. The night before the series began, many in the entertainment industry came out to support the Mets. The gathering looked more like a Hollywood premiere. Despite the pageantry, baseball was played the next day.

Shea Stadium hosted the first two games, but for all intents and purposes that was the highlight for New York for the next 48 hours. The pitchers: Bruce Hurst against Ron Darling.

The temperature at the start of the series was 50 degrees, which allowed both pitchers to blow on their pitching hands.

Hurst and Darling pitched shutout ball until the top of the seventh, when Darling walked Rice with nobody out. Evans was at bat when Darling threw a wild pitch that sent Rice to second. After Darling retired Evans, Rich Gedman stepped to the plate and hit a ground ball straight to second baseman Tim Tuefel, who held the glove a few inches from the grass. But the ball did not bounce or roll into his glove. Instead the ball traveled into right field allowing Rice to score from second. That run was all Bruce Hurst needed as he went all the way and held on to defeat the Mets 1–0.

By winning the first game, Boston had achieved what any visiting team would want in the first two games of the World Series: win at least a game on the road to guarantee at least a spilt.

Game 2 was the matchup that every baseball fan was waiting to see. The pitchers: Dwight "Doctor K" Gooden against Roger (Rocket) Clemens, two strikeout specialists who threw heat. Both men stood 6'4". Gooden had a 24–4 record the previous year; Clemens had the same record this year.

Boston drew first blood in the top of the third. Spike Owen walked and McNamara ordered Clemens to lay down a sacrifice. Mets first baseman Keith Hernandez came charging in and fielded the ball, but he made an errant throw in mid-air to shortstop Rafael Santana and Clemens was safe on the play. With runners on first and second and no outs, Boggs stepped to the plate and doubled home Owen and moved Clemens to third to give the Red Sox a 1–0 lead. Next, Barrett and Buckner both singled, which gave the Red Sox two more runs. Boston now led 3–0.

The Mets came back in the bottom of the second. Santana singled and Mets manager Davey Johnson ordered Gooden to sacrifice. Gooden bunted the ball too hard, but as Buckner dove to make the catch, he fell down and allowed the ball to roll to his right and Gooden, like Clemens before him, was safe at first on an error. Backman followed Gooden with a single up the middle to score Santana with the Mets first run of the Series. Keith Hernandez then hit a ball back up the middle that ricocheted off of Clemens' foot to Boggs at third who fielded the ball. Boggs made a great play to nail Hernandez at first, but Gooden scored on the play to make the score 3–2 in favor of the Red Sox.

In the top of the fourth, Henderson kept up his October surprise with a home run. The Red Sox's offense did not stop, for in the top of the fifth, Rice singled and Evans brought him home with a two-run home run to make the score 6–2. New York scored their final run in the bottom of the fifth on back-to-back singles by Hernandez and Carter to drive home Backman who had walked.

But Boston would answer back by scoring three more runs in the seventh and ninth innings to win the game 9–3. The pitching matchup did not come to fruition as Gooden was in a hole from the start, and Clemens left the game with one out in top of the fifth; therefore, he could not qualify for the win. Nevertheless, Boston led the Mets 2–0 in the Series.

On the off day, on the sports talk radio, some Met detractors remarked that the NY logo on the Mets cap meant next year. But the New York Mets were not like their National League predecessors, the Brooklyn Dodgers, who always cried, "Wait til next year" after each World Series defeat to the New York Yankees. The Series shifted to Fenway Park for the next three games. The Mets knew that if they lost the third game, the Series would virtually be all but over as no team had ever come back from a 0–3 deficit.

Game 3 would be better for New York. The pitchers were Bob Ojeda against Dennis "Oil Can" Boyd. This was Ojeda's first start at Fenway Park since he was traded for Calvin Schiraldi during the off season. Lenny Dykstra began the game with a line drive into the right field seats for a home run. Next, Backman and Hernandez came up and singled to continue the Met attack. Carter kept the assault going with a double to score Backman and the Mets led 2–0. After "Oil Can" Boyd fanned Strawberry for the first out, the next play revealed how the Red Sox ignored the fundamentals of baseball. Knight came up and hit the ball back to Boggs at third, who now had Hernandez caught in a rundown. Boggs threw to Gedman at home, but Hernandez managed to run past Boggs and dive safely back to third. Carter, who was now trapped between second and third, made it back to second when shortstop Spike Owen, now with the ball, could not make up his mind and botched the play. Hernandez, Carter, and Knight were all safe at third, second, and first base.

With the bases full of Mets, Danny Heap, the designated hitter, singled home Hernandez and Carter to give the Mets a 4–0 lead. Boston scored its only run of the game when Barrett singled home Henderson in the bottom of the third. As for the Mets, they scored three more runs in the seventh and eighth innings to win their first game of the series 7–1.

In Game 4 the pitchers were Ron Darling and Al Nipper. Boston loaded the bases against Darling in the bottom of the first, but Darling got out of the inning without any runs scored. During the game a bunch of balloons with a sign that read "GO SOX" descended on Fenway Park. The Mets made a statement of their own and picked up where they left off in Game 3. In the top of the fourth, Backman singled up the middle just out of the reach of Nipper. With one out and a man on, Carter brought Backman home with a home run to give the Mets a 2–0 lead. The Mets added another run in the fifth to make the score 3–0.

New York kept up the attack in the top of the seventh when Wilson singled and Dykstra followed with a long fly ball deep in right field. Dwight Evans ran back and made a snow cone catch, but Evans lost the ball when his arm hit the fence and Dykstra and Wilson scored for a 5–0 Mets lead. For Evans it was similar to what Henderson had experienced two weeks before against the Angels. In the top of the eighth, Carter hit his second home run of the game to give the Mets a 6–0 lead. Boston made a late charge when they scored two runs in the bottom of the eighth, but the rally was too little, too late as the Mets won the game 6–2 to even the Series at two games apiece. By taking games three and four, the Mets assured themselves of going back to Shea Stadium.

Pitchers Dwight Gooden against Bruce Hurst faced off in Game 5.[16]

The Red Sox didn't start Game 5 any better than they began Game 4. Boston loaded the bases in the bottom of the first, but like the night before, they came up empty. But in the bottom of the second, Henderson hit a ball to right center which eluded Strawberry. As Dykstra came up with the ball, he slipped, which allowed Henderson to race around the bases with a triple. He then scored on Owen's sacrifice fly to give Boston a 1–0 lead. The Red Sox added another run in the top of the third when Santana's error allowed Buckner to reach first. After Rice walked, Evans came through with a single to score Buckner from second. Boston scored two more runs in the fifth when Rice hit a ball to the gap in center that got caught up in the wind and nearly went out of the park. The ball bounced off the fence, eluding Dykstra and Rice, like Henderson before, raced around the bases and ended up on third.

Baylor came up and fisted the ball into right field for a single to score Rice. Evans kept the rally going with a single moving Baylor to third, and drove Gooden out of the game. Sid Fernandez replaced Gooden on the mound, but Henderson greeted Fernandez with a double down the third base line to score Baylor with Boston's fourth and final run of the game.

With New York trailing 4–0, the Mets got on the scoreboard in the eighth on Teufel's home run and added another run in the top of the ninth. Hurst didn't allow another run and pitched his second complete game. The Red Sox won 4–2, and for the first time, the home team won a game in the World Series; more importantly, the Red Sox were one win away from the World Series and Roger Clemens was the starting pitcher for the sixth game.

Roger Clemens and Bob Ojeda took the mound in Game 6. On a cold night in New York City, no one could be found walking the streets, as all of Gotham were glued to their television sets to watch this memorable sixth contest.

Ojeda's first pitch to Boggs was a strike. Shea Stadium eagerly cheered their beloved Mets, but the stadium became quiet when Boggs hit a ball that ricocheted off of Knight's glove to Santana who fielded the ball cleanly. Boggs was safe at first. After Barrett flied out to Dykstra in center field, the stadium became alive again when an enthusiastic Met fan parachuted on the field with his sign that read "GO METS." This was a response to Boston's sign in Game 4. This token of appreciation lifted 55,073 fans at Shea Stadium and probably everyone in New York City who were still mindful that the Mets needed to win this game to stave off elimination.

After the police escorted the parachute fan off the field, Buckner flied out to Dykstra for the second out, but Ojeda did not settle down. He walked Rice and surrendered a double to Evans in left center to score Boggs and the Red Sox took an all important 1–0 lead. But that was all the scoring for Boston in the top of the first as Ojeda retired Gedman to get out of the inning with the Mets trailing by one run.

Shea Stadium applauded as Dykstra came to the plate in the bottom of the first, but Clemens immediately quieted the stadium as he fanned both Dykstra and Wally Backman and got Hernandez to fly out to center field to end the inning.

With one out in the top of the second, Owen singled up the middle. Ojeda fanned Clemens for the second out, then Boggs stepped in the batter's box. McNamara signaled for a hit and run play and as Backman went to cover second, Boggs seized the opportunity and singled to move Owen to third. Barrett came up and kept the rally going with a single to score Owen. Boston now led 2–0. The Red Sox did not score any more runs that inning as Buckner flew out to Strawberry for the third out.

Strawberry led off the bottom of the second with a walk, stole second base, and scored the Mets' first run of the game on Knight's single. Wilson followed Knight and battled Clemens for a single, and when Evans bobbled the ball in right field, Knight raced to third. Though Clemens induced Danny Heep to hit into a double play, Knight scored from third to tie the game at 2–2. Clemens got out of the inning when Ojeda grounded out to Barrett for the third out.

The game remained unchanged until the top of the seventh. Roger McDowell, now pitching for the Mets, walked Barrett to start the inning. McNamara ordered Buckner to sacrifice Barrett to second. Buckner failed on the sacrifice attempt, but Barrett made it to second as McNamara took off the bunt sign and employed a hit-and-run play as Backman retired Buckner on a fielder's choice. Rice then stepped up to the plate and hit a one hopper at third to Knight, who charged the ball and fielded it on one hop; however, Knight's throw sailed over Hernandez, who had to jump in the air to keep the ball from going into the stands. The error allowed Rice to reach first and Barrett to reach third. Evans took his turn at bat and worked McDowell to a full count. On the payoff pitch, Evans chopped a grounder to Backman at second, but McNamara employed another hit-and-run play and Rice was safe at second. Though Evans was out at first, Barrett scored the go-ahead run to put the Red Sox in front 3–2. The Red Sox tried to pad their lead when Gedman singled, but Rice made a wide turn around third. Wilson charged the ball and made a perfect throw to Carter at home to gun down Rice. This play would haunt the Red Sox later in the game.

The Mets did not score off of Clemens in the bottom of the seventh. Yet, in the top of the eighth, McNamara decided to take Clemens out of the game. Clemens had developed a blister in the fifth inning and he could no longer throw his slider. Clemens insisted that he could still get the Mets out with his fastball. We will never know.

The Red Sox still had a chance to add to their lead as Boston loaded the bases with one out in the top of the eighth. McNamara had decided to pinch-hit for Clemens. Since the designated hitter could not bat in a National League ballpark in the World Series, this would have been a perfect time to use Don Baylor as a pinch-hitter. Instead McNamara sent up rookie Mike Greenwell, who promptly struck out.[17] Baylor, visibly upset, sat on the bench. Buckner

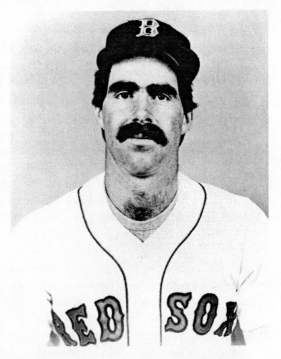

Bill Buckner: **A consummate contact hitter who set fielding records while playing first base. How ironic that Buckner's fielding error in Game 6 of the 1986 World Series etched his name in baseball lore and belied a fine baseball career. (Photograph courtesy of the National Baseball Hall of Fame Library, Cooperstown, N.Y.)**

fared no better as he flied out to center field to end the eighth.

Schiraldi replaced Clemens on the mound and New York knew Schiraldi all too well. Schiraldi came up through the Mets organization with such high expectations as a starting pitcher and his career seemed boundless until he was injured. After he returned from the disabled list, Schiraldi's ineffectiveness led the Mets to trade him for Bob Ojeda during the 1985 off season. When he arrived in Boston, the team convinced Schiraldi to become a reliever and after some initial hesitation, Schiraldi accepted the position and adjusted to his new role with the Red Sox.[18] The acquisition proved fruitful, as Schiraldi won four games and saved nine down Boston's stretch run for the Eastern Division.

Lee Mazzilli, who began his career with the Mets ten years before, and was reacquired in August from the Pirates, singled off Schiraldi to open the eighth. Dykstra followed Mazzilli with a sacrifice back to Schiraldi who threw the ball to Barrett at second. Schiraldi's throw landed in the dirt, and Mazzilli was safe at second and Dykstra was safe at first.

Backman came up and also laid down a sacrifice, but this time Schiraldi took the sure out at first to retire Backman. Next, McNamara intentionally walked Hernandez to load the bases. Shea Stadium was back in the game as the fans were up and cheering for the Mets to tie the score.

Carter reciprocated as he stepped up to the plate, worked the count to 3–0, got the green light, and laced into Schiraldi's fourth pitch to deep left field. Rice caught the ball for the second out, but Mazzilli tagged up and easily scored from third to knot the game at 3–3. Schiraldi got out of the inning when he retired Strawberry on a fly out to center field.

In the top of the ninth, Rick Aguilera was now pitching for the Mets. Kevin Elster replaced Santana at shortstop and Mazzilli replaced Strawberry in right field. Despite Elster's two errors, the Mets survived the ninth when Aguilera induced Gedman to hit into a double play.

The Mets had a chance to win the game in the bottom of the ninth. Schiraldi walked Knight and everyone knew that Wilson would try to sacrifice Knight to second. On Wilson's bunt, Gedman pounced on the ball, but for the second time in two innings, an errant throw allowed a Met runner to reach second as Barrett was pulled off the bag. Knight was safe at second as Barrett and McNamara began arguing that Knight was out, but the television replay confirmed that Barrett had lifted his foot off the bag. The Mets had two men on and no outs when pinch-hitter Howard Johnson, no relation to the manager, tried unsuccessfully to bunt the runners over. With two strikes on Howard Johnson, manager Davey Johnson took off the bunt sign and told Johnson to hit. The strategy backfired as Johnson struck out. Mazzilli came up and hit a fly ball deep to Rice in left field. If Howard Johnson had been given the chance to sacrifice the runners over, Mazzilli's fly ball would have won the game for the Mets. Instead Schiraldi escaped without any damage when Dykstra flied out to Henderson in center field for the third out. The game went to the top of the tenth.

Since Babe Ruth was purchased by the Yankees every Red Sox team has failed to win the Fall Classic. Thus the "Curse of the Bambino" was born. Up to this point some baseball fans might not have believed in such talk. It sounded rather pretentious and didn't do anything to enhance the player or the game, but after Game 6 of the 1986 World Series, baseball players began to think otherwise, or just said it was bad luck.

Rick Aguilera was still on the mound and as Dave Henderson came up to the plate, NBC replayed his now famous home run that he hit off of

Donnie Moore two weeks earlier. Vin Scully remarked how the Angels were one strike away from the World Series when Henderson stepped to the plate. Aguilera's first pitch blew by Henderson for strike one, but on Aguilera's second offering, Henderson jumped all over it and launched the ball out of Shea Stadium. It bounced off the scoreboard in left field.

The Red Sox ran out of the dugout and gave each other high fives. Shea Stadium became as quiet as a library; the fans were completely taken out of the game.

Aguilera struck out Owen for the first out and for the second time in the game, Baylor did not pinch-hit for Schiraldi, who promptly struck out. Boggs then stepped to the plate and doubled off the wall in left center and came around to score on Barrett's single to give the Red Sox a 5–3 lead. Barrett's hit seemed to ruffle Aguilera as he plunked the next batter, Buckner, in the ribs, before finally retiring Rice on a fly out to Mazzilli in right field to end the inning.

Scene: Shea Stadium

In 1957, rumors were rampant that the Dodgers might leave Brooklyn. Robert Moses, who was the chairman of the mayor's Committee on Slum Clearance and also served as the Parks Commissioner, proposed building a baseball stadium in Flushing Meadows, Queens, New York, for the Brooklyn Dodgers.[19] Walter O'Malley, the Brooklyn Dodgers owner, was cool to this idea and took his team to Los Angeles, California, to join the Giants, who had recently transferred their franchise to San Francisco.

It was difficult to believe that National League baseball did not exist in New York. The next year, New York mayor Robert Wagner created a commission headed by attorney William A. Shea to bring National League baseball back to New York.[20] Shea tried, but without success, to lure the Cincinnati Reds, Pittsburgh Pirates, and Philadelphia Phillies to New York.

Shea then formed a third baseball organization called the Continental League, which consisted of eight cities. New York, being one of the eight municipalities, would have another baseball team. Branch Rickey would be the league's new commissioner.

By 1960, with the threat of anti-trust suits and the other major leagues afraid the Continental League would raid their rosters, the National League decided to expand from eight to ten teams: Houston was included and New York was back in baseball.

One of the deciding factors that led to New York's franchise was a deal for a new stadium to be constructed by the 1963 season. On October 28, 1961, the city of New York broke ground on a new stadium in Queens near the site of the 1939 World's Fair, on Flushing Meadow Park.

Until then, the New York Mets, named after the nineteenth century baseball team, the Metropolitans (see Chapter 1), would play their games in the Polo Grounds for one season in 1962. New York City spent $250,000 refurbishing the Polo Grounds, and baseball once again was played at Coogan's Bluff after a five year absence. But the Mets' play at the Polo Grounds lasted for two seasons and the team won less than one hundred games and lost more than two hundred.

Shea Stadium opened on April 17, 1964. The new facility, which cost $28 million to construct, was named after William Shea, who was credited with bringing National League baseball back to New York.

Shea Stadium immediately witnessed baseball history on Father's Day in June of that year as the Philadelphia Phillies' Jim Bunning pitched a perfect game. The next month, the National League triumphed 7–4 as Shea Stadium witnessed its first and only All-Star game. Fans went delirious in 1965 and 1966, but not because the Mets won a title — rather, it was for the Beatles, who played two sold out concerts. But fans would cheer for their beloved Mets who won the World Championship in 1969 and the pennant in 1973.

As they did two generations earlier, the Yankees played their home games in a National League ballpark, this time at Shea Stadium, from 1974 to 1975. The New York Jets also played there from 1964 to 1983.

Left and right field foul lines stand at 338. The power alleys are at 371. The deepest part of center field is 410 with an 8 foot fence comprising the entire outfield wall of the stadium.

Bottom of the tenth: Many times when the Red Sox were ahead during the late innings in the playoffs, McNamara would replace Buckner with Dave Stapleton.[21] Since the Red Sox were three outs away from the World Championship, it has been speculated that McNamara wanted Buckner to be on the field to celebrate with the team if the Red Sox won the World Series.[22] If true, McNamara's generosity would be questioned for years, since Buckner was hobbling on the field throughout the game. His ankles were so bad that his body moved back and fourth each time he went to field a ball or ran down to first.[23]

Wally Backman led off the bottom of the tenth for the Mets. Shea Stadium made some noise to spur the team on, but most of the stadium was quiet. Schiraldi's first pitch caught the outside corner for a strike. Backman fouled the next pitch for strike two, then lofted Schiraldi's third pitch to left field to Rice for the first out. Vin Scully began reading off the names of the NBC staff that had helped televise the World Series. NBC then sent its television crew along with Bob Costas, one of the announcers of the World Series, to interview the Red Sox in the visitors' locker room.

As with the California Angels on October 12, plastic covering was applied to all of the Boston locker room to prevent any champagne from wetting the room.

A podium was set up to present the World Series trophy to Jean Yawkey, widow of Tom Yawkey, the long-time owner of the Red Sox who died a decade before. Bruce Hurst was chosen as the MVP of the Series.[24] The most ironic moment occurred when the camera focused on Tom Seaver. Seaver, as most fans know, was a member of the 1969 World Series champion New York Mets. Now "Tom Terrific" was about to win the World Series in a Red Sox uniform.

Davey Johnson got up from his bench, walked a few feet, then sat back down. He was resigned that his Mets were about to lose the Series. Hernandez came up to bat and Schiraldi's first pitch was a strike. Henandez worked Schiraldi to a 2–1 count in his favor, then hit Schiraldi's fourth pitch to deep center field. Henderson ran back and caught the ball on the warning track for the second out.

Vin Scully read some more names as Marty Barrett was chosen as the player of the game.[25] Carter came up representing the third out and Boston's championship. Carter fouled Schiraldi's first pitch and for a moment it looked like Gedman had a chance to make the play for the final out, but the ball went into the stands for a foul ball. Though Carter fouled off the last pitch, the first two outs were line drives that might have been hits if the ball had landed in another part of the field. Carter took the next two pitches and like Hernandez before him, had a 2–1 count in his favor. However, this time Carter lined Schiraldi's fourth pitch into left field for a hit.

Kevin Mitchell was so sure that the Mets would go down in the tenth inning that he was making travel arrangements to fly back home to California.[26] Davey Johnson had other plans as he sent Mitchell to pinch hit for Aguilera. Mitchell had been Schiraldi's teammate when both men played for the Tidewater Tides, the Mets' triple A farm team. It was with the Tides that Schiraldi kidded Mitchell that if he ever faced him on the mound, Schiraldi would start Mitchell with a fastball, then would throw a slider on his second pitch. Mitchell stepped up to the plate and fouled Schiraldi's first pitch, a fastball, for a strike one. Then remembering Schiraldi's warning to him, Mitchell reached out over the plate and poked Schiraldi's second pitch — a slider — for a single. Carter stopped at second.

Shea Stadium made a little more noise hoping that the Mets could mount a comeback. Knight was now the batter and he took the first pitch for a strike. Schiraldi threw another pitch inside that Knight managed to hit for a little dribbler down the third base line. Boggs wisely let it go foul. One more strike. The game seemed to be over, but it was only two weeks ago that Angels were in this same situation.

The Mets took a page out of the Red Sox's playbook as Knight fought off Schiraldi's next offering and dunked it into center field. Carter raced around third and scored. Now the game was 5–4 in favor of the Red Sox.

Mitchell went to third base on Knight's single and Shea Stadium became electric. McNamara came out to the mound and signaled for another relief pitcher, Bob Stanley, who came in to replace Schiraldi.

Mookie Wilson stepped up to the plate, fouled Stanley's first pitch for a strike, took the next two pitches that were balls and ran the count to 2–1, and then fouled the ball off of his foot for strike two. The Red Sox were again one strike away from the championship. Wilson fouled off two more pitches. Stanley's seventh pitch to Wilson was inside, but Gedman wasn't in position to handle the pitch and barely reached for the ball. Wilson fell to the ground and eluded the pitch as the ball sailed to the backstop. Wilson then jumped up and waved Mitchell home with the tying run.

Unbelievable! The Mets had tied the game 5–5. Shea Stadium exploded with joy as Knight went to second base on the passed ball. Wilson kept battling Stanley by fouling off two more pitches. Marty Barrett kept yelling in vain at Stanley to throw the ball to him; Knight had taken a big lead and was well off second base.[27] Joe Garagiola, the other announcer in the World Series, commented that Knight could have been picked off, as Knight was nearly picked off in the bottom of the ninth, before he dove back to second just in time. Since Barrett had vacated his position at second base, Buckner moved away from his position at first and began to move towards second to cover some of the ground that was lost due to Barrett's pick-off attempt.[28] Before Stanley made his fateful ninth pitch, he checked the runners and then threw. Wilson made contact and the ball rolled towards Buckner down the first base line. Buckner hobbled to the base line, but as he went down to make sure that the ball did not get by him, he pulled himself over to his left as the ball went to his right over his glove, and traveled into right field. Knight came around and scored and the Mets won the game 6–5. *Amazin'!*

Yogi Berra was right for the second time in this 1986 post season. "It's déjà vu all over again."

Mike Torrez was in the stands when the Red Sox lost that night. After Buckner's error, Torrez walked up to the Boston media and declared that he was now off the hook for giving up Bucky Dent's home run.[29] But Torrez was wrong. Though the Red Sox were within one strike of winning the World Series in Game 6, as we know, baseball fans have long memories and Buckner's error would go along with Torrez's pitch as a reminder of Boston's failure to win the World Series.

Buckner met with the media after the game.[30] "It was bouncing and bouncing and then it just went underneath me. It skipped or something. I can't remember the last time I missed the ball like that, but I'll remember that one."

Objectively, the Mets made one of the greatest comebacks in World Series history. The Red Sox made a similar comeback in Game 6 of the 1975 World Series against the Cincinnati Reds when pinch-hitter Bernie Carbo hit a three-run home run to tie the game at 6–6. And every Red Sox and baseball fan knows that Calton Fisk's home run in the bottom of the twelfth won the game 7–6. But Carbo's home run came in the eighth inning. The Mets' comeback began with two outs in the tenth with the Red Sox one strike from winning the championship.

For Bill Buckner, his error would live on in baseball history. Buckner is blamed for losing the game; had he made the play, whether Wilson would have been safe is all speculation.

Rain postponed Game 7 for one day. The rainout allowed the Red Sox to regroup after the devastating loss on Saturday.

Ron Darling started for the Mets. Oil Can Boyd wanted to pitch this game, perhaps to atone for his poor performance in Game 3.

But Oil Can Boyd would not get that chance. McNamara used the rainout to bring back Bruce Hurst on three days' rest.[31]

John Feinstein of the *Washington Post* wrote what all sports fans knew.[32] "In a game that will be remembered as one of the strangest in World Series history, Stanley and Buckner wrote themselves into the legacy of New England's disasters forever. If the Boston Red Sox recuperate and win Game 7 from the New York Mets, all will be forgiven."

Could the Red Sox shake off their heartbreaking defeat like the Reds did after their Game 6 defeat in the 1975 World Series? Boston quickly answered that question as Evans led off the second with a home run.[33] Gedman stepped to the plate and laced the ball into right field. Strawberry raced to the fence and suffered the same mishap as Evans and Henderson in this post season: as all three men got their gloves on the ball, they could not come down with it when they hit the fence. Gedman trotted home and the Red Sox led 2–0. Darling then proceeded to walk Henderson. After Henderson was sacrificed to second, Boggs kept the inning going with a single to score Henderson and increase the Red Sox lead to 3–0.

Unlike the Reds, Boston was unable to hold the lead and win Game 7. Or like every Boston team dating back to the 1946 World Series, they would lose Game 7.

Momentum shifted back to the Mets when Rice was again thrown out after trying to stretch a single into a double. Davey Johnson went to the mound and replaced Darling with Sid Fernandez. Fernandez came in and restored order by shutting down the Red Sox with his high rising fastball that kept the Mets' deficit at three runs.

The game remained the same until the bottom of the sixth with one out when singles by Mazzilli and Wilson, coupled with a walk to Tuefel, loaded the bases.

After Backman went in to run for Tuefel, McNamara went to the mound to settle down Bruce Hurst. Hernandez spoiled that notion with a single to score Mazzilli and Wilson to cut the lead 3–2 in favor of Boston. Carter came up next and lofted a fly ball to shallow right field that hung up for awhile. Evans dove for the ball and made the catch, but he could not hold on to it. The ball rolled out of his glove, Backman scored, and the game was tied at 3–3.

Roger McDowell replaced Hernandez on the mound in the top of the seventh and retired the Red Sox without much of a sweat. In that inning, the injured Tony Armas pinch-hit for Bruce Hurst and struck out.

In the bottom of the inning, Schiraldi was summoned by McNamara to keep the game at 3–3. However, Schiraldi looked as if he were about to be sacrificed to the gods. Knight wasted no time and homered to put the Mets in front 4–3. Schiraldi gave up two more hits and a walk, then left the game. Joe Sambito and Stanley could not quell New York's offense as the Mets scored two more runs to make the score 6–3.

Boston made one valiant attempt to win the series. In the top of the eighth, Buckner and Rice singled off of the new Met pitcher, Jesse Orosco. Evans then doubled home Buckner and Rice to cut New York's lead to 6–5. Surprisingly, Gedman was not instructed to bunt and lined out to Backman. Henderson had no more October surprises left and struck out.

When Baylor finally batted, it was too late — he grounded out to end the eighth. The Mets added another run on Strawberry's home run off of Al Knipper. Bedlam roared throughout Shea Stadium; it began to rock as fans were standing in their seats. New York was not satisfied. Knight singled and reached second when Knipper walked Santana. The Mets scored their final run when Jesse Orosco singled home Knight to make the score 8–5.

When Jesse Orosco fanned Marty Barrett for the third out in the top of the ninth and threw his glove in the air, he was covered by the rest of the Mets, who ran to the pitcher's mound. The new World Champions of baseball were joined by the rest of Shea Stadium singing "We Are the Champions" by the rock group Queen.

The World Series was over, but for Bill Buckner, the scapegoating had begun. Buckner should never have been at first base after the Red Sox took the lead in the tenth. Stapleton had a fresh pair of legs in contrast to Buckner's damaged Achilles tendon and all of Boston's post season victories happened when Dave Stapleton was at first base. As the saying goes, "If it ain't broke, don't fix it."

Ten years later, every Yankees fan can recall that Wade Boggs was the starting third baseman when the Yankees clinched the 1996 World Series over the Atlanta Braves in Game 6. Boggs even celebrated the Series win by riding around Yankee Stadium on a mounted policeman's horse, but he was not the third baseman who caught the final out. Joe Torre had inserted Charlie Hayes at third for defensive purposes in the bottom of the ninth inning.

McNamara's magnanimity towards having Buckner on the field if the Red Sox won the World Series was noble in nature; however, it was costly considering that Stapleton was available. Ironically, it was Stapleton who was the starting first baseman for the Red Sox two years before, before he was injured and replaced by Bill Buckner.[34] Had McNamara brought Stapleton into Game 6, both teams of that Fall Classic agreed that Stapleton would have beaten Wilson to first base and preserved the tie score.

Maybe the Red Sox could have won the championship if they had survived the tenth inning. If Boston had lost the game, at least Buckner, who gallantly played in constant pain throughout his whole career, would have avoided the constant reminder of his error at first.

We must also remember that Buckner did not give up those two runs to tie game at 5–5. Calvin Schiraldi and a passed ball by Gedman allowed the Mets to get even.

Also, McNamara was too deliberate in making decisions that might have changed the outcome of the game. Baylor, a good contact hitter, stood on the bench in the eighth, ninth, and tenth innings of Game 6. Finally, people conveniently forget that the Red Sox led in Game 7, until the Mets rallied and won the game.

Bill Buckner returned to the Red Sox lineup the next year and on Opening Day, he and Bob Stanley were serenaded with boos when their names were announced.[35]

Buckner played in 75 games for Boston before he was released in July of 1987. Still, it was not without the jeering that accompanied Buckner when he took the field, or when he went on the road. After Buckner was released by the Red Sox, he signed on with the California Angels. Still, Buckner was booed when he returned to Fenway Park as the fans and the media never let him forget that error. Ironically, as a California Angel, Buckner became Donnie Moore's teammate.[36] But Buckner was able to go on with his life whereas Moore, who was still reeling from the pitch he threw to Dave Henderson in 1986, could not go on with his life and committed suicide in 1989. After Moore's suicide, a reporter contacted Buckner and asked if he thought about taking his own life. Buckner did not. Instead, he went on playing baseball.

With both teams, Buckner batted a respectable .290, with 74 RBIs and 134 hits. In April 1988, the Angels released Buckner. Buckner then bounced back with the Kansas City Royals for two seasons before finally ending his career with the Boston Red Sox in 1990.[37] This time Buckner received a standing ovation from Red Sox fans on Opening Day, but his second tour of duty with Boston ended after 22 games, when he was released for good in June of that year.

For two baseball seasons, millions of baseball fans who watched NBC's *Game of the Week* on Saturday saw Boston's best and worst moments in the World Series—Calton Fisk using his "body English" to will his home run in the 1975 Series followed by Buckner's error in the 1986 Series. If Buckner were an actor, he would have made a million dollars in residuals. In 1989, NBC replaced Buckner's error with Kirk Gibson's home run off of Dennis Eckersley in the 1988 World Series. In Game 1 of the 1988 Series an injured Kirk Gibson could not play in the outfield. Eckersley, now pitching for the A's, was the best reliever in baseball that year and faced the Dodgers with the A's leading 4–3 in the bottom of the ninth. Gibson took a 3–2 slider and hit a two-run home run to give the Dodgers an improbable 5–4 win. Ironically, it was like a Hollywood movie.

This is what Buckner endured throughout the years—the videotape of the error, the articles in the sports pages, the sniping by the fans. He did interviews regarding Game 6 of the 1986 World Series, all the while living in the Boston area. Still Buckner endured, managing to get on with his life.

However one incident did occur in late July 1993, when Buckner was working as a minor league hitting instructor for the Syracuse Chiefs, the Toronto Blue Jays' Triple A team. On this day Buckner was signing a few autographs when a fan asked him to sign a ball. Suddenly, a young man blurted out, "Don't give him the ball. He'd just drop it anyway."

After the comment, Buckner put his belongings in the truck. He had lived with that error for nearly seven years.[38] Buckner had had enough and went back and grabbed the man by his collar, but the melee was broken up by several bystanders who separated the two and the young man was not injured. Buckner's wife, Jody, remarked in the *Wall Street Journal* how the press nearly crucified her husband over that error.[39] No one can blame Buckner for his actions; after all, how much can one person take?

Pedro Martinez, today the star pitcher for the Red Sox, has commented that Bill Buckner can't live in Boston anymore, which is the reason why Buckner moved his wife and three children to Meridian, Idaho, in 1993. But Jody Buckner has commented on television that her husband purchased some property in Idaho years before and has said that the error in Game 6 did not drive their family from New England.[40]

In 1996, after his stint with the Blue Jays farm system, Buckner became the hitting instructor for the Chicago White Sox,[41] a job that he held until August of 1997.[42] Throughout the rest of 1990s the Buckners have lived in Idaho, and the people of Meridian seem to respect Buckner and realize that no one is perfect and everybody makes mistakes. Buckner is involved with the community by doing charity work, and he also runs a local hitting clinic and coaches his son's little league team and has ventured into real estate.[43]

Bill Buckner is a hero of the highest form as he played despite the constant pain he endured for years. His credentials speak for themselves, yet he is not in the Hall of Fame, though he has more hits than 70 percent of all Hall-of-Famers. There are at least two certain requisites that will allow a hitter to gain entry into the Hall of Fame as a hitter: (1) 3,000 base hits or (2) 500 home runs. The lone exception is Pete Rose, who has been banned from baseball.

There are some Hall-of-Famers who have failed to get 3,000 base hits, but have been inducted into the Hall. Billy Williams, for example, has four fewer hits than Buckner, and a higher batting average by one point. If Billy Williams is in the Hall of Fame due to his 400 plus home runs, then what about Hall of Famer Joe Morgan? Morgan, like Buckner, played most of his 21 seasons as an infielder with some games in the outfield. Morgan was selected to the Hall of Fame in his first year of eligibility, but Morgan only leads Buckner in home runs with 268 to 174. Buckner leads Morgan in every other statistical category. Buckner out hit Morgan 2715 to 2517, a total of 198 more hits. Buckner batted .300 seven times as compared to Morgan who batted .300 twice. Buckner has 1208 RBIs to Morgan's 1133, and his average stands at .289 in contrast to Morgan's .271 average. The numbers don't lie, and these statistics should be good enough for any player to be admitted into the Hall of Fame. Maybe then baseball fans will begin to appreciate Buckner as a player. More importantly he should be appreciated as a human being, for what Buckner has gone through is inhuman.

A few days after the 1986 World Series, the Mets celebrated their World Series triumph with a ticker tape parade and a visit to City Hall.

Mookie Wilson declared on the steps of New York's City Hall: "Dynasty 1986, Dynasty 1987, Dynasty 1988."

That would not happen. During the off season, the Mets traded Kevin Mitchell for outfielder Kevin McReynolds of the San Diego Padres. Mitchell was nicknamed "World" for the five positions he covered in the infield and outfield. The Mets traded Mitchell because they feared that he would be a negative influence on star pitcher Dwight Gooden. Coincidentally, Gooden missed the parade the next day. It was reported that he overslept. In reality, Gooden was dealing with a substance abuse problem.

Gooden tested positive for cocaine the following spring and was suspended from baseball for the first sixty days of the 1987 baseball season. After his stay at the Smithers Rehabilitation Center, Gooden joined the Mets in June and was received warmly by Met fans. But Gooden wasn't the only person dealing with difficulties: outfielder Daryl Strawberry had to deal with domestic problems, and Ron Darling went 14 games without a decision. Ray Knight, MVP of the World Series, was offered a contract from the Mets for $850,000 for one year. Knight wanted a two year contract and he would not budge from his demand and neither did the Mets. The end result: Knight would not be around to receive his World Series ring at Shea Stadium. Instead he wound up playing for the Baltimore Orioles. What a way to treat the MVP.[44]

Despite the on and off field problems, the Mets managed to get back into the race for the Eastern Division crown, but the Cardinals held on and won the division and the pennant before finally losing the World Series to the Minnesota Twins. The following year, the Mets won the division; however, they lost the pennant to the eventual world champion Los Angeles Dodgers.

The Red Sox fared no better. Probably no team could have returned to the World Series after the devastating loss in Game 6. Although the Yankees lost the World Series in 1960 to the Pittsburgh Pirates on Bill Mazeroski's home run in the ninth, and won the series the next year, no team lost the World Series like the Red Sox in 1986.

Aside from the loss, Gedman decided to test the free agent market; to his surprise, Gedman, like other free agents in the mid–1980s, drew little or no interest from any other clubs. He re-signed with the Red Sox on May 1. The pitching suffered[45] as Oil Can Boyd was injured and won only one game in 1987. Clemens was ineffective in the beginning of the year, but he rebounded with 20–9 season and won his second Cy Young Award. Buckner would be released in June and Baylor and Henderson would also leave by year's end. Both men would appear in the World Series with the A's in 1988.

Like the Mets, the Red Sox would not win the Eastern Division in 1987. But Boston would win the division the next year and they too would lose the pennant to a California team, the Oakland A's. That year, Gedman and many other free agents found out why they hardly received any offers from the other clubs. After a lengthy three-year investigation, baseball owners were found guilty of collusion in an attempt to break free agency. The owners paid $280 million to compensate the players for the three years of estimated lost income.[46]

The Red Sox would win the Eastern Division in 1990 and 1995 and the Wild Card in 1998 and 1999. Since 1986, however, Boston has yet to appear in the World Series. Hopefully one day the great people of Boston will hoist a World Series flag. Red Sox fans can only hope that the Curse of the Bambino is a twentieth century phenomenon.

CHAPTER 9

Mitch Williams

The year 1976 looked bleak for the San Francisco Giants.[1] The team's fortunes had waned during the last few years. With low attendance and with most of their top stars sold, the Stoneham family, who had owned the Giants since they were in New York City, wanted to sell the team. It was speculated that the Giants would end up in Toronto. But unlike New York City, San Francisco mayor Frank Masconie went to court and blocked the sale. Later, Masconie found two investors to buy the team and the Giants remained in San Francisco.[2]

Baseball inevitably came to Toronto as the city was awarded a franchise for the 1977 season. The Toronto Blue Jays defeated the Chicago White Sox 9–5 in the team's first game at Exhibition Stadium, but the Blue Jays did not win many games as Toronto lost 100 or more games during the first three seasons. The team started to improve after Toronto finished strong in the second half of the strike season in 1981.

The Blue Jays, under their second manager, Bobby Cox, enjoyed their first winning season in 1983 with a 89–73 record. Toronto finished the next year with the same record, and in 1985 the Blue Jays held off the Yankees and won the Eastern Division with a 99–62 record. Also that year, the League Championship Series modified its rules from a best three out of five to four out of seven games to advance to the World Series. Toronto won the first three out of four games against the Royals in the LCS and would have qualified for the World Series, but the Royals took advantage of their new life, winning the next three games and the pennant.

The Blue Jays wound up in fourth place the next year. Nineteen eighty-seven would bring more bad news as Toronto went into the last week of the season with a six game lead over the Tigers with seven left to play. The Blue Jays lost four games to reduce their lead over the Tigers to two games. Toronto went head-to-head with the Tigers on the last weekend of the regular season. The Blue Jays had to take 2 out of the 3 games for the Eastern Division crown or win at least a game to insure a tie for the Division and force a one game playoff, but the Tigers swept the Blue Jays and won the Division by a single game.

Over the next four years the Blue Jays would finish either in first or second. Coincidentally, in odd years—1985, 1989, 1991—Toronto would win 90 or more games and the Eastern Division. And if it weren't for their collapse during the final week of 1987, the Blue Jays would have won that year as well. Equally frustrating was Toronto's inability to win the pennant. The Blue Jays lost the LCS to the A's and Twins. During this time, Toronto moved into a brand new stadium, the SkyDome, which paid dividends. Attendance soared to more than four million during the stadium's first two years of operation.

In 1992, under new manager Cito Gaston, Toronto finally won the Eastern Division on an even year. The Blue Jays also awarded their fans with the pennant, avenging their 1989 loss to the A's. With newly acquired stars like sluggers Dave Winfield and pitching aces Jack Morris and David Cone, Toronto went all the way and became the first non–American team to win the World Series.

In 1993, the defending World Series champs again revamped their lineup. Dave Winfield, catcher Kelly Gruber, and pitchers David Cone and Jimmy Key were gone. Those stars were replaced by shortstop Tony Fernandez, infielder-DH Paul Molitor, outfielder Ricky Henderson, and pitcher Dave Stewart. Rookie John Olerud batted .363 to lead the league with 17 home runs and 107 RBIs. Returning Blue Jays Joe Carter smacked 33 home runs and 121 RBIs, and Roberto Alomar batted .326 with 17 home runs and 93 RBIs.

The pitching staff was led by Pat Hentgen who went 19–9 with a 3.87 ERA. Juan Guzman chipped in with a 14–3 record and a 3.99 ERA. Dave Stewart, 12–8, 4.44 ERA, Al Lieter, 9–6, 4.11 ERA and Todd Stottlemyre, 11–12 , 4.84 ERA, rounded off the pitching staff.[3]

Throughout the 1993 season, Toronto and New York again vied for the Eastern Division crown. On September 4, Yankee pitcher Jim Abbot tossed a Labor Day no-hitter against the Cleveland Indians,[4] but that would be the last hurrah for New York as Toronto hung on and won the Eastern Division for the fifth time in eight years. In the LCS, Dave Stewart kept his perfect streak of 6–0 as the Blue Jays defeated the Chicago White Sox in six games to win the pennant.

In the National League, the Atlanta Braves' 104 wins were just enough to edge the San Francisco Giants by one game to win the Western Division. The Braves were trying to win the pennant for the third straight year, but in the NLCS the Phillies shocked the Braves in six games to win the pennant.

The Phillies, who entered the National League in 1883, won their first pennant in 1915 but lost the World Series to the Boston Red Sox.[5] It would take Philadelphia another 35 years before the team won its next pennant, and in 1950, the Phillies, then known as the Whiz Kids, lost the World Series again — this time to the New York Yankees in four games. In 1964, as every baseball fan knows, the Phillies blew a 6½ game lead with twelve games to play to the St. Louis Cardinals, who overtook the Phillies and won the pennant and World Series that year.

In the late 1970s the Phillies, like the Kansas City Royals, would lose the pennant three times in the LCS. Finally, in 1980, the Phillies won the pennant in five thrilling games over the Astros. Coincidentally, the Royals also won the pennant that year and the Phillies won the battle of the runners-up by besting Kansas City in six games for the World Championship. The Phillies won the pennant in 1983, but lost the World Series to the Baltimore Orioles in five games.

The 1993 Phillies were a cast of characters who blended together and reminded everyone of a modern day Gas House Gang. The team wore long hair, dirty uniforms, and scratched and clawed their way to each victory. Philadelphia was led by first baseman John Kruk, a slightly overweight, but athletic, player. The players once said, "The game wasn't over until the fat man swings." Kruk batted .316, 14 home runs, and 85 RBIs.[6] Center fielder Len Dykstra batted .305, with 19 home runs, and 66 RBIs. Dykstra came over to the Phillies from the Mets in a trade for Juan Samuel in 1989. Dykstra, known as "Nails" with the Mets, was now "the Dude" with the Phillies. Catcher Darren "Dutch" Daulton hit .246 with 24 home runs and 105 RBIs. Slugger-outfielder Pete "Incky" Incaviglia hit .274 with 24 home runs and 89 RBIs.

The Phillies pitching staff was led by Curt Schilling, who went 16–7 with a 4.02 ERA. Tommy Greene went 16–4, 3.42 ERA, Danny Jackson 12–11, 3.77 ERA, and Terry Mulholland rounded off the staff going 12–9 with a 3.25 ERA. Finally, reliever Mitch Williams, who entered every home game with the song "Wild Thing" by the sixties rock group the Troggs blaring in the background, led the team in saves. But, the official song of the Phillies was "Whoomp! (There It Is)" from the group Tag Team. As the post season began, most baseball fans fell in love with this rag tag team and rooted for the Phillies, the underdogs of the 1993 World Series. The Phillies were managed by Jim Fregosi.

Mitchell Steven Williams was the second of three sons born to Geoffrey and Larrie Williams on November 17, 1964, in Santa Ana,

California.[7] Williams left California with his father, Geoffrey, and his older brother, Bruce, for West Linn, Oregon, after his parents divorced in the mid–1970s.

Williams starred as a pitcher for West Linn High School and was drafted by the San Diego Padres in 1982. Williams began his professional career as a starting pitcher with the Reno Padres, in the California League, but would never throw a pitch for the San Diego Padres. In December of 1984, Williams was claimed by the Texas Rangers.[8] The deal was completed in the following spring when Williams was traded for Randy Asador.[9]

Williams moved up from A ball to Double A in the Texas League. The Texas League moved from the Midwest to the Southwest in the mid 1970s.

For four years as starting pitcher, Williams' record was below .500 and he sported an ERA above 5. Then there was the incident when Williams first arrived in the big leagues. In a spring training game, Williams hit three of the first five batters, sending them from the batter's box to the trainer's room.[10] Despite this, Williams skipped triple A and won a spot on the Rangers roster in 1986. Rangers pitching coach Tom House suggested that Williams become a reliever.[11] Coming out of the bullpen, Williams appeared in 80 games that year and established a rookie record as he went 8–6 with eight saves. Williams topped his record with five more appearances the next year and his won-loss record remained the same with two less saves, but he fanned 129 batters. Also that season, Williams was involved in an incident that has only added to his character.

As described in his autobiography *I Ain't an Athlete, Lady*, former teammate John Kruk described Williams as a man with a good heart who means well, but sometimes is wrapped too tight.[12] Kruk could have been referring to an incident on August 15, 1987, when Williams came on in relief against the Red Sox. The game was tied 6–6 with a runner on first base. Williams immediately walked the next two batters and with the bases loaded, Wade Boggs, the reigning batting champion who also possessed the best batting eye in the game, was up next. Boggs took Williams' first pitch for a ball, and Williams became flustered as Boggs took the next pitch for ball two, thereby prompting Williams to curse at the Red Sox third baseman. Boggs never wavered, and Williams, yelling invectives, walked Boggs to score the winning run.[13]

But these attributes were not the only traits that fueled Williams' fire. Williams was a serious competitor who always wanted the ball, and in 1988, Williams developed a better rapport with his teammates who were put off by his incessant need to pitch. More importantly, Williams learned to control his blazing fastball and saved 18 games for the Rangers. Despite those saves, the following year Williams was involved in an eight player deal that sent him to the Chicago Cubs.[14] Cubs fans would question the trade for two of the three players that went to Texas, Rafael Pamiero and Jaime Moyer, are still in the big leagues.

Cubs fans got to know Williams right away. In a game against the Phillies on Opening Day 1989, Chicago was leading the Phillies 5–3 when Mike Schmidt homered off of Calvin Schiraldi to make the score 5–4. Manager Don Zimmer brought in Williams to keep the Phillies at bay. Williams did, but in the eighth inning, he walked two men and committed a balk. The Phillies did not score. In the ninth inning, Williams walked the bases loaded before a chorus of boos that filled Wrigley Field. Williams then gathered himself and fanned the next three batters to get the save.[15] Williams was dubbed "Wild Thing" from the movie *Major League* while he was with the Cubs.[16]

In the movie, actor Charlie Sheen portrays Ricky Vaughn, a pitcher named "Wild Thing," who throws the ball with amazing speed but little control. Despite those heart stopping, Maalox moments, Williams saved 36 games for the Cubs, a record for left hand relievers.

As mentioned in Chapter 1, the Cubs won the Eastern Division and faced the San Francisco Giants in the NLCS. The Giants won the Series in five games. In Game 5 Giants first baseman Will Clark stroked a hit off Williams with the bases loaded to give the Giants the pennant. It would not be the last time Williams would yield a decisive hit in the post season.

But 1990 was another story. In June of that year, Williams was trying to cover first base on a play when he injured himself.[17] Although he came back to pitch later in the year, he was ineffective that season as he went 1–8 with a 3.93 ERA and his save total dropped by 20 games. And when the Cubs signed right hand reliever Dave Smith over the off season, Williams' days as a Cub were numbered. The Cubs, who had been trying to trade Williams during the off season to the Phillies, finally consummated the deal on April 7, 1991. That evening Chicago swapped Williams for reliever Chuck McElroy and minor leaguer Bob Scanlon.[18] Williams rebounded with the Philadelphia Phillies in 1991 where he went 12–5 with 30 saves and a 2.34 ERA. But wherever he went, Williams remained the same on the mound. He would throw the ball all over the plate, yet he hid the ball so well and by falling off the mound deprived the batter an opportunity to pick up the ball.

Williams, who once said he pitched as if his hair were on fire, admitted that even he did not know where the ball would end up once it was released from his hand. To compound matters, Williams still continued to flirt with danger as he rarely retired the side in order, which meant a 1-2-3 inning was null and void. For in Philadelphia, Williams would walk a batter, then strike out a batter, give up a hit or two, before finally retiring the side to get the save. This would drive some of his teammates crazy, especially Curt Schilling, the star pitcher of the team, who would put a towel over his head so he did not have to watch Williams pitch. And if Williams ever saved three or four ball games in a row, then blew the next one, the Phillies fans, notoriously known for riding their own home team, would shower Williams with boos.

Despite Williams' mechanics on the mound, he saved 29 games the next year and in 1993 made 65 appearances and saved 43 games for the Phillies, a club record. The Phillies led the second place Cardinals by five games at the All-Star Break and held on to clinch the Eastern Division with a 10–7 win over the Pirates on September 28.

In the NLCS, Williams appeared in four games, winning and saving two games for the National League Champions

Game 1 was held at the Sky-Dome in Toronto, Canada, and featured Curt Schilling against Juan Guzman.

Mitch Williams: **Never a dull moment when the "Wild Thing" was on the mound and he never changed, despite his detractors. But in the end, Williams' constant flirtations with danger — walking too many batters and yielding too many hits — finally caught up with him. (Photograph courtesy of the National Baseball Hall of Fame Library, Cooperstown, N.Y.)**

After five innings, both teams were tied at 4. The Blue Jays scored one run in the sixth and three runs in the eighth on back-to-back doubles by Devon White and Roberto Alomar. The Phillies added another run in the ninth, but Toronto held on and won the game 8–5.[19]

The *New York Times* headline read, "Too close for comfort" following Game 2.[20] Terry Mulholland went up against Dave Stewart.

The game was scoreless until the top of the third, when the Phillies had two runners on and Kruk singled to score Dykstra with the first run of the game. Up came Phillies third baseman Dave Hollins who hit Stewart's offering into shallow center field. The ball dropped between center fielder Devon White and shortstop Tony Fernandez, allowing Mariano Duncan to score and increase the Phillies lead to 2–0. Stewart retired Darren Daulton, but rightfielder Jim Eisenreich kept the assault going with a three-run home run to make the score 5–0.

Toronto's offense woke up in the bottom of the fourth when Molitor singled and came home on a towering home run by Joe Carter to trim the score to 5–2 in favor of Philadelphia before Toronto pushed across another run to make the score 5–3.

In the top of the seventh, Dykstra welcomed reliever Tony Castillo with a home run to give the Phillies a 6–3 lead. Toronto, however, was not finished, for in the bottom of the eighth, Molitor doubled off of Phillies reliever Roger Mason. This led Fregosi to bring in Williams, much to the delight of Molitor, who immediately took advantage of Williams' erratic delivery to the plate and easily stole third and scored on a sacrifice fly to make the score 6–4 in favor of Philadelphia.

The drama was not over yet as Williams walked Alomar, who also took advantage of Williams' erratic delivery and easily stole second. Williams was sure that Alomar would steal again and stepped off the mound. His hunch was right. Alomar broke towards third when Williams fired to the bag and nailed Alomar at third base to retire the side. Alomar had breached the most sacred rule in baseball: never get thrown out at third base to make the first or third out.

Williams still flirted with danger in the bottom of the ninth when he walked Tony Fernandez. Williams gathered himself and induced Toronto third baseman Ed Sprague to hit a tailor-made double play ball to Kim Baptiste at third, but Baptiste threw the ball in the dirt and although Duncan held onto the ball for the second out, Sprague was safe on the relay to first. Williams finally got catcher Pat Borders to hit into a double play to end the game and the Phillies won 6–4 to tie Series was tied at 1–1.

Game 3, the gamble at Veterans Stadium, pitted Pat Hentgen against Danny Jackson.[21]

The third contest began after an hour and a half rain delay. With no designated hitter in the National League ballpark, manager Cito Gaston took a gamble and inserted Paul Molitor at first base instead of batting champion John Olerud. Many Toronto fans questioned Gaston's strategy and sanity.

In the top of the first, the Blue Jays had runners on first and second courtesy of a single by Henderson and a walk to Devon White. Up came Molitor, who tripled into right field and scored on Carter's sacrifice fly to give the Blue Jays an early 3–0 lead. The Phillies threatened in the bottom of the first, when they had runners on second and third with one out, but Hentgen fanned both Hollins and Daulton to get out of the inning unscathed.

In the top of the fourth, Molitor stepped up and homered to left. Molitor would get three hits on this night, and Toronto never looked back. The Blue Jays won the game going away 10–3. Gaston's critics were silenced as Toronto led 2–1 in the Series.

Todd Stottlemyre and Tom Greene faced off in Game 4.[22]

The Blue Jays picked up where they left off in Game 3 and scored three runs in the first. Greene aided Toronto's cause when he gave up a double to Rickey Henderson and a walk to Devon White. Greene retired Alomar on a fly out, but Joe Carter came up next and rifled a shot down to third that Hollins managed to corral. Hollins had trouble getting the ball out of his glove, allowing Devon White, who overslid second base, to dive safely back to the bag. With the bases full of Phillies, Greene reached back and retired Olerud on an infield fly rule at first, but walked the next batter, Paul Molitor. When Rickey Henderson scored the first run of the game, it was the start of the longest and most poorly played game in the World Series to date. The Blue Jays were not content with just one run. Shortstop Tony Fernandez came up and laced a double to drive in two more runs to give the Blue Jays another early 3–0 lead before Greene finally retired Pat Borders to get out of the first inning.

Todd Stottlemyre, whose father Mel is the current Yankee pitching coach, duplicated Greene's generosity in the first inning. Dykstra led off the bottom of the first with a walk, and although Stottlemyre retired Duncan on a fly-out and fanned John Kruk, he walked Hollins, Daulton, and Eisenrich to send Dykstra home and cut the Blue Jays' deficit to 3–1. Unlike the night before, the Phillies took advantage of their scoring threat in the bottom of the first — Milt Thompson tripled to give the Phillies a 4–3 lead. Dykstra's two-run home run in the bottom of the second upped the Phillies' lead to 6–3.

However, the game was far from over as Toronto answered with a rally of its own. In the top of the third, after Carter popped out, Greene could not hold the lead as he walked Olerud and surrendered singles to Molitor, Fernandez, and Borders which netted Toronto two runs and trimmed Philadelphia's lead to 6–5 and knocked Greene out of the game. Mason relieved Greene and retired Borders on a force-out at second, but he could not put out the fire. He walked Henderson to load the bases, then up came White who singled in two runs. The Blue Jays reclaimed the lead 7–6.

In a light drizzle, the Phillies tied the game in the bottom of the fourth when Duncan singled home Dykstra who had doubled with two outs. The game seesawed back to the Phillies, who pushed across five runs in the bottom of the fifth on two two-run home runs by Daulton and Dykstra, and Thompson's RBI double.

With Philadelphia leading 12–7, Veterans Stadium fans began chanting the team theme song "Whoomp! (There It Is)." The Blue Jays scored two runs in the sixth, but the Phillies answered Toronto with a run in the sixth and another run in the seventh, retaining their five run lead at 14–9.

In the top of the eighth, Larry Anderson was on the mound for the Phillies and when Roberto Alomar grounded out to first for out number one, it looked like the Phillies had the game under control. Philadelphia needed only five more outs and they were still in good shape with a five run lead, but again the game was far from over. Larry Anderson, who appeared in 64 games for the Phillies that season, ran out of gas as he gave up a single to Carter and a walk to Olerud. With one out and men on first and second, Molitor came up and hit a high hopper to Hollins, who moved back and tried to field the ball between hops, but the ball bounced past him and rolled into left field. Hollins' error was the turning point of the game. Carter scored easily, Molitor wound up on second, and Olerud went to third. Now the Phillies led 14–10.

Phillies manager Jim Fregosi brought Mitch Williams in with one out in the eighth. Veterans Stadium gave Williams a standing ovation. With a four run lead, Veterans Stadium knew that Toronto might score a run off of Williams, but most of the Stadium was confident that Williams could get out of the eighth with the lead.

Shortstop Tony Fernandez had other plans. He singled off of Williams to score Molitor with Toronto's eleventh run. Williams then walked Blue Jays catcher Pat Borders to load the bases. With the bases full of Blue Jays, Williams struck out pinch-hitter Ed Sprague for the second out, and the Veterans Stadium crowd roared their support.

Had Hollins turned a double play or at least a force-out, Philadelphia would have gotten out of the eighth inning with at least a three-run lead and the entire complexion of the game would have been different. But Henderson capitalized on the situation with a single to send home Molitor and Fernandez. Now the score was 14–13 in favor of Philadelphia.

The fans at Veterans Stadium knew that the game was slipping away from them and were hoping, even trying, to will the last out. Some fans could no longer watch the game; they buried themselves in their coats, or covered their eyes.

Still, the Phillies had the lead and Veterans Stadium once again began cheering for one more out, but Devon White tripled to score Borders and Henderson. Toronto's bench was in a state of ecstasy. Incredibly, the Blue Jays rallied for six runs with one out in the eighth inning to take a 15–14 lead.

Relievers Mike Timlin and Duane Ward came in for the Blue Jays and, surprisingly, shut down the shell-shocked Philadelphia Phillies to preserve the 15–14 score and win the game. More importantly, the Blue Jays took a commanding 3–1 lead in the Series.

Game 5 was now or never, and Juan Guzman went up against Curt Schilling.[23]

The Blue Jays hoped to wrap up the Series in Philadelphia. Toronto had hit Schilling hard in the first game and they were confident the Phillies were still reeling from last night's devastating loss. Although the Phillies trailed the Blue Jays three games to one, Philadelphia was still confident they would come back and win three games in a row — something that had not been done since the 1985 Kansas City Royals.

The Phillies had the right man for the job. Curt Schilling wanted to show the baseball world that his Game 1 start was an anomaly. Schilling did. Backed by Veterans Stadium, Schilling sailed through the first seven innings, but, in the top of the eighth, he ran into trouble. Borders started the inning off with a single and was replaced by Willie Cinate at first base. Pinch hitter Rob Butler singled just out of the reach of Duncan, moving Cinate to third base. The Blue Jays now had runners on first and third with no outs. Henderson, who represented the winning run, was now the batter. Schilling threw a fastball in on Henderson, who swung and hit the ball back to Schilling who knocked it down and threw to Daulton as Cinate was sprinting towards home plate. Cinate, caught in a rundown, tried to get back to third, but Hollins ran him down and applied the tag for the first out. Butler stood camped at second, but Toronto still threatened with one out and runners on first and second.

Schilling then fanned Devon White for the second out. Alomar came up next and Veterans Stadium rose to cheer Schilling, who did not let the fans down. He induced Alomar to ground out to Duncan at second to retire the side, and ended Toronto's scoring threat as the Blue Jays went down in order in the top of the ninth.

Like a big game pitcher in the mold of Sandy Koufax, Bob Gibson, Whitey Ford, Juan Marichal, Catfish Hunter, and others before, Schilling shut down the Blue Jays and gave the Phillies relievers and every baseball fan an efficient and well pitched ball game in just under three hours. Under today's standards, less than three hours is pretty economical.

The Phillies eked out a run in the first and second innings, and behind Shilling's 134 pitches, Philadelphia held on and won the game 2–0 to send the World Series back to Toronto. The Blue Jays still led the Series 3–2.

Unfortunately, some narrow-minded baseball fans did not learn anything after Donnie Moore's death. After Schilling's victory over the Blue Jays, Williams returned to his home and was met by a policeman who informed him that his life had been threatened.[24] Williams reported that he did not sleep that night or go to the SkyDome to work out the next day. "Fan" comes from the word "fanatic," and there are those fanatics who love baseball so much that they take this baseball club to heart like their own family members. One can understand the disappointment with Williams' performance, but it was the first time in recent memory that someone's life was threatened over a blown save.

In Game 6, played October 23, 1993, Terry Mulholland and Dave Stewart faced each other again.[25]

In the bottom of the first, White walked with one out and Molitor followed with a triple to score Toronto's first run of the game. Molitor then scored on Carter's sacrifice fly to net Toronto another run, but the Blue Jays were not through. An Alomar single and an Olerud double gave Toronto their third run for an early 3–0 lead.

The Phillies pushed across a run in the top of the fourth inning, but the Blue Jays countered with single runs in the bottom of the fourth and fifth innings to take a 5–1 lead.

Just as in the 1986 Series, before the top of the sixth inning, WCBS, who televised the 1993 World Series that year, replayed Buckner's error. Play-by-play announcers Tim McCarver and Will McDonough mentioned not only the former Red Sox first baseman, but Bucky Dent's home run as well. Was this a bad omen? For which team? The Phillies began to make a comeback as the 1978 Yankees and 1986 Mets did, when in the top of the seventh, Dykstra stepped up to the plate with two men on and homered to right field to trim Toronto's lead to 5–4.

Stewart was replaced by Danny Cox, who promptly gave up a hit to Duncan, who wasted no time and stole second. Hollins came up and singled up the middle to score Duncan and tie the game at 5–5. Cox then walked Daulton to load the bases. Then up came Pete Incaviglia who hit a sacrifice fly that sent home Hollins with the go ahead run and the Phillies led 6–5.

Roger Mason, who entered the game in the sixth, had retired all six batters, but after Mason retired Joe Carter on a pop-up in the bottom of the eighth, Fregosi took out Mason and brought in David West. Though West had a lively fastball, he walked Olerud. Next Larry Anderson came in and struck out Alomar, but he hit Tony Fernandez and walked Ed Sprague to load the bases before finally retiring Pat Borders on a pop fly to the infield. More importantly, the Phillies had gone through relievers Mason, West, and Anderson, and the top of Toronto's order was due to bat in the bottom of the ninth.

The Phillies went down in order in the top of the ninth. Philadelphia still led 6–5 when Fregosi again turned to Williams to retire the Blue Jays and force a seventh game.

As Williams took the mound, Blue Jays fans cynically cheered his arrival.[26] Williams proceeded to walk Henderson, then got Devon White to pop out to Morandini for the first out. Up came Molitor who singled to move Henderson to second.

The stage was set for Joe Carter. Carter came up through the major leagues a decade ago, in 1983, for the Chicago Cubs. After playing a quarter of the season for Chicago, Carter went to the Cleveland Indians where he remained for the next six seasons. It was with Cleveland in 1986 that Carter had a break-out year playing in all 162 games and batting .302 with 200 hits, 29 home runs, and 121 RBIs.[27]

In 1990 Carter moved to the San Diego Padres, but he did not enjoy his stint with the Padres manager Larry Bowa, and his average dipped well below .300. Carter, along with his Padres teammate, Roberto Alomar, wound up with the Toronto Blue Jays in 1991.

With the Blue Jays, Carter again played in all 162 games, and had a good year at the plate as he raised his average some forty points to a respectable .273. Although his average slipped a bit over the next two years, due to his 100-plus strikeouts, his productivity did not; he drove in over 100 runs and hit over 30 home runs.

Scene: The SkyDome[28]

Astroturf, or artificial turf, originated when the Houston Astros opened the Astrodome in 1965, and became synonymous with many of the new stadiums that were constructed in the 1960s, 1970s and 1980s. The cookie cutters, or "concrete doughnuts," which looked like a giant circle from an aerial view, changed the way fans viewed a ball game. Gone were the small, intimate ballparks. As former Brooklyn Dodger announcer Red Barber has said, "When you [the fan] were in Ebbets Field, you were in the ballpark. You could see the perspiration on the Dodger players' faces." If baseball fans thought the cookie cutters were a departure from tradition, then they pale in comparison to the SkyDome.

The SkyDome was a new breed of stadium, packed with amenities and distractions. After breaking ground in April of 1986 the stadium opened on June 5, 1989, at a cost of $500 million.

Though the Milwaukee Brewers defeated the Blue Jays 5–3 on Opening Day, Toronto won at the end of the season by drawing over four million fans.

The SkyDome is equipped with an electronic roof to protect the fans from the elements, be it snow or rain. And unlike stadiums of the past, where advertisements were seen on the outfield walls, the SkyDome is an advertisement itself. It is complete with 348 hotel rooms situated in back of center field, although only 70 patrons can actually see a game from their rooms, but then again, some hotel guests have been seen engaging in extracurricular activities instead. There are 161 private skyboxes, or visitors may try the Windows on the SkyDome, a restaurant that seats up to 650 people, or Sightlines, a 300-foot long bar, or the Hard Rock Café. Each place is located in back of center field.

However, if you just want to take in the ball game, then you can watch the replays and other features on the Jumbotron. At 33 by 115 feet, the Jumbotron is the largest scoreboard in the world. Yet, there are downsides to this multiplex stadium: there are no bleachers and the opposing team must view the relief pitcher from a television monitor when he is warming in the bullpen. Like other symmetrical ballparks, the SkyDome's left and right field foul lines are 330 feet, the power alleys are at 375 feet, and center field is 400 feet, with the outfield fence at 10 feet. After the baseball season ends, the Toronto Argonauts of the Canadian Football League play at the SkyDome.

Carter took Williams' first two pitches in his favor and worked for a 2–0 count before Williams came back and got two strikes to even the count at 2–2. Yet, Carter was ready. Williams' last pitch was a slider in the dirt that fooled Carter.

Carter was thinking that Williams would throw another slider and on the fifth pitch, Williams, as usual, fired. But since Toronto had two men on, Williams, who would normally use his high kick when he delivered the ball to the plate, went into a slide step, and although the pitch was down and in, the ball arrived at the plate with less velocity.[29] Carter followed the ball with his head down, connected, and swatted Williams' offering over the left field fence for a three-run home run. Toronto won the game 8–6 and became the first team since the 1977-1978 Yankees to repeat as back-to-back champions.

Carter jumped up and down around the bases as if he just won the million-dollar lottery. Fireworks lit across the SkyDome as a congregation of his teammates crowded home plate to meet him. Carter was then carried off the field like the other conquering heroes of baseball lore. For baseball, it was the second walk-off home run to end the World Series since Bill Mazeroski's home run in 1960.

Champagne flowed in the Blue Jays' clubhouse. In the Phillies locker room, Williams sat on the stool with his head down.

At least the players understood. After all, only a player can know the pressure of performing in front of thousands of fans every day and millions more on television.

Fregosi came to Williams' defense. He reminded the Phillies that Williams' 43 saves were essential to the team winning the pennant. Fregosi also did not regret putting Williams back there on the mound when he could have chosen someone else.[30] Back in Philadelphia, though, a restaurant owner put up a sign that read "Patrons permanently banned from this restaurant: Mitch Williams."[31]

Philadelphia took exception to the questions that were being asked Williams, and when the Phillies thought that Williams had had enough of the questions, they took him inside for a meeting that everyone knew was an excuse to stop what must have felt like torture. Williams took a separate plane back to his home in Texas; if he had traveled with the team back to his New Jersey residence, he would have discovered that his windows were broken and eggs had been thrown at his home by some fanatics over his pitch to Joe Carter.[32] Williams confided to Kruk that he did not have a dead arm, he just didn't have his usual velocity and his pitches didn't have any life on them. Kruk admired Williams for trying to pitch without his best stuff in conjunction with the death threats that he endured before Game 6.[33]

Williams sat and answered every question directed to him as he did after Game 4 when he blew the save. Of course he felt terrible after he gave up a Series ending home run to Joe Carter.

Despite the death threats, pelted eggs, and jeers, Williams did receive some measure of respect. Days after the World Series about 200 townspeople from Mitch's home town of Hico, Texas, honored the beleaguered reliever with a cake for his 29th birthday and a key to the city.[34]

No one knows how the threats on Williams' life affected his performance in Game 6. To his credit, Williams said that the threats had no effect on him — it was just a bad pitch. But it was a good pitch, and Joe Carter should get the credit as a good baseball player who hit a home run. In fact the threats did have some effect, in that Williams did not work out the day after.

Williams vowed that he would not curl up and die, but that's exactly what happened. Before Williams could face the Phillies fans and prove that he was a still a good reliever, he was traded to the Houston Astros for reliever Doug Jones and minor leaguer Jeff Juden.[35]

The Phillies organization thought they were doing Williams a favor by getting him far away from the fans that might turn on him the way they did Donnie Moore.

Unfortunately, Williams did not resurrect his career with the Astros. Terry Collins, in his rookie season as the Astros' manager, needed to win as many games as possible. Thus, he could not be as patient with Williams as Fregosi had been. In 25 games with the Astros, Williams went 1–4 with six saves and a 7.65 ERA.[36]

After his stint with the Astros in 1995, Williams signed on with the California Angels, but he was ineffective with the Angels as well. In 20 games, Williams went 1–2 with a 6.75 ERA.[37] In 1997, Williams made one more attempt at a comeback with the Kansas City Royals, but that stint was short lived as well. In seven games he was 0–1 with a 10.80 ERA.[38]

In the late 1990s he moved to Pennsauken, New Jersey, and opened up the Maple Bowl Bar with his father-in-law; he became the sole owner of the bar a year later. Still physically fit, Williams thought about another return to the game, but he was still in pain from a torn shoulder tendon he had endured the last time he was on the mound and knew it would take another operation if he thought about pitching again.[39] But in 2001 Williams made his triumphant comeback to the game with the Atlantic City Surfs of the Independent Atlantic League as the team's pitching coach. Williams even managed to throw 3⅔ innings as he helped his team defeat the Long Island Ducks 9–8.[40]

Williams was a good reliever. From 1988 to 1993 he saved over 172 games (an average of thirty games per year). In total, Williams saved over 192 games in his nine-year career. In 2002, Williams became the manager of the Atlantic City Surfs.[41]

Like the other scapegoats in this book, Williams has appeared on television to talk about the pitch. Years after his home run to Joe Carter, he appeared with his old nemesis on ESPN.[42] Both men participated in a bowling game and sat down to talk about their famous confrontation. Williams and Carter, like Owen and Henrich, Branca and Thomson, and Dent and Torrez, talked about their confrontation at ease and joked about their moment in baseball history. Since that pitch nearly ten years ago, Williams is not bitter, which also makes him a hero.

As for the Toronto Blue Jays, the team has not returned to the post season since their World Series appearance in 1993.

Epilogue

After Joe Carter's home run ended the 1993 World Series, baseball began the 1994 season by splitting into three divisions: American and National League Eastern, Central, and Western divisions, and for the first time, a Wild Card team could qualify for the post season, which meant eight teams now would have a chance to win the pennant come October.

The Veterans Committee elected Phil Rizutto, former Yankee shortstop and longtime Yankee broadcaster, to the Hall of Fame. The New York Rangers finally won the Stanley Cup after 54 years. The New York Knicks nearly won the NBA Championship before falling to the Houston Rockets in seven games. After the Rangers and Knicks finished their season in June, the sports scene was dominated by the indictment of former Buffalo Bills football great O.J. Simpson on murder charges. Millions of Americans watched as he rode in a white Bronco on a California freeway proclaiming his innocence. Americans were divided over his role in his ex-wife's murder, and although many thought he was guilty, O.J. was found innocent the following year.

The Yankees made the prognosticators look like geniuses when they ran away with their division. The pleasant surprise in baseball was the Montreal Expos, who led the heavily favored Atlanta Braves by six games in the Eastern Division. The last time both teams qualified for the post season was in 1981, the year of the strike season.

Coincidentally, there was talk throughout the summer of another baseball strike. This strike focused on salary caps and was similar to the one that existed in basketball and football. The players were adamantly against the salary cap, and the owners were for it. Baseball fans kept hoping that a settlement could be reached before the August 9 deadline approached. This would not happen. The top two teams in baseball — the Yankees at 70–44 and the Montreal Expos at 76–38 — would not face each

157

other in the post season as the owners and players held their ground. On August 9, 1994, the players went on strike.

For the first couple of days the box scores remained the same, reminiscent of the All-Star break, but soon the box scores disappeared. The feeling was like the end of October, only it was August and the weather was hot. Pre-season football was on only on Sundays, which meant no sports on television. The only way to view baseball games was on the Classic Sports Channel, which replayed old baseball games on cable television. At first, it was a treat to relive classic ballgames, but it was a reminder of when baseball could manage its affairs, as most fans succumbed to a pervading feeling of doom regarding the rest of the season.

A month later, the players and owners met in New York City to try salvage the rest of the season. Unfortunately, on September 7, the baseball owners voted to cancel the baseball season and for the first time in 90 years, there would be no World Series. It seemed inconceivable in the late twentieth century, when baseball had experienced four labor strikes since 1972 season, including the strike in 1981, that there would be no World Series that year.

In 1995, baseball began experimenting with replacement players in an attempt to continue the season. Unlike the Second World War, when replacement players substituted for the regular players who were in the service, these players donned a uniform due to the stubborn owners who did not wish to enter into a labor agreement with the players. And the only war was that between the players and the owners.

The lack of regular players allowed anyone the opportunity to become a major leaguer. Baseball was turning into a joke as the replacement players made errors; soon fans remarked about the shoddy play on the field. The owners knew that this would be a long season and without major league talent, gate receipts would certainly fall. Also at stake was Cal Ripken, Jr.'s pursuit of Lou Gehrig's most consecutive games played record of 2,130 games. Ripken said that if the season started, and he was replaced as a Baltimore Oriole, he would stay with his players and not cross the picket line. Thus, he would risk losing his record.

The problem was averted in April of 1995 when Judge Sonia Sotomayor issued an injunction against baseball, forcing the owners and the players to go back to the bargaining table and work on a revenue sharing agreement. The strike was officially over. Cal Ripken would break Lou Gehrig's consecutive game streak on August 10, 1995, when he played in his 2,131st game.

In 1998, two teams debuted: the Arizona Diamondbacks in the National League and the Tampa Devil Rays in the American League. The Yankees would win the World Series after going 125–50 in the regular season and playoffs. But the main attraction was the home run race between St. Louis Cardinal first baseman Mark McGwire and Chicago Cub rightfielder Sammy Sosa.

Millions of Americas tuned in on September 7, as McGwire broke Roger Maris' 37-year-old record. He hit home run #62 on his way to 70 that year. As for Sosa, he ended up with 66. Many baseball experts agreed that the 1998 home run race between McGwire and Sosa brought baseball back after the disastrous 1994 baseball strike which had alienated many baseball fans. Barry Bonds would break this record with 73 in 2001.

If fans can forgive baseball for going on strike in 1994, if Americans can forgive Richard Nixon for Watergate, then fans should realize that Fred Merkle, Fred Snodgrass, Mickey Owen, Ralph Branca, Mike Torrez, Tom Niedenfuer, Donnie Moore, Bill Buckner, and Mitch Williams were only doing their jobs and let bygones be bygones and give them the credit for the people they are: men who dared to achieve what every baseball fan in his lifetime wishes—to become a ball player—and they succeeded.

We have come to the end of this book. It was never intended to rewrite baseball history; what's done is done and nothing can alter the scores in the record book. If anything, I hope the reader will take into consideration that ballplayers, like all of us, are still human and will make mistakes now and then. And it still takes 25 men and 27 outs to win a ball game. Not one person can get an entire team out by himself. Yes, we have seen Roger Clemens and Kerry Wood retire 20 batters in a game, but this has happened only three times: Clemens in 1986 and 1996 and Wood in 1998.

So when the writers or a commentators label a player a goat the minute a player makes a mistake or a bad pitch, to make a point, just think for a minute of the death of Donnie Moore. Yes, one might say that Moore carried with him demons that he never exorcised; however, when one thinks of Moore, or the attacks on Merkle, or the constant reminder of Branca's pitch to Thomson, or the viewing of Buckner's error on television, and the threats on Williams' life, it tells us that there is a better way to report a ball game so fans can live with a disappointing loss. As sportswriters create heroes to honor and villains to vilify, let us at least do this by constructive criticism. Let us remember that the ball player, like all of us, is human, but those ball players are also endowed with a remarkable ability to play this grand game of baseball. Writers should keep in mind that they wield a pen, not a bat, and should strive to maintain the same level of professional quality as the men they write about.

Thomas Boswell, sports columnist for the *Washington Post*, is one such writer. Three days after Donnie Moore's death, Boswell wrote a column titled "The Sorrowful Truth: Nothing to Forgive."[1] It was dedicated to Bill Buckner, Ralph Branca, Tom Niedenfuer, Donnie Moore, and any other player who was branded as "Goat." In the column, Boswell wrote that the players never did anything wrong and gave their best effort, but failed. Boswell also reminded baseball fans that one team had to win and one team had to lose. Lastly, Boswell pointed out, if not accurately, then tellingly, "The flaw [is] in our attitude — perhaps it is even an American predisposition with puritan roots to equate defeat with sin. The unspoken assumption is that those who lose must do so because of some moral flaw."

It is not sinful to lose a game, and certainly no player is flawed because that player did not perform up to our expectations. And if he was involved in a significant loss during or at the end of the season, that player is no less of a person than he was the day before. What would have been sinful, or to use a better word, shameful, is if these players had retreated from their professions and quit due to their infamous moments in baseball. As we know, this did not happen, as each player in this book continued with his career.

What should also be noted is that if we are to hold each player responsible for his actions, then we can acknowledge that each person was willing to take such responsibility, which is admirable and honorable because this desire came from the heart.

Notes

Chapter 1

1. www.Merkle.com: The Sporting News Archives: *Daguerreotypes*: January 12, 1939.
2. Robinson, Ray. *Matty: An American Hero*. New York: Oxford University Press, 1993, p. 57.
3. Ibid., pp. 89–90.
4. DeValeria, Dennis, and Jeannie Burke DeValeria. *Honus Wagner: A Biography*. New York: Henry Holt, 1995, p. 173.
5. Ibid., p. 175.
6. Christensen, Chris. "Merkle Revisited." *Elysian Fields Quarterly*, vol. 15, no. 4, 1998, p. 40.
7. Ibid., p. 41.
8. Robinson. *Matty*, p. 91.
9. DeValeria and DeValeria. *Honus Wagner*, p. 187.
10. Schott, Tom, and Nick Peters. *The Giants Encyclopedia*. Champaign, Illinois: Sports Publishing Company, 1999, p. 3.
11. Christensen. *Elysian Fields Quarterly*, p. 42.
12. Robinson. *Matty*, p. 98.
13. Ibid., p. 100.
14. Hynd, Noel. *The Giants of the Polo Grounds*. New York: Doubleday, 1988, p. 148.
15. Anderson, David M. *More Than Merkle*. Lincoln: University of Nebraska Press, 2000, p. 143.
16. Robinson. *Matty*, pp. 103–104.
17. DeValeria and DeValeria. *Honus Wagner*, p. 193.
18. Robinson. *Matty*, p. 106.
19. Robinson. *Matty*, p. 107.
20. Christensen. *Elysian Fields Quarterly*, pp. 46–47.
21. *The Baseball Encyclopedia*, 8th edition, 1990. New York: Macmillan, p. 2455.
22. Ibid.
23. *The Sporting News*: January 12, 1939.
24. Ibid., March 14, 1956.

25. *The Sporting News*: January 12, 1939.
26. Aulick, W. W. *New York Times*: September 24, 1908.
27. Olberman, Keith. *Baseball America*: October 13–26, 1997.
28. Christensen. *Elysian Fields Quarterly*, p. 50.
29. *The Sporting News*: January 12, 1939.
30. Barber, Red. *Christian Science Monitor*: February 26, 1987, p. 18.
31. Christensen. *Elysian Fields Quarterly*, p. 50.
32. *Sporting News*: March 14, 1956.

Chapter 2

1. Author interview with Spencer Garrett, grandson of Fred Snodgrass.
2. Light, Jonathan Fraser. *The Cultural Encyclopedia of Baseball.* Jefferson, NC: McFarland, 1997, pp. 172, 332.
3. Ritter, Lawrence S. *The Glory of Their Times.* William Morrow, 1966, pp. 92–93.
4. Ibid., p. 106.
5. Robinson. *Matty,* p. 140.
6. Ibid., pp. 141–142.
7. Lieb, Fred. *Baseball as I Have Known It.* University of Nebraska Press, 1977, p. 93.
8. Smith, Curt. *Our House: A Tribute to Fenway Park.* Masters Press, 1997, p. 8.
9. Shaughnessy, Dan. *At Fenway.* Crown Publishing, 1999, p. 22.
10. Stout, Glenn & Johnson, Richard. *Red Sox Century.* Houghton Mifflin, 2000, p. 69.
11. Shaughnessey. *At Fenway,* p. 24.
12. Stein, Fred, and Nick Peters. *Giants Diary.* North Atlantic Books, 1987, p. 256.
13. Robinson. *Matty,* pp. 143–149.
14. *The Sporting News*: April 9, 1942.
15. *New York Times*: October 17, 1912.
16. Ritter. *The Glory of Their Times,* p. 114.
17. Ibid., p. 116.
18. *The Sporting News*: April 9, 1942.
19. *New York Times*: April 6, 1974.
20. Author interview with Spencer Garret.

Chapter 3

1. Author interview with Charles Owen, son of Mickey Owen.
2. Paul Stubblefield. *The Sporting News*: October 16, 1971.
3. *The Baseball Encyclopedia,* p. 2508.
4. Creamer, Robert W. *Baseball in 1941.* University of Nebraska Press, 1991, p. 269.
5. www.BaseballReference.com. New York Yankees.
6. www.BaseballReference.com. Brooklyn Dodgers.
7. Creamer. *Baseball in 1941,* pp. 295–6.

8. Ibid., p. 297.
9. Ibid., pp. 303–5.
10. Sullivan, Neil J. *The Dodgers Move West*. Oxford University Press, 1986, p. 5.
11. Ritter, Lawrence S. *East Side, West Side,* Total Sports, 1998, p. 44.
12. Sullivan. *Dodgers Move West,* p. 4.
13. Ritter, Lawrence S. *East Side, West Side,* p. 44.
14. Golenbock, Peter. *Bums*. Pocket Books, 1984, p. 4.
15. Ritter, Lawrence, S. *East Side, West Side,* p. 48.
16. http://www.ballparks.com:EbbetsField.
17. *The Sporting News*: October 16, 1971.
18. Creamer. *Baseball in 1941,* p. 294.
19. *The New York Daily News*: October 16, 1941.
20. Salant, Nathan. *This Day in Yankee History*. New York: Stein Day Publishers, 1983, p. 250.
21. *New York Herald-Tribune*: October 6, 1941.
22. *New York Daily News*: October 6, 1941, p. 40.
23. *The Sporting News*: October 16, 1971.
24. Ibid.
25. Van Hyning, Thomas. *Puerto Rico's Winter League: A History of Major League Baseball's Launching Pad*. Jefferson, NC: McFarland, 1995, pp. 176–77.
26. *The Sporting News*: October 16, 1971, p. 43.
27. Author interview with Thomas Henrich, former outfielder for the New York Yankees, 1937–1950.

Chapter 4

1. Ward, Geoffrey C., executive producer and telescript, narration by Will Lyman. 1990 "The American Experience: Nixon."
2. Ron Firmitte. *Sports Illustrated*, September 18, 1991.
3. Golenbock. *Bums*, pp. 96–97.
4. Westcott, Rich. *Splendor on the Diamond: Interviews with 35 Stars of the Baseball Past*. University Press of Florida, 2000, p. 190.
5. Firmirte, Ron. *Sports Illustrated*, September 16, 1991.
6. Thorn, John, and Pole Palmer. *Total Baseball*. Warner Books, 1999, p. 1358.
7. Westcott. *Splendor on the Diamond,* p. 192.
8. Ibid.
9. Golenbock. *Bums,* p. 314.
10. Ibid., p. 354.
11. Getz, Mike. *Brooklyn Dodgers and Their Rivals*. Montauk Press, 1999, p. 37.
12. *New York Times*: May 25, 1951.
13. Ibid., May 26, 1951, Section 5, p. 1.
14. Author interview with Carl Erskine, former pitcher of the Brooklyn and Los Angeles Dodgers, 1948–1959.
15. *New York Times*: June 16, 1951, p. 1.
16. Ibid., June 22, 1951, p. 17.
17. Ibid., July 20. 1951, p. 13.

18. Ibid., August 2, 1951, p. 24.
19. Ibid., August 4, 1951, p. 9.
20. Ibid., August 6, 1951, p. 26.
21. Getz. *Brooklyn Dodgers*, p. 51.
22. *New York Times*: Aug. 14, 1951.
23. Golenbock. *Bums*, p. 345.
24. *New York Times*: August 25, 1951, p. 14.
25. Ibid., August 28, 1951, p. 26.
26. Ibid., August 29, 1951, p. 29
27. Ibid., September 2, 1951, Section 5, p. 1.
28. Ibid., September 6, 1951, p. 40.
29. Ibid., September 10, 1951, p. 25.
30. Ibid., September 21, 1951.
31. Ibid., September 28, 1951.
32. Ibid., October 1, 1951, p. 26.
33. Ibid., October 2, 1951, p. 1.
34. Interview with Carl Erskine.
35. *New York Times*: October 3, 1951, pp. 1, 42.
36. Robinson, Ray. *Matty*, pp. 121–122.
37. Thornley, Stew. *Land of the Giants*. Temple University Press, 2000, pp. 65–66.
38. http//www.ballparks.com.PoloGrounds. 2001.
39. Thornley. *Land of the Giants*, pp. 92–93.
40. http//www.ballparks.com.PoloGrounds. 2001.
41. Ritter, Lawrence S. *Lost Ballparks*. New York: The Penguin Group, 1992, p. 163.
42. Ritter, Lawrence S. *East Side, West Side*, pp. 132, 136.
43. Khan, Roger. *Sports Illustrated*. October 10, 1960.
44. Golenbock. *Bums*, p. 372.
45. Author interview with Carl Erskine.
46. Anderson, Dave. "Sports of the Times." *New York Times*: Feb. 1, 2001.
47. Thorn. *Total Baseball*.
48. Kahn. *Sports Illustrated*: October 10, 1960.
49. *New York Daily News*: October 4, 1951.
50. Smith, Ron. *Sporting News 25 Greatest Moments*. St. Louis, Mo.: *Sportings News*, 1999, p. 18.
51. Golenbock. *Bums*, p. 376.
52. *Baseball Encyclopedia*, p. 2345.
53. Gilman, Kaye. *New York Daily News*: October 6, 1974, p. 142.
54. *New York Times*: Malcolm Moran. October 7, 1987.
55. *New York Times*: September 18, 1951.
56. *New York Times*: February 7, 1987.
57. *New York Times*: September 26, 1951.
58. Prager, Jonathan. *Wall Street Journal*: Reprinted in *Newsday*, February 1, 2001.

Chapter 5

1. Television Bureau of Advertising, Inc., statistics found at www.tvb.org/tvfacts/tvbasics/basics1.html.

2. Game 6 of the 1986 World Series. "NBC Sports." 1986 Major League Baseball.

3. Ward, Geoffrey C., and Ken Burns. *Baseball: An Illustrated History*. New York: Knopf, 1994, p. 390.

4. *New York Times*: December 29, 1975.

5. Solomon, Burt. *The Baseball Timeline*. New York: DK Publishing, 2001, p. 125.

6. Shaughnessy, Dan. *The Curse of the Bambino*. Penguin Books, 1990, p. 1, 30.

7. Ibid., p. 47.

8. Ibid., pp. 51–52.

9. Salant. *This Day in New York Yankees History*, p. 1.

10. Ibid., p. 371.

11 Allen, Maury. *New York Post*: April 17, 1983.

12. Thorn. *Total Baseball*, p. 1795.

13. *Baseball Encyclopedia*, p. 2522.

14. Ibid.

15. Ibid.

16. Ibid.

17. Salant. *This Day in New York Yankee History*. Stein & Day, 1979, 1983, p. 82.

18. *New York Times*: June 18, 1978.

19. Stout, Glenn, and Richard Johnson. *Red Sox Century*. Houghton Millflin, 2000, pp. 379–380.

20. Salant, Nathan. *This Day in New York Yankee History*, p. 356.

21. *New York Times*: April 8, 1978.

22. *New York Times*: April 9, 1978.

23. Salant. *This Day in Yankee History*, p. 357.

24. Smith, Curt. *Our House: A Tribute to Fenway Park*, Masters Press, 1999.

25. Salant. *This Day in New York Yankee History*, p. 359.

26. *New York Times*: June 18, 1978.

27. *New York Times*: June 19, 1978.

28. *New York Times*: June 20, 1978.

29. *New York Times*: June 21, 1978.

30. Smith. *Our House*, p. 148.

31. Salant. *This Day in Yankee History*, p. 360.

32. Riley, Dan. *The Red Sox Reader*, p. 213. Reprinted from *The New Yorker*, Roger Angell, 1978.

33. Salant. *This Day in New York Yankee History*, p. 362.

34. *New York Times*: July 18, 1978.

35. *New York Times*: July 24, 1978.

36. *New York Times*: August 3, 1978.

37. Salant. *This Day in New York Yankee History*, p. 366.

38. Ibid., p. 366.

39. *Los Angeles Times*: August 19, 1978.

40. Stout & Johnson. *Red Sox Century*, p. 382.

41. Shaughnessy. *The Curse of the Bambino*, p. 137.

42. *Los Angeles Times*: September 3, 1978.

43. Ibid., September 5, 1978.

44. Ibid., September 6, 1978.

45. Ibid., September 7, 1978.

46. Salant. *This Day in Yankee History*, pp. 368–369.

47. Ibid., p. 370.

48. Ibid., pp. 370–371.

49. *Los Angeles Times*: October 2, 1978.

50. Whiteside, Larry. *Boston Globe*: March 11, 1979, p. 52.

51. "Baseball's Greatest Games." 1978 AL East playoff. 1992 Major League Baseball. The Phoenix Communications Group.

52. Thorn. *Total Baseball*, p. 725.

53. Shaughnessy. *The Curse of the Bambino*, p. 14.

54. Ibid., p. 38.

55. Ibid., p. 14.

56. Ibid., p. 46.

57. Ibid., p. 14.

58. Reidenbaugh, Lowell. "Take Me Out to the Ballpark." *The Sporting News*: pp. 52–54.

59. Shaughnessy. *At Fenway*, p. 40.

60. http://www.ballparks.com:FenwayPark.

61. Pepe, Phil. *Talkin' Baseball: An Oral History of Baseball in the 1970s.* Ballentine Books, 1998, p. 333.

62. Salant. *This Day in Yankee History*, p. 367.

63. Shaughnessy. *The Curse of the Bambino*, p. 139.

64. Whiteside, Larry. *The Boston Globe*: October 3, 1978.

65. Ibid.

66. Coutros, Pete. *New York Post*: September 8, 1989.

67. *Denver Post*: July 18, 2000.

68. Shaughnessy. *The Curse of the Bambino*, p. 145.

69. Ibid., p. 147.

Chapter 6

1. McNeil, William F. *The Dodgers Encyclopedia*. Sports Publishing, 2001.

2. Ibid., p. 15.

3. Ibid.

4. Ibid.

5. Washington State University Sports Information. Tom Niedenfuer. Pullman, WA, 99164.

6. *The Sporting News*: September 5, 1981, p. 47.

7. *The Dodgers Encyclopedia*, p. 79.

8. Ibid.

9. *The Sporting News*: November 28, 1983, p. 63.

10. *The Sporting News*: June 8, 1985, p. 24.

11. *The Sporting News*: July 15, 1985.

12. *The Sporting News*: September 30, 1985, p. 16.

13. Peter, Golenbock. *The Spirit of St. Louis: A History of the Cardinals and Browns*, pp. 557–559.

14. *Los Angeles Times*: October 14, 1985.

15. "Greatest League Championship Series." Narrated by Warner Fusselle. Phoenix Communications Group, 1994.

16. ESPN Classic. Game 6 of the 1985 N.L.C.S.
17. *Total Baseball*, p. 675.
18. Sullivan, Neil. *The Dodgers Move West*. Oxford University Press, 1986, pp. 42–43.
19. Ibid., pp. 47–48.
20. Ibid., p. 48.
21. Ibid., p. 51.
22. Ibid., pp. 110–112.
23. Golenbock. *Bums*, p. 571.
24. Sullivan. *The Dodgers Move West*, p. 84.
25. Ibid., p. 100.
26. Ibid., p. 160.
27. *Los Angeles Times*: June 5, 1958.
28. Ibid., July 15, 1958.
29. Sullivan. *The Dodgers Move West*, p. 172.
30. Ibid., p. 183.
31. Ibid., p. 188.
32. Reidenbaugh. "Take Me Out to the Ballpark," p. 142.
33. *Los Angeles Times*: October 17, 1985.
34. Ibid.
35. Ibid.
36. Ibid., March 10, 1986.
37. Ibid., April 26, 1990.
38. *The Baseball Encyclopedia*, p. 2467.
39. *Los Angeles Times*: April 26, 1990.
40. "2001 Where Are They Now?" *People Magazine*.

Chapter 7

1. Riess, Steven A. *Touching Base*. University of Illinois Press, 1999, p. 134.
2. Ibid., p. 146.
3. *Total Baseball*, p. 11. Anaheim Angels.
4. Ibid.
5. Ibid.
6. Ibid.
7. Ibid.
8. Ibid.
9. Feldman, Loren. *GQ Magazine*. February 1990, p. 220.
10. Ibid., p. 255.
11. Ibid., p. 221.
12. Ibid., p. 221.
13. *The Baseball Encyclopedia*, p. 2460.
14. Sowell, Mike. *One Pitch Away*. McMillan Sports Books, 1995, p. 102.
15. Chass, Murray. *New York Times*: January 25, 1985.
16. Newman, Ross. *Anaheim Angels*. New York: Hyperion Books, 2000, p. 251.
17. Sowell. *One Pitch Away*, pp. 102–104.
18. Newman, Ross. *Anaheim Angels*, p. 263.

19. http.www.baseball reference.com/teams CAL/1986 shtml. 1986 California Angels Statistics.

20. *Los Angeles Times*: April 1, 1988.

21. Sowell, Mike. *One Pitch Away*, pp. 10, 105–106.

22. Shaughnessy. *The Curse of the Bambino*, pp. 150–151.

23. http.www.baseball reference.com/teams BOS/1986 shtml 1986 Boston Red Sox Statistics.

24. Shaughnessy. *The Curse of the Bambino*, p. 158.

25. Ibid., p. 160.

26. *Los Angeles Times*: October 7, 1986.

27. Ibid., October 8, 1986.

28. Ibid., October 10, 1986.

29. Ibid., October 12, 1986.

30. ESPN Classic Sports. Game 5 of the 1986 A.L.C.S.

31. Sowell, Mike. *One Pitch Away*, pp. 25–26.

32. Newman, Ross. *Anaheim Angels*, p. 267.

33. http://www.ballparks.com. Edison International Field of Anaheim.

34. *Los Angeles Times*: October 13, 1986.

35. Sowell. *One Pitch Away*, pp. 33–35.

36. Ibid., pp. 143–144.

37. *Los Angeles Times*. October 17, 1986.

38. Sowell. *One Pitch Away*, pp. 106–107.

39. Ibid., p. 107.

40. *Los Angeles Times*: April 1, 1988.

41. Sowell. *One Pitch Away*, p. 108.

42. *Los Angeles Times*: August 27, 1988.

43. *One Pitch Away*, p. 110.

44. *The Star Ledger*: July 19, 1989.

45. *The Sporting News*: July 31, 1989.

46. *One Pitch Away*, pp. 111–112.

47. *The Sporting News*: July 31, 1989.

48. Ibid.

49. *New York Times*: July 20, 1989.

Chapter 8

1. Buckner, Bill. *Beyond the Glory*. Fox Sports Net. Narrated by Jay Mohr, 2001.

2. Porter, David L. *Biographical Dictionary of American Sports*. Greenwood, 1988.

3. *The Sporting News*: January 10, 1970.

4. Ibid., April 10, 1971.

5. *Total Baseball*, p. 641.

6. Sowell, Mike. *One Pitch Away*, p. 246.

7. *The Baseball Encyclopedia*, p. 2349.

8. Ibid.

9. Sowell. *One Pitch Away*, pp. 71–72.

10. Halberstam, David. *October 1964*. New York: Ballantine Books, 1994, pp. 71–72.

11. *Los Angeles Times*: October 14, 1986.

12. *New York Times*: October 20, 1986.

13. Lang, Jack. *New York Mets: Twenty-five Years of Baseball Magic*. H. Holt, 1987, pp. 218–22.

14. http://www.Baseball-Reference.Com. 1986 New York Mets Statistics.

15. http://www.Baseball-Reference.Com. 1986 Houston Astros Statistics.

16. *New York Times*: October 24, 1986.

17. Shaughnessy. *The Curse of the Bambino*, p. 165.

18. Sowell. *One Pitch Away*, p. 267.

19. Sullivan, Neil. *The Dodgers Move West*, p. 110.

20. Reindenbaugh. "Take Me Out to the Ballpark," pp. 184–187.

21. Sowell. *One Pitch Away*, p. 258.

22. Ibid., p. 260.

23. *New York Times*: October 20, 1986.

24. *Baseball: A Film by Ken Burns*. "Inning 9," 1994.

25. Game 6 1986 World Series. NBC Sports.

26. Shaughnessy. *The Curse of the Bambino*, p. 167.

27. Gammons, Peter. *Sports Illustrated*. April 6, 1987

28. Buckner, Bill. *Beyond the Glory*. Fox Sports Net.

29. Shaughnessy. *The Curse of the Bambino*, p. 172.

30. Feinstein, John. *Washington Post*: October 26, 1986.

31. Shaughnessy. *The Curse of the Bambino*, p. 173

32. *Washington Post*: October 26, 1986.

33. *New York Times*: October 28, 1986.

34. Sowell, Mike. *One Pitch Away*, p. 258.

35. Layden, Tim. *Albany Times*: April 1, 1987.

36. Prager. Joshua Harris. *Wall Street Journal*: July 24, 1998.

37. Thorn. *Total Baseball*. Stats on Buckner with the Angels/Royal, p. 641.

38. Sowell. *One Pitch Away*, pp. 238–239.

39. Prager. *Wall Street Journal*: July 24, 1998.

40. Buckner, Bill. *Beyond the Glory*.

41. *Detroit News*: December 13, 1995.

42. *Chicago Tribune*: August 17, 1987

43. Prager. *Wall Street Journal*: July 24, 1998.

44. Sowell. *One Pitch Away*, p. 216.

45. Shaughnessy. *Curse of the Bambino*, p. 179.

46. Burns, Ken. *The Baseball an Illustrated History*, p. 451.

Chapter 9

1. Thorn. *Total Baseball*. Team Histories— Toronto Blue Jays, pp. 66–67.

2. *The Giants: A Tale of Two Cities*. 1986 Scotch Video.

3. http://www.BaseballReference.Com-Toronto Blue Jay.

4. *New York Times*: September 5, 1993.

5. Thorn. *Total Baseball*. Team Histories— Philadelphia Phillies, pp. 49–51.

6. http://www.BaseballReference.Com-Philadelphia Phillies.

7. Telander, Rick. *Sports Illustrated*: August 24, 1989.

8. *Sporting News*: December 17, 1984.

9. *The Baseball Encyclopedia*, p. 2535.

10. *Sports Illustrated*: May 4, 1992.

11. Telander, Rick. *Sports Illustrated*: August 24, 1989.

12. Hagan, Paul, with John Kruk. *I Ain't an Athlete, Lady.* Simon and Schuster, 1994, p. 228.

13. *Sports Illustrated*: August 24, 1989.

14. *The Baseball Encyclopedia*, p. 2535.

15. *Chicago Tribune*: April 5, 1989.

16. Telander. *Sports Illustrated*: August 24, 1989.

17. *Chicago Tribune*: April 8, 1991.

18. Ibid.

19. *New York Times*: October 17, 1993.

20. *New York Times*: October 18, 1993.

21. *New York Times*: October 20, 1993.

22. "ESPN Classic: Game 4 1993 World Series."

23. *New York Times*: October 21, 1993.

24. *St. Louis Post Dispatch*: October 24, 1993.

25. "ESPN Classic: Game 6 1993 World Series."

26. *New York Times*: October 25, 1993.

27. Thorn. *Total Baseball*, p. 661.

28. http://www.ballparks.com. SkyDome.

29. McCullough, Bob. *My Greatest Day in Baseball*, p. 52.

30. *New York Times*: October 25, 1993.

31. Ibid.

32. *Houston Chronicle*: October 27, 1993.

33. Hagan. *I Ain't an Athlete, Lady*, p. 233.

34. *Los Angeles Times*: November 14, 1993.

35. *USA Today*: December 3, 1993.

36. Thorn. *Total Baseball*, p. 2535.

37. Ibid.

38. Ibid.

39. *New York Daily News*: Jan. 17, 1999.

40. Associated Press: June 25, 2001.

41. *New York Daily News*: July 18, 2002.

42. "ESPN Classic: Game 6 1993 World Series."

Epilogue

1. Boswell, Tom. *Washington Post*: July 21, 1989.

Bibliography

Anderson, David W. *More Than Merkle: A History of the Best and Most Exciting Baseball Seasons*. University of Nebraska Press, 2000.

The Baseball Encyclopedia, 9th edition. Macmillan, 1990.

Cramer, Robert C. *Baseball in '41*. Penguin Group, 1991.

DeValeria, Dennis, and Jane Burke DeValeria. *Honus Wagner: A Biography*. Henry Holt, 1995.

Firmite, Ron. *Sports Illustrated*. Vol. 75, September 16, 1991.

Getz, Mike. *The Brooklyn Dodgers and Their Rivals*. Montauk Press, 1999.

Gillete, Gary C. *The Great American Stat Book 1994*. Harper Collins, 1994.

Golenbock, Peter. *Bums*. Pocket Books, 1984.

Hagan, Paul, with John Kruk. *I Ain't an Athlete, Lady*. Simon and Schuster, 1994.

Kennedy, John F. *Profiles in Courage*. Simon and Shuster, 1957.

Lang, Jack. *The New York Mets: Twenty-five Years of Baseball Magic*. H. Holt, 1987.

Lieb, Fred. *Baseball as I Have Known It*. University of Nebraska Press, 1977.

Light, Jonathan Fraser. *The Cultural Encyclopedia of Baseball*. McFarland, 1997.

McCullough, Bob, ed. *My Greatest Day in Baseball, 1946–1997*. Taylor, 1998.

McNeil, William F. *The Dodgers Encyclopedia*. Sports Publishing, 1997.

Newman, Ross. *The Anaheim Angels: A Complete History*. Hyperion, 1999.

Porter, David L. *Biographical Dictionary of American Sports*. Greenwood, 1998.

Riley, Dan. *The Red Sox Reader*. Houghton Mifflin, 1991.

Ritter, Lawrence S. *East Side, West Side*. Total Sports, 1998.

Ritter, Lawrence S. *The Glory of Their Times: The Story of the Early Days of Baseball Told by the Men Who Played It*. William Morrow, 1966.

Ritter, Lawrence S. *Lost Ballparks*. Penguin, 1992.

Robinson, Ray. *Matty: An American Hero*. Oxford University Press, 1993.

Salant, Nathan. *This Date in New York Yankees History*. Stein & Day, 1979, 1983.

Shaughnessy, Dan. *The Curse of the Bambino*. Penguin, 1990.

Smith, Curt. *Our House: A Tribute to Fenway Park*. Masters Press, 1999.

Sowell, Mike. *One Pitch Away*. Simon & Schuster/Macmillan, 1995.

Stein, Fred, and Nick Peters. *Giants Diary*. North Atlantic Books, 1987.

Stout, Glenn, and Richard A. Johnson. *Red Sox Century*. Houghton Mifflin, 2000.

Sullivan, Neil J. *The Dodgers Move West*. Oxford University Press, 1986.

Thorn, John, and Pete Palmer. *Total Baseball*. Warner Books, 1999.

Thornley, Stew. *Land of the Giants: New York's Polo Grounds.* Temple University Press, 2000.
Westcott, Rich. *Splendor on the Diamond: Interviews with 35 Stars of Baseball Past.* University Press of Florida, 2000.

Video

Baseball's Greatest Games. 1978 American Eastern Division Playoff, 1993.
Forever Fenway: 75 Years of Red Sox Baseball. Magnetic Media Division 3/M, 1987.
The Greatest League Championship Series. Phoenix Communications Group, 1994.
1986 World Series Game Six. Property of Major League Baseball, 1987.
1993 World Series. Phoenix Communications Group, 1993.

Television

Fox Sports. Bill Buckner — "Beyond the Glory," 2001.

Periodicals

CHAPTER 1

The Christian Science Monitor: February 26, 1987.
The Sporting News: Daguerreotypes: Jan 12, 1939.
The Daily News: March 25, 1986.
Elysian Fields Quarterly: Vol. 15, No. 4, 1998.
The Sporting News: March 14, 1956.

CHAPTER 2

The Sporting News: April 9, 1942.
The Sporting News: May 18, 1974.

CHAPTER 3

New York Post: June 24, 1975.
The Sporting News: October 16, 1941.
The Sporting News: October 16, 1971.

CHAPTER 4

Boston Sunday Globe: March 11, 1979.
The Daily News: October 6, 1974.
The Denver Post: September 18, 2000.
New York Post: May 17, 1983.
New York Post: September 8, 1989.
New York Times: April 9, 1979.
The New York Times: February 7, 1987.
Sports Illustrated: October 10, 1960.
The Sporting News: October 22, 1966.
The Sporting News: October 1, 1986.

CHAPTER 5

Los Angeles Times: October 9–17, 1985.
Los Angeles Times: March 30, 1986.
Los Angeles Times: April 26, 1990.
The Sporting News: September 5, 1981.
The Sporting News: November 28, 1983.
The Sporting News: July 8, 1985.
The Sporting News: July 15, 1985.
The Sporting News: November 4, 1985.

CHAPTER 6

The Los Angeles Times: September 16, 1987.
The Los Angeles Times: April 1, 1988.
The Los Angeles Times: April 27, 1988.
New York Post: July 20, 1989.
New York Times: January 25, 1985.
New York Times: July 20,1989.
The Sporting News: July 31, 1989.

CHAPTER 7

Albany Times: April 11, 1987.
Biographical Dictionary of American Sports.
The Sporting News: May 21, 1990.
Wall Street Journal: July 24, 1998.

CHAPTER 8

New York Daily News: January 17, 1999.
USA Today Baseball Weekly: April 15–21, 1998.

Index